T0283645

REVOLUTION
to EVOLUTION

The Story of the Office of Minority Affairs & Diversity
at the University of Washington

By Emile Pitre

REVOLUTION TO EVOLUTION:
The Story of the Office of Minority Affairs & Diversity
at the University of Washington

By Emile Pitre

First Edition
Printed in South Korea

Published by Documentary Media LLC
books@docbooks.com
www.documentarymedia.com
(206) 935-9292

Author: Emile Pitre
Editing and book production: Tori Smith
Book Design: Marilyn Esguerra
Editorial Director: Petyr Beck

Available through the University of Washington Press
uwapress.uw.edu

ISBN: 978-1-933245-67-6

Library of Congress Control Number: 2022917708

_____

*This book is dedicated to
the founders of the 1968 Black Student Union
whose unapologetic actions
changed the University of Washington forever.*

_____

———————

"The Board of Regents considers it to be one of the highest educational priorities of the University to provide special educational opportunities to persons from minority groups which have been historically denied access to higher levels of higher education, and to women in those professional and academic fields where they have been traditionally grossly underrepresented (and directs) the Office of Minority Affairs to continue to recruit minorities and provide such special educational opportunities as it deems necessary in order that more persons from underrepresented minorities may qualify for admissions into graduate and professional schools."

—Board of Regents Policy Statement, January 13, 1975

———————

Table of Contents

Foreword

R ace still casts a long and cogent shadow on the past, present, and future of this nation, including on schools, colleges, and universities. Alarming indications of the extent to which the United States is painfully reckoning with its racial legacy include the Black Lives Matter movement, the killings of African Americans such as George Floyd and Breonna Taylor by police in 2020, the heightened visibility of inequities revealed by the COVID-19 epidemic, and the tragic murder of 10 African Americans at a grocery store in Buffalo, New York, in 2022, by a White teenager endorsing White supremacist ideology known as replacement theory (Burch & Vander Ploeg, 2022).

This timely and illuminating book by Emile Pitre describes how structural and cultural racism were manifested at the University of Washington in the late 1960s and early 1970s, the establishment of the Office of Minority Affairs & Diversity, and the program's 50-year legacy. The struggles and protests students initiated on the UW campus to increase the enrollment of students of color, obtain more faculty of color, and reform the curriculum to reflect the racial and ethnic diversity within American life, parallel the experiences that Black and other students of color had on other White-serving institutions' (WSIs) campuses at that time. The book is an important case study of the efforts of students of color to diversify WSIs' campuses and the costs and benefits of social protest and action on a university campus. Shaun Harper (2020), a past president of the American Educational Research Association, perceptively states that student uprisings "made campuses better, more diverse, more inclusive, more responsive, and more accountable" (p. xvi).

Racism had rarely been challenged or recognized by UW administrators and faculty since the founding of the University in 1861. Joyce King and

Chike Akua (2012) call the kind of racism that existed at the UW in the late 1960s and early 1970s "dysconscious racism," which is "an uncritical habit of mind (including perceptions, attitudes, assumptions, and beliefs) that justifies the existing order of things as given." It is also "an uncritical habit of mind that lacks any ethical judgment regarding critique of systemic racial inequity" (p. 723). The institutionalized racism at the UW in the late 1960s and early 1970s was neither as blatant nor as egregious as the racism I experienced as a Black Southerner growing up in the racially segregated Arkansas Delta in the 1950s and 1960s, where a statue of Robert E. Lee dominated the town square in Marianna, Arkansas. Rather, racism at the University of Washington was subtle, the kind of racism Robin Di Angelo (2021) refers to as "nice racism."

The small number of African American and other students of color on campus, as well as the tiny percentage of faculty and administrators of color, were indications of the institutional, structural, and dysconcious racism at the UW. The statistics on faculty, students, and administrators of color were comparable to their representation at other WSIs. In the 1967–1968 school year, there were five Black faculty members in a UW faculty of 1,900.

Pitre describes, with riveting and engaging details from extensive participants interviews, how the African American students who organized and constituted the Black Student Union took actions destined to diversify the student body, the faculty, and the curriculum in significant ways. Their sober and determined social action culminated in the occupation of the office of President Charles Odegaard in 1968, and ultimately resulted in the establishment of the Office of Minority Affairs & Diversity and the appointment of Samuel E. Kelly as the first vice president for Minority Affairs (Kelly & Taylor, 2010).

As Pitre astutely points out, the outcome of the students' occupation of Odegaard's office resulted, in part, from Odegaard's democratic values and commitment to creating an environment at the university that respected and honored diversity (Odegaard, 2000). Odeggard was also an adept and perceptive administrator. He refused, for example, to have the police intervene in the office occupation incident, as had President Grayson L. Kirk at Columbia University when students occupied his office. The result was catastrophic when Kirk turned 1,000 police officers in riot gear against student protesters. Student protest intensified and Columbia closed for the reminder of the semester.

Pitre amply documents the successes of the Office of Minority Affairs & Diversity, including the ways in which it established nationally recognized tutorial and counseling programs, the Ethnic Cultural Center, the Ethnic Cultural Theater, and the successes of its graduates and their impact and leadership across the nation. He describes how ethnic tensions, suspicions, and interethnic conflicts, characteristic of ethnic groups throughout the nation, were also reflected among ethnic and racial groups within the Office of Minority Affairs & Diversity. Pitre also details the challenges of establishing and securing funds to sustain a program designed for students who have the *potential* for academic success but, because of structural, racial, and class inequality, need institutional help, support, and encouragement to be successful in a large research state university environment.

Pitre describes why leaders with knowledge, political acumen, administrative skills, and a commitment to diversity have been essential for the survival of the Office of Minority Affairs & Diversity. During its 50 years, the program has been led by several visionary and effective vice presidents, including Samuel E. Kelly, the first individual to lead the office. Kelly, with rich administrative experiences during his military career, wisely asked President Charles Odegaard to make the head of the Office of Minority Affairs & Diversity a vice president so that the individual could interact and negotiate directly with the university president. Other able and creative leaders who effectively led the Office of Minority Affairs & Diversity during its 50 years include Herman Lujan, Rusty Barceló, Myron Apilado, Shelia Edwards Lange, and Rickey Hall, who currently holds the position.

I am personally grateful for the actions the Black Student Union took to increase diversity at the University of Washington. As a result of the robust national movement in the late 1960s and early 1970s to reduce institutionalized racism within the nation writ large, including within colleges and universities, and as a result of student action and protest at the University of Washington, various colleges and departments hired their first Black professors. James A. Goodman was hired in 1967 as the first African American vice-provost with an academic appointment in the School of Social Work. John W. Macklin became a faculty member in the chemistry department in 1968. In 1969, I was the first Black professor hired by the College of Education (Brown, 2018). Jacob Lawrence, the eminent artist, was recruited and joined the art faculty in 1971. Thaddeus Spratlen (2021) was hired in the School of Business in 1972. Albert W. Black Jr. joined the sociology department faculty in 1973.

The University of Washington, like other WSIs, also responded to student protest by establishing programs in Black Studies, Asian/Pacific Islander Studies, Chicano/a Studies, and American Indian Studies. David Llorens, a writer and an associate editor of *Ebony* magazine in Chicago, was recruited to direct the newly established Black Studies program.

I extend warm congratulations and deep appreciation to Emile Pitre for researching and writing this historically significant and landmark book chronicling the origins, struggles, and triumphs of the Office of Minority Affairs & Diversity at the University of Washington. His effort is a true gift to the UW, the regional community, and scholars interested in diversity throughout the nation. This book is inspiring and hopeful because it describes how student activism played a decisive role in challenging cultural and institutional racism and diversifying the UW's students, faculty, administrators, and the curriculum, a process that continues still fifty years later.

—*James A. Banks, University of Washington, Seattle*

James A. Banks is Kerry and Linda Killinger Endowed Chair in Diveristy Studies Emeritus at the University of Washington, Seattle. He was the Russell F. Stark Univeristy Professor at the UW from 2000 to 2006 and founding director of the Center for Multicultural Education from 1992 to 2018, renamed the Banks Center for Educational Justice.

Garry Owens (second from left), Jimmy Groves (third from front), and other UW students march in front of the UW administration building.

Introduction

I have often wondered if you know what a profound difference you made in my life. Almost 30 years ago now I was a street kid, my parents were on drugs, I had no resources, and very little education. I had attended an alternative high school that required little effort to graduate, and I applied to the UW and was admitted through the EOP. I would not have graduated without the instructional center and your guidance in particular. I don't know if you remember me, but I spent all day every day at the IC. . . . After a few years I was hired by the IC where I tutored chemistry for several years. It felt amazing to help other students, and I loved being at the IC.

—Corey Ray Thomas, high school chemistry teacher of 25 years, writing to the author, Emile Pitre, 2015

My IC tutors [instructors] supported me when the difficulties of being a first-generation college student became overwhelming and celebrated with me when I reached my accomplishments. I CANNOT say enough about how special this place was and how much it contributed to levelling the playing field."

—Anisa Ibrahim, former Somalian refugee, Harborview Pediatrics Clinic Medical Director and UW Department of Pediatrics clinical assistant professor

How the University of Washington (UW) Office of Minority Affairs & Diversity (OMA&D) and its signature program, the Educational Opportunity Program (EOP), came into being is a complicated story. It's Corey Ray Thomas's story, Anisa's story, and the story of so many others like them at the UW and within the UW's embrace—students, faculty, staff, administrators, community members—dedicated and driven individuals pushing ever forward and together for a better future.

Over the past 50 years, the program established to serve minority and economically/educationally disadvantaged students has grown from the Special Education Program with a staff of 10 and a budget of $50,000, to the Office of Minority Affairs & Diversity with a staff of 124 and an annual budget of $18M. In addition to the family of programs that support the Educational Opportunity Program (from 1970 to today), another 22 programs are subsumed under the aegis of OMA&D, 13 of which are federally funded. Many of these programs have been added to facilitate access to the University and to urge students and their families to start thinking about college as early as middle school. The number of student recruiters, who are among the most successful advocates for OMA&D, has increased five-fold, from eight in 1968 to 40 in 2017.

At the core of this story lies a movement fueled by the unwavering desire of a passionate group of individuals to face head-on the issues of educational equity and social justice. Like many campaigns in predominantly white institutions (PWIs) in 1968 and beyond, it was born from student movements generally and Black student movements in particular—a phenomenon that fomented the Black Revolution.

If not for the catalytic role played by students in transforming the landscape on these campuses, change likely would have occurred incrementally at best, over many years. After all, many PWIs had been in existence for more than a century and the landscape remained virtually homogeneous even in

Demonstrations by UW students against the Vietnam War and social injustices mirrored protests on campuses across the nation.

northern cities. In most instances, a revolutionary mindset and a strong sense of urgency was required to bring about substantive change. Such was the case at the University of Washington in Seattle.

Through intellectual analysis and an innate sense that something was not right, a small cadre of individuals at the UW became increasingly aware of contradictions that were reaching heights of undeniable blatancy. It was time for change and a movement at the University of Washington.

The need led to the transformation of an essentially apolitical student organization—the Afro-American Student Society—into a highly politically conscious group—the Black Student Union (BSU). The students were inspired by the revolutionary language of Black Power espoused by Stokely Carmichael and by readings about the history of oppression and exploitation of Black and Third World people in the US and worldwide.

The stirrings culminated in a set of circumstances and events that reached a critical mass and demanded a turning point: a revolution. Even though this journey was not revolutionary in the true sense of the word, the fact that activists with a revolutionary mindset, and without fear of reprisal, boldly insisted on changes to the curriculum, on how a subset of applicants was recruited and admitted to the University, and on how support should be provided to facilitate their matriculation once admitted *was* essentially revolutionary.

Their efforts led to the establishment of a program that grew to become the finest program of its kind in the land. The growth was sometimes by leaps and bounds and at other times slow but steady; the movement sometimes encountered bumps in the road and at other times smooth stretches. At all times, it moved forward with optimism and a determination.

To tell this story, it is necessary to go back to 1960 with the founding of the Student Nonviolent Coordinating Committee (SNCC) and the subsequent years. SNCC provided the training ground for two field workers who, equipped with knowledge of the organization's major tenets, would have the vision to take the movement from the South to college campuses on the West Coast. The first stop was San Francisco State College where the first Black Student Union was established and where the first Black Studies program was created. They then took the movement to other universities in the state of California, and later all the way up to the northwest corner of the contiguous United States at the University of Washington.

Abbreviations

ACE Asian Coalition for Equality

AISA American Indian Student Association

BSU Black Student Union

CAMP Central Area Motivation Program

ECC Ethnic Cultural Center

ECT Ethnic Cultural Theater

EDW Enterprise Data Warehouse

EOP Educational Opportunity Program

FEOP Friends of the Educational Opportunity Program

HBCU Historically Black Colleges and Universities

MEChA Movimiento Estudiantil Chicano de Aztlan

OMA Office of Minority Affairs

OMA&D Office of Minority Affairs & Diversity

PWI Predominantly White Institution

SAB Student Advisory Board

SCLC Southern Christian Leadership Conference

SEP Special Education Program

SNCC Student Nonviolent Coordinating Committee

UMAS United Mexican American Students

URM Underrepresented Minority

UW University of Washington

UWLSC University of Washington Libraries Special Collections

LA SNCC Director Jimmy Garrett, at a Selma Bloody Sunday demonstration, 1965.

Kathleen Halley (Nafasi), (center, top) Black Panther member and a BSU founder, 1969.

Revolution to Evolution details the irrepressible efforts of the BSU, with support from white students and selected faculty, to insist that the University take definitive steps to answer the call of social justice and educational equity for a people who had been virtually overlooked and neglected during the institution's first 107 years. This account describes the actions of the BSU and its supporters leading up to and during the cornerstone confrontation with the University administration, as well as the eventual resolution and plans to address the equity and justice issues, thus ending the revolutionary journey and beginning the evolutionary journey of OMA&D over the next 50-plus years.

The evolutionary journey of OMA&D developed in phases coinciding with the tenure of each of the UW's eight vice presidents. These phases highlight events of historical importance, significant controversies and their root causes and resolution strategies, salient contributions and accomplishments of the students and staff, and the directing and redirecting of focus and priorities over a 50-year time span.

It's a story of recruitment, enrollment, retention, staffing, budgetary challenges, educational outcomes graduation rates, academic performance, degrees earned, and best practices, but never a bend in commitment or persistence.

Ultimately, it is a journey about people and the intersection of OMA&D with other campus entities, the communities from whence students served by OMA&D came, and the communities those students later stepped out into. It's about staff and alumni who serve as models of success, not only giving back but also paying it forward to help others reach their maximum potential.

Revolution to Evolution is a story of how a minority program progressed from the margins of an educational institution to become a significant

Black Panther founder Bobby Seale speaks at the UW HUB, with Seattle activist Tony Orange (left) and Chicago Black Panther Billy Che Brooks (right), circa 1972.

contributor to the educational outcomes of the greater student body with reach far beyond the campus. The OMA&D community's steadfast attention to student-focused relevancy paved a path for programs that are considered national models, that have garnered countless achievements and awards, and that have elevated OMA&D to the distinction of a program of firsts. *Revolution to Evolution* brings the program's history to the table and makes the case not only for why the program still exists after more than a half a century, but also for why its continuing into the next is imperative.

A Note: The original name of the Office of Minority Affairs, headed by Vice President Sam Kelly, is referred to as OMA, the abbreviation that was used until Rusty Barcelo's term as vice president. When her duties expanded to include a vice provost title responsible for broader university-wide programs to encourage diversity, the name became Office of Minority Affairs & Diversity to recognize that change. When Sheila Edwards Lange became vice president and vice provost in 2007, the abbreviation became OMA/D. The abbreviations changed, but the fundamental missions remained constant as programs, staff, and responsibilities evolved.

A Program of Firsts

Addressing the needs that are unique to students served by the Office of Minority Affairs & Diversity requires being innovative and willing to implement strategies and programs that may not be preceded by anything done before with programs at peer institutions.

This means that, in many instances, OMA&D became a program of "firsts." The following examples distinguish the UW as a national leader.

- *OMA&D was the first minority program in the country to be led by a vice president, a level where this individual would not be buffered by an executive director, dean, or even the provost, but would have direct access to the president of the University.*
- *OMA&D was the first minority-serving program to serve economically disadvantaged white students.*
- *OMA&D was the first to implement a prison education program allowing inmates to be under the supervision of the Department of Corrections while living in a campus residential building to pursue their college education. What was even more impressive was the bold decision to implement this high-risk program just two years after Dr. Sam Kelly was appointed vice president of OMA. The program lasted for 10 years and during that period at least 268 Resident Release Project participants earned bachelor's degrees. One earned a doctorate degree.*
- *The OMA&D Instructional Center (IC) was the first academic support program to be established on the UW campus:*
  - The IC was the first to employ discipline-specific professional instructors along with a large cadre of peer tutors to provide academic support in the form of multifaceted teaching strategies, including teaching students to learn how to learn—in essence, "teaching them to fish."
  - The IC was the first program to electronically track student usage by course and duration of each visit.

Students using IC services to strengthen their learning strategies.

- In addition to providing support in UW undergraduate courses, the IC was the first to offer professional exam preparatory classes, including the Medical College Admission Test (MCAT), Dental Admission Test (DAT), Graduate Record Exam (GRE), Law School Admission test (LSAT), PCAT (Pharmacy College Admissions Test), and OAT (Optometry Admissions Test). At least three programs on the UW Seattle campus and one each on the UW Bothell and Tacoma campuses adopted this model.

- The Ethnic Cultural Center was the first (and largest) cultural center in the country to provide social and leadership development support to students of color in a multi-ethnic environment. Also, the Ethnic Cultural Center was the first building on the UW campus to be named for a person of color, Samuel E. Kelly, the founding vice president for Minority Affairs.

- The OMA&D Early Identification Program was the first to host and sponsor a research conference, held on the University of Washington campus.

CHAPTER 1

Setting the Stage: Building Toward that Defining Moment

There was a festive aura that night. The balcony, and every seat and every place to stand was filled to capacity, and everywhere you could look in and around the school, and inside the huge auditorium was bathed in the harsh glare of flashing bulbs and TV lights illuminating crowds of civilians and the uniformed cops, firemen, school security guards, plain-clothed cops, and reporters. The authorities and the press were like schools of sharks nervously overwhelmed and temporarily rendered impotent by the enthusiasm and excitement of a new sea full of dark and light faces all laughing and applauding someone they were trained to despise.

The speech was brilliant, well-crafted, rehearsed, and delivered at a rapid-fire pace with lilting singsong repeats for emphasis. The audience, including a goodly number of young women, treated him like a rock star clinging to his every word and cheering wildly

—Carl Miller's description of evening of Stokely Carmichael's speech at Garfield High School, April 1967

The civil rights movement and the Vietnam protests were the impetus for the Black student movements on campuses at predominantly white institutions (PWI) across the nation in 1968 and 1969. In the case of the Black student movement at the University of Washington, events in the fall of 1967 and spring of 1968 were born out of the Student Nonviolent Coordinating Committee (SNCC) that was founded almost a decade earlier in 1960. According to Stanford University's Martin Luther King Research and Education Center, an SNCC youth conference was held at Shaw University, Raleigh, North Carolina. Organized by Ella Baker, a longtime activist, the conference included students who had participated in lunch-counter sit-ins as well as college students affiliated with the Southern Christian Leadership Conference (SCLC). The purpose of the conference was to motivate participants to take more aggressive action steps than those of the SCLC. At the time, the group's main emphasis was participating in sit-ins and voter registration drives. Later, some SNCC members participated in the Freedom Rides organized by Congress of Racial Equality (CORE). The Rides were aimed at integrating buses traveling from the North to the South. The disruption of the status quo by staging sit-ins, became an important strategy in effecting change on college campuses regardless of PWI and Historically Black Colleges and Universities (HBCU) status (Stanford University).

One of the tenets of the SNCC was the concept of participatory democracy, which emphasized consensus decision making. The SNCC also emphasized the concept of the principles of self-education, self-respect, and self-determination, especially under Stokely Carmichael's leadership. At the forefront of the Black Power movement and leader of the SNCC, Carmichael encouraged students on college campuses, as well as community folk, to learn their history and not to be duped by the notion that integration was a panacea. He insisted that integration could be a threat to the integrity of the culture and lifestyles of Black people. Thus, his clarion call to Black people was to embrace Black Power.

So, how did the SNCC make its way to Seattle and the University of Washington? In 1966, Carl Miller was discharged from the army and then enrolled at Seattle Central Community College. What the SNCC was doing nationally resonated with him, so much so that he decided to establish an SNCC chapter in the city. Not knowing exactly how to go about making the group functional, he contacted SNCC headquarters for help. They sent Emanuel James Brisker, Jr., universally known as E.J., a brilliant activist and experienced organizer, to provide consultation.

It was in Atlanta where Brisker participated in his first sit-in at Woolworth's. He was just 17 years old. At the time, Brisker was a student at Morehouse College, a Historically Black College, where he met Julian Bond. This was Brisker's first involvement with political activism and with the SNCC. He would later meet John R. Lewis, Robert Moses, and James Forman. For the next six years, he participated in the Freedom Rides, gaining valuable insights into the struggle, as well as first-hand organizing experience. In 1964, he met Jimmy Garrett who had joined SNCC in 1963. They both participated in the Mississippi voters registration training in Oxford, Ohio. It was during this period the news came that two previous trainees, Schwerner and Chaney, had been kidnapped and murdered in Philadelphia, Mississippi. Profoundly shaken by the news, he wrote a piece described by *Jet Magazine* as eloquent. It read:

> *I am crying—crying for three people missing in action in what promises to be one of the most brutal wars in history. . . . But the tears . . . and the hollow feeling in my stomach are not for (the three) who, as I write, might be suffering from anything from castration to death. My cry is also for the parents of these three people who wait alone with fear in their hearts. And in a true and vivid sense I cry for America . . . because Americans in general do not yet realize the seriousness of the situation in Mississippi. . . . It is as if police are saying that if your daughter or son tries to help Negroes in Mississippi, I will beat your son, and if necessary, I will kill your daughter* (Preparing for Miss., 1964, p. 6).

Perhaps Brisker was crying tears of gratitude for his life being spared; he was scheduled to accompany the three civil rights activists on their trip to Mississippi but did not show up in time.

Brisker and Garrett again crossed paths a year later by way of James Hill, who led the Arkansas state project aimed at recruiting people to work in the SNCC.

After consulting with Brisker, Miller became chair of the Seattle chapter. The popular myth was that Miller and Brisker met while they were serving as field workers for SNCC down south, and that they came to Seattle to establish a SNCC chapter. But Miller was already in Seattle and had reached out to SNCC for help. So much for rumors. Together, they were successful in attracting both students and community members to the Seattle chapter. A roster of active members was not kept for fear that the names of members would end up in FBI and Counterintelligence Program (COINTELPRO) files, and result in constant scrutiny by these agencies that considered groups such as the SNCC to be "subversive." Based on oral accounts, which by no means are exhaustive, other members of the chapter included Elmer and Aaron Dixon, Kathy Halley, Garry Owens, Sam Sneed, Chester Northington, Louis Keith, Kathy Jones, Jeri Ware, Anthony Ware, Gwynn Morgan, Bobby Morgan, Rose Young, Sylvia Young, and Infanta Spence.

For some of the SNCC charter members, it was imperative that the organization evolve to the next phase of the movement. According to Garrett, a key idea was to create Black Student Unions on PWI campuses, especially on the West Coast. In addition to Garrett, Bob Moses and Charlie Cobb participated in this effort. The idea came to fruition in March 1966 when Garrett and two other activists, Tom Williams and Jerry Varnado, founded the first BSU in the country at San Francisco State College (now San Francisco State University). The primary purpose of this organization was to recruit Black students and work toward the creation of a Black Studies program. To achieve these goals, Garrett moved to forge a working relationship with the president of the college providing the group access to key decision makers. The next phase was to begin organizing BSUs in middle and high schools, as well as community colleges.

The Makings of a Revolutionary Organization

In 1964, Larry Gossett, a graduate of Benjamin Franklin High School in Seattle, enrolled at the UW. Gossett noticed there were very few students on campus who looked like him. By his count, there were just 63 Black students in a student body of 21,000. That same year, Lee Leavy, who had experienced

UNIVERSITY OF WASHINGTON DAILY

C18   SEATTLE, WASHINGTON, THURSDAY, FEBRUARY 10, 1966   No. 61

Governor Blames States For Federal Ascendancy

By GREGG HERRINGTON

Gov. Dan Evans b l a m e d states, not the federal government, for continued usurpation of state and local power by the national administration in a speech delivered in the HUB Auditorium yesterday.

Evans said the states will be forced to streamline their governments and show an ability for getting things done themselves if they want to retain traditional state powers.

"I believe strongly in a state-local-federal government partnership, but the state and local governments are becoming junior partners or not partners at all," he said.

"You can't complain about this drift of power," he continued, "you've got to do something about it."

EVANS ALSO talked about "The Blueprint for Progress," his four-year plan for Washington State government which he began to initiate upon assuming the governor's office last January.

Evans said he hoped a call for a state constitutional convention would receive top priority on the 1967 state legislative agenda. He said there is a definite need for a more flexible state constitution.

The 40-year-old University engineering graduate-turned-politician said the Design for the Washington Conference last December recommending several changes in the state executive branch was also a step toward making the state government more efficient.

Evans kicked off his speech by declaring the major problem that faced him when he took office was the provision of jobs for the growing number of people entering the work force.

"The situation has changed almost 100 per cent, we now need people to fill the jobs," he said.

EVANS CITED rapid industrial expansion at Boeing and throughout the state as the reason for the about-face in the employment situation.

He said reduction of the business and occupation tax in m a n y Washington industries and increased efforts to pro-

(Continued on Page 13)

staff photo by jim loomis

Gov. Dan Evans outlined his "Blueprint for Progress" in a speech in the HUB Auditorium yesterday.

staff photo by dave hatfield

No, it's not a pick-in. Lee Leavy is dressed like a slave to bring attention to National Negro History Week and a speech by Seattle Negro leader Keve Bray in the HUB auditorium at 12:30 p.m. today. He succeeded.

Nobel Prize Winner Named Danz Lecturer

Dr. F. H. Compton Crick, British Nobel Prize winner in turer in other American uni-

The *UW Daily* features Lee Leavy's enactment of a slave scene intended to draw attention to Negro History Week.

racially motivated brutality by the San Diego police, transferred to the UW. He, too, was bothered by the fact that he seldom crossed paths with other "Negro" students. Although these men were not pleased with the circumstances, no viable solution to this problem was seen.

Two years later, Larry Gossett prepared to leave the University to join VISTA (Volunteers in Service to America). Before leaving, however, he witnessed the first harbinger of Black consciousness at UW during what was then called Negro History Week. Leavy enacted a slave scene in front of the Husky Union Building (HUB). The slave was picking cotton and singing Negro spirituals. According to Leavy, he wanted to draw attention to a campus where Black students were virtually invisible. He further stated, "Black people should not be ashamed of where we came from and never turn our backs on our ancestors who sacrificed a great deal in order to ensure that the race survived." He went on to say that "We should not relinquish this stance no matter how out of place it may appear to others, even other Black people."

This act created a buzz on campus. Gossett found himself placed in the position of having to explain to UW administrators and other "Negro" students what was going on here. Word spread as far as the Governor's office. Dan Evans, governor at the time, asked to meet with Leavy, but Leavy declined. Leavy's actions served as a springboard that led to a small number of Black students coming together to organize for, in the minds of some of the students, psychological and social support. Dan Keith, along with Onye Akwari, who organized the group, stated, "The organization's purpose was to bring about better cultural understanding among Black students" (Doctor, 1968, p. 6). Others who were present included Patsy Mose, Pauline Alley (now known as Royal Alley-Barnes), and James Ashford. According to Leavy, fewer than 10 students met. Three names for the group were proposed: Africa dela America, Afro-American Student Society, and Black Student Association. Afro-American Student Society was chosen.

In the fall of that same year, Eddie Demmings, Verlaine Keith, and Eddie Walker, classmates at Seattle's Cleveland High School, enrolled at the University of Washington. All three were very capable students and were eager to pursue higher education. Eddie Walker was salutatorian of his graduating class. During his salutatory speech, he spoke about injustices faced by Black people in America. Demmings entered the University anticipating that it would be overwhelmingly white, but he had no idea how profoundly he would be affected by that fact. He said, "I absolutely hated it. It affected me physically." He went on to say, "I was angry, and a big part of what fueled this anger was the fact that my parents paid taxes. Why were there not more of us here?" The disproportionality was a blatant contradiction. It was a sign that something was very wrong. It was at this point that the seed of Black consciousness was planted. Demmings asserted, "In the words of Malcom X, we have been had." For Verlaine, the experience was totally different. She initially experienced no adverse effects. Her pathway to an emerging Black consciousness would crystallize a year later.

The next sequence of events would provide the soil needed for the seed of Black consciousness to germinate. It began with Stokely Carmichael coming to Seattle. So how did that happen? Rumor had it that E.J. Brisker and Carl Miller were front men for Carmichael and had set it up. Not exactly. Once the Seattle SNCC chapter was firmly established, the group inquired about what it would take to have Carmichael come to Seattle. The response was not very encouraging. The cost was prohibitive—at least $1,000. A short time later, another call came from SNCC headquarters in Atlanta informing the Seattle leadership that Carmichael was scheduled to give a speech at the University of Washington. According to Miller, all they knew was that a white anti-war group financed the visit and talk. No one from the BSU knew the name of the individual or group. Neither did anyone from the Students for a Democratic Society (SDS) nor the Young Socialist Alliance (YSA) have any idea. It was later learned that a group called The Political Union, supported by UW history professor Giovanni Costigan and Michael Lerner of the Seattle Liberation Front, sponsored the event. It was financed by the Associated Students of the University of Washington (ASUW) with approval from the Board of Control. Carmichael was paid $500 and half the receipts from a 25-cent admission fee.

The *University of Washington Daily* follows up Carmichael's April 19, 1967, speech held at Hec Ed Pavilion.

More than 3,000 students, faculty, and staff attended the UW event held at the Hec Edmundson Pavilion. Carmichael spoke about "the Negro need to reclaim his history and identity from the cultural terrorism and depredation of self-justifying white guilt." He criticized the press for its biased coverage of the Black Power movement. Carmichael asserted that integration was meaningless if it is not accompanied by power—that is, the power to maintain racial and cultural identity. He divided racism into two types—individual and institutionalized. He spoke about the lack of control of such things as resources, political decisions, law enforcement, and housing, including standards as well as physical structures. Carmichael spoke of the leadership not being beholden to the white press and power structure, which implies white superiority. That it should, instead, work toward collective power in the Negro community—an overarching goal of the SNCC.

Regarding how whites could participate in the Black Power Movement, Carmichael suggested they could either challenge whites who speak against Negroes or teach whites to be more civil toward Negroes. He emphasized that whites could only be committed at an intellectual level, but never at an emotional level because "they just don't understand what it is to be Black" (Todd, 1967).

In addition to Carmichael speaking at UW, SNCC headquarters informed the Seattle chapter that it would only charge the chapter one dollar to sponsor Carmichael if the chapter would pay for transportation and lodging and schedule a talk in the Black community. The necessary funds were garnered with the help of prominent members of the community, including the Reverend Samuel McKinney and Cliff Hooper. Garfield High School auditorium was selected as the venue. However, there was resistance to the notion of an activist speaking at a Seattle Public Schools' facility. The School Board denied the request. The American Civil Liberties Union (ACLU) intervened, and Judge Frank James overruled the Board's decision citing the right to free speech (Stevens, 2015).

A crowd estimated at around 4,000 reportedly was captivated by Carmichael's words throughout his entire talk (Smith, 1967).

The speech set the tone for the movement and, according to Miller, contained coded instructions for activists including, as expected, an emphasis on:

- *Black pride (Black is Beautiful, no attacking brothers and sisters)*
- *Black power and economics (We don't own a single Caddy Dealership)*
- *Higher education (not one Black face in the UW audience)*
- *A new emphasis on Ethnic Studies (want to read about people like you and me)*
- *An end to Police Brutality through Political power (Register and Vote)*
- *Militant direct action (We got to stick it to the man) and,*
- *A surprising new stance against the war in Vietnam (Ain't no Viet Cong ever called me Ni**er).*

According to the UW student newspaper, *The Daily*, "As he spoke a number of Negroes who had accompanied him began to form a circle around the edges of the building's ground floor and balcony" (Todd, 1967, p.1). These were SNCC members.

In his speech, Carmichael referred to readings about people "like you and me." He specifically mentioned Frederick Douglass, Denmark Vesey, W.E.B. DuBois, Leroi Jones (aka Amiri Baraka), Richard Wright, J.A. (Joel Augustus) Rogers, Countee Cullen, Malcolm X, and Martin Luther King. He also mentioned George Washington Carver, but only in a negative light. Carmichael emphasized the need for Black children to know about Africa and the exploits of Hannibal. To drive his point home he stated emphatically, ". . . because a people without its roots, a people without its history, is like a tree without its roots and we have been floating for 400 hundred years" (Stevens, 2015).

As can be seen from these accounts, Carmichael's talk was markedly different at Garfield than the one he gave at UW. A *Seattle Times* reporter described Carmichael's speech at UW as scholarly, whereas at Garfield his speech was more on an emotional level where he was described as "warm, more smiling—theatrical at times" (Smith, 1967, p. 7; Cour & Evans, 1967, p.1).

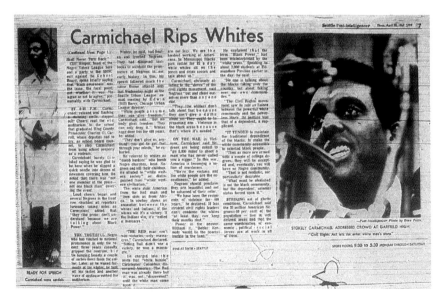

Carmichael's April 1967 speech for the community at Garfield High highlighted in *Seattle Post-Intelligencer*.

According to Eddie Demmings, who witnessed the event, Stokely Carmichael's Garfield speech had a profound effect on the Black community. Larry Gossett later asserted, "Before Stokely spoke, community members referred to themselves as Negroes. Afterwards, they called themselves Black. It was a transformative experience for Aaron Dixon, who at the time was a high school student at Garfield. From then on, he would view Black people and the Black community through a different set of lenses. It truly was a defining moment.

Those members of the UW's Afro-American Student Society who were in attendance left the event inspired and further motivated to cultivate their growing political/Black consciousness. On a personal note, I was not yet at the UW. As a senior at Southern University, an HBCU, I had the opportunity to hear Carmichael speak in early spring of 1967, and I can attest to the effect he had on his audiences. What he had to say further catalyzed the embryonic stage of a transformation toward a well-defined Black political consciousness. "Black" rather than "Negro," and challenging the 350 years of social injustices that had been perpetrated against oppressed people, resonated strongly with everyone who heard him speak.

Compared to Carmichael's speech at UW's Hec Edmundson Pavilion, little was reported by the media about the Garfield speech, except that the event drew a crowd of about 4,000, and that Carmichael stated, "No one is talking about the blacks taking over the country, but about taking over our own community" (Cour and Evans, 1967).

The further cultivation of the UW Black students' political and Black consciousness came about as a result of studying the works of a myriad of writers, many of whom were activists/revolutionaries. This budding consciousness was nurtured by students reading and analyzing books about Black history from Africa to the Jim Crow era; the struggle for civil rights in America; critiques of integrationists and Black Nationalists; the history of Black people as told through their music; contradictions of the American Dream for Black people; a history of exploitation in America; the relationship between ethnocentrism, racism, and capitalism; racism and Black identity; and societal disowning.

These readings, discussions, and analyses provided a strong foundation for understanding what was missing in the education available to Black students at the University and the realization that the issues were broader than what was happening at the UW, in Seattle, and in the United States for that matter. Their consciousness expanded to a Third World view. Intellectual fodder for this growth came from readings on colonialism; racial difference and revolutionary struggle; Black identity and critical race theory; revolutionary struggles against colonialism in Africa, Asia, and South America; unity; and vanguardism. The reading lists were diverse, and covered writings by revolutionaries from around the world, providing students an understanding of the intersection of oppression, exploitation, and racism, and their relationship to politics and economics.

It became clear that the struggle involved other races and ethnicities. E.J. Brisker was the revolutionary theorist who stimulated the group's revolutionary conscience by encouraging the group to read such works as *The Autobiography of Malcom X* (Alex Haley) and *Before the Mayflower* (Lerone Bennett). Carl Miller said he read each of the two books in one night.

While the seeds of political/Black/Third World consciousness were germinating among some members of the Afro-American Student Society and the Seattle chapter of SNCC, Larry Gossett was becoming politicized and radicalized while serving in VISTA (Volunteers in Service to America) in Toledo, Ohio, and New York City (Harlem) between March 1966 and

Brisker's Early Reading List

Other books Brisker encouraged people to read included *The Souls of Black Folk* (W.E.B. DuBois); *The Crisis of the Negro Intellectual* (Harold Cruse); *A People's History of the United States* (Howard Zinn); *Blues People: Negro Music in White America* (Leroi Jones); *The Wretched of the Earth* (Frantz Fanon); *Up from Slavery* (John Hope Franklin); *Black Skin White Masks* (Frantz Fanon); *Diary of Che Guevara* (Ernesto Guevara); *Class Struggle in Africa* (Kwame Nkrumah); *Caste, Class and Race* (Oliver Cox); *The Spook Who Sat by the Door* (Sam Greenlee); along with articles by Amilcar Cabral, Jomo Kenyatta, and Ho Chi Minh to name a few.

In addition to recommendations by Brisker, others who offered recommendations that resulted in a list of at least 35 books included Miller, Gossett, Demmings, Owens, and Keith-Miller. A quasi-exhaustive list is included as Appendix A.

September 1967. Gossett stated, "So by the time I came home [to Seattle], my name had changed, my thought patterns had changed, my value system had completely changed, my ideology had changed, and my commitment to the struggle of oppressed Black and other people was absolutely cemented within my being. Because, I said, in my country, nobody should have to live like this, and I was going to do all I can." He, too, became involved with the Seattle chapter of SNCC, looking to further expand his consciousness. It was around this time, he encouraged Brisker and Miller to enroll at the University of Washington.

While speaking at Garfield, Carmichael mentioned there had been no Blacks in the audience when he spoke at the UW, but there also was no mention of the need to increase the number of Black students attending college at PWIs. In fact, such a notion would have seemed counterintuitive since the emphasis of Carmichael's speech was about Blacks creating their own destiny. However, some charter members of SNCC had other ideas.

Taking a page from the SNCC-founding play book, the group planned and organized a conference to be held in a large metropolitan area of California, such as Los Angeles or San Francisco, and invited youths from the western states to get involved. For more than a year, Jimmy Garrett, along with such SNCC members as H. Rap Brown, James Forman, and George Ware (SNCC campus traveler) proposed a West Coast Black student conference in Los Angeles, CA. Other organizers included Harry Edwards, a professor at San Jose State, whom Garrett credited with having a definitive strategy; Angela Davis, Communist Party member; Elaine Brown, a Black Panther Party member; Ron Maulana Karenga, founder of Organization Us, "US Black People," and Kwanzaa; and Erica Thompson, a UCLA student. Some well-known athletes at the time, including Lew Alcindor (Kareem Abdul-Jabbar), Jim Brown, and Tommy Smith, also helped plan the event. A chief goal was to organize around a boycott of the 1968 Olympics, scheduled for Mexico City.

Garrett, who had known Brisker since 1964 when they both were field workers in SNCC, informed Brisker about the conference and urged him to recruit a group of Black college students to participate. Needed funds were contributed by individuals such as Robby and Susan Stern and Carla Fraser of Students for a Democratic Society, as well as Valarie Rubiscz and Linda Corr, Black members of the Communist Party.

Revolution to Evolution

More than 30 students from Seattle, chaperoned by Jerline Ware and one other parent, rented a Greyhound bus and traveled to the conference during the Thanksgiving break, November 23rd through 25th, 1967. It was reported that, overall, more than 800 youth were in attendance. Plenary sessions focusing on different topics were held in the basement of a church on 42nd Street and Avalon Boulevard. One of those sessions was led by Garrett. At the time of the conference, Garrett was a member of the Black Panther Party and coordinator for the Western Regional Alliance for Black

Jimmy Garrett sharing the *BSU Weekly Campus* update in front of the Student Center at San Francisco State College, spring 1967.

Student Unions (BSU), which boasted a membership of 27 BSUs.

The mandate for action was to establish BSUs at middle and high schools, community colleges, as well as at other universities along the West Coast; establish Black Studies Programs; recruit Black students for enrollment; and call for the establishment of Black cultural centers on white college campuses. The idea for cultural centers was influenced by Sonia Sanchez who led the Black Arts Movement plenary. There was no mention of efforts to increase Black faculty, administrators, and staff at PWIs.

On their return trip to Seattle, many of the participants were highly energized and ready to work for the above goals. Reflecting on the experience, Eddie Demmings stated that he was most impressed by the diversity of opinions. He felt that the conference provided the conduit for Black brothers and sisters to unite and work together to change the situation at UW. The one idea that was most impressive to him and others was that of forming a Black Student Union. Many on the bus ride from LA back to Seattle felt that forming a UW BSU was virtually a done deal.

Fewer than six weeks later, members of the Afro-American Student Society, after much debate, voted to change the name of the group to the Black Student Union.

30

With respect to the gender composition of the group, males outnumbered females by a ratio of two-to-one. Except for Verlaine's role as secretary, women held no other formal leadership position in the BSU. Regarding this visible lack of formal leadership, Larry Gossett (later) stated:

We rarely talk about their role in organizing these historic events and actions and institutions—we're not documenting enough about the historical role that women played into the effort. That is absolutely something that we have not done with the Black Student Union because women were always in the forefront but kind of in the back. But they did the majority of the work consistently, and absent their fundamental commitment, loyalty to the movement, hard work, looking past a lot of the foolishness of some of us crazy Black men, we could have never made the progress that we made.

In particular, Kay Coleman, Verlaine Keith-Miller, Kathy Halley, Leathia Stallworth, Charlotte Moore McAllister, Kathleen Russell, and Frances Johnson should be "lauded for their work ethic, being great spokespersons, and stalwart, respectively" (Gossett, 2016). Along similar lines, Eddie Walker credited the women BSU founders with making things happen when they needed to happen, particularly Kathy Halley, whom he called "a general." Kathy Halley's perspective on the role women played in the revolution was that it was complementary, as well as supportive. Above all else, worthy of note is that all decision-making was collective rather than controlled by formal leaders, and consensus ruled.

It is important to point out that the racial/ethnic composition of the BSU was not homogeneous. At the time, the BSU at UW was believed to be the only Black Student Union in the country that was not all Black. So, how did two American Indians and one Chicano end up as founding members of the BSU at the University of Washington? The common connections were a Black participant named Richard Brown who befriended them, and the Upward Bound Program. Brown was gregarious, engaging, intelligent, and quite articulate. The three non-Black students gravitated to him. They entered UW in the fall of 1966 as a subset of a larger cohort and were inseparable. At the UW, the American Indian women did not encounter anyone who looked like them. They felt left out and were bothered by the way they were being treated on campus—either largely ignored or treated as though they did not

Garry Owens (second from right), Jesus Crowder (left of center), and Eddie Demmings (center) march outside the UW Administration Building.

belong. Jesus Crowder had a similar initial experience, but Brown was his friend, and Crowder wanted to stay connected. In fact, he lived at Brown's home while enrolled at UW.

So, when Brown began attending the Afro-American Student Society meetings, the three joined him. In this environment, they felt accepted and welcomed with open arms. They felt that Brisker was a brilliant and open leader who often relied upon the opinions of others, especially the women (participatory democracy actualized). He welcomed criticism. Along with Eddie Demmings' friendship, they were impressed with his ability to articulate ideas and concepts. Marcie Hall said of Demmings, "If anything needed to be summed up, he would put it into beautiful words."

1968: The Transformative Confrontation

On January 6, 1968, the new name of the Black student organization was announced on the steps of the main entrance of the Husky Union Building (HUB) with Eddie Walker serving as spokesperson.

Eddie, in a very expressive fashion, said something like: "From now on we will be representing Black folks of America and from the African Diaspora on this campus. We have the audacity and the mendacity to state that we will be the only true representatives of Black folks on the University of Washington campus. We choose to represent the Black voice in whatever means that we deem necessary, and we will be effective, and our voice will never, ever be silent. We are the UW's Black power warriors" (Gossett, 2016).

It was not until almost six weeks later that *The Daily* announced the establishment of the new group. In the article there were quotes from William "Dan" Keith, E.J. Brisker, Larry Gossett, and Eddie Demmings. Brisker spoke about a Black studies curriculum that would define Black culture as determined by the Black community. Increasing Black enrollment on campus was one goal. The use of the term "Negro" was rejected. According to Brisker, "'Negro' is an American term that cut off our cultural link to our African Brothers." Gossett spoke about conditional minority enrollment and Demmings emphasized the need to apply pressure to bring about change.

The entire membership of the BSU played an integral role in challenging the issues of racism perpetrated by enclaves of the University toward Black students as well as the Black community at large. Brisker pointed out that the institution was racist, and that the athletic department was the worst of all. Keith spoke about not being absorbed into, but rather maintaining, cultural identity. Brisker's battle cry was, "Power to the People. Black Power to Black People" (Doctor, 1968, p. 6).

The next political and ideological step was to move toward establishing Black Student Unions outside of UW. This strategy, led by Gossett, achieved considerable success with the formation of BSUs at Washington, Meany, Sharples, and Asa Mercer middle schools, as well as Garfield, Franklin, Cleveland, and Rainier Beach high schools. In addition, a BSU was established at Seattle Central Community College. The ease and swiftness of this accomplishment can be attributed to the organizing abilities of Gossett, Brisker, and Miller, coupled with the communal connections many of the members had with the middle and high schools where they, family members, and friends had grown up and had attended.

Concurrent with the organizing efforts, the BSU leadership also examined the University's history of recruitment of non-white students and their subsequent enrollment. Efforts were expanded to conduct an analysis of the status of non-white students (mainly Afro-Americans, American Indians, and Mexican Americans) on the UW campus. Their findings corroborated their suspicions. According to Larry Gossett's estimates, 63 Black students were enrolled at UW between 1964 and 1966. That number had increased to 200 out of the 30,000 students enrolled at UW during the 1967–1968 school year. For American Indians and Mexican Americans, the numbers were a dismal 20 and 10, respectively. It is important to note that there was no way of verifying or disputing these numbers, since the University did not previously keep student records based on race. It was not until Spring Quarter's pre-registration for Fall 1968 that students were asked to voluntarily identify their race/ethnicity, by filling out a census card. Although the University was required to report the ethnic/racial distribution in order to be in compliance with the Civil Rights Act of 1965, the BSU leadership was suspicious of how this information might be used.

BSU leaders' research also revealed that of the more than 1,000 courses offered in the College of Arts and Sciences, none required textbooks written by minority authors—not to mention the fact that the course offerings were not relevant to the experiences and history of Black, American Indians, Chicanos and Third World people (from countries that were colonized) in general. Nor were the lifestyles and cultures of these groups taught. Their findings also revealed that of the hundreds of academic counselors employed at UW, none were from underrepresented groups, i.e., American Indian, Afro-American, and Mexican American.

Leaders in the BSU also investigated the UW's recruitment and hiring practices of Black faculty, staff, and administrators. In all instances, their findings were disappointing. There were no Black administrators, and only five Black faculty members, a few of whom were hired one year earlier—a tiny percent of the total number of UW faculty of almost 1,900. Their findings also revealed that while African American staff were visible, almost all held semi-skilled positions. Moreover, there was not one Black person on the Board of Regents. Armed with these disturbing and unacceptable findings gathered over a four-month period, the BSU leadership began meeting with administrators, including President Charles Odegaard, Dr. Eugene Elliot, members of the Faculty Senate, the admissions director, and the Office of Financial Aid.

About three months after the inception of this newly formed organization, the BSU's political consciousness and radicalization steered it in a direction that led to the reorganization of the leadership. E.J. Brisker became president and Larry Gossett became vice president. Afterwards, activities intensified, compelled by a strong sense of urgency.

The University's administration appeared to be receptive to the need

Thur MAY 9th '68   —P-I Photo by Cary Tolman
BLACK STUDENT UNION LEADERS PRESENTED FIVE DEMANDS AT RALLY AT UW
From left: Eddie Demmings, Carl Miller, Jesse Crowder, E. J. Brisker, Larry Gossett, Ricado Markuma

Black Student Union leaders present their letter
and five demands at a rally.

for change; however, the pace toward acting on its part was slow. The BSU leadership felt that the administration was not sincere and essentially was using stalling tactics to lead the students to give up. Sensing that an impasse was imminent, members drafted a letter and submitted it to President Odegaard on May 6, 1968. The first line of the letter read: "The University of Washington has been and is a racist institution." The letter emphasized that the notion of white superiority and non-white inferiority needed to be dispelled. The letter contained five demands with commentary that led with the following:

(1) All decisions, plans, and programs affecting the lives of black students, must be made in consultation with the Black Student Union . . .

(2) The Black Student Union should be given the financial resources and aids necessary to recruit and tutor non-white students . . .

(3) We demand that a Black Studies Planning Committee be set up under the direction and control of the Black Student Union . . .

. . . We make this demand because we feel that a white, middle-class education cannot and have not met the needs of non-white students. . .

(4) We want to work closely with the administration and faculty to recruit black teachers and administrators . . .

(5) We want black representatives on the music faculty. Specifically, we would like to see Joe Brazil and Byron Polk [Pope] hired . . .

—Black Student Union Letter, 1968, p. 4.

Although not listed in the five demands, the need to change low enrollment of poor white students was noted in a BSU position paper.

So, what was the rationale for demanding that Pope and Brazil join the faculty of the School of Music? Byron Pope, an alto saxophonist, was at the time a professor of jazz and blues at Simon Fraser University, Burnaby, British Columbia. He also was the leader of a jazz ensemble. His major influence was John Coltrane. Joe Brazil was an accomplished musician who had played with John Coltrane, a virtuoso saxophonist. Brazil appeared on the Coltrane album "Om" playing flute and on the Roy Ayers album "Ubiquity." He also played in jazz sessions with well-known musicians such as Donald Bird, Sonny Red, and Joe Henderson.

University of Washington
Black Student Union
Room 92 - Husky Union Bldg.
May 6, 1968

President Charles Odegard
University of Washington
Seattle, Washington

Dear President Odegard:

The University of Washington has been, and is a racist institution. Its function has been, and is to preserve and extend a racist status quo.

Through its administration, faculty, curriculum, and admission policies, the University has sent white and black students into society with the racist notion that white, middle-class, Western ideals and practices are superior.

The average white student leaves the University with the absurd notion that he is superior. The average black student leaves the University with an equally absurd notion that he is inferior.

The phenomenon in the last paragraph can be understood by taking a look at key aspects of the University.

First, the administration. Psychologists talk about the need for youth to have adult models. At this point a non-white student has no model at a high administrative level to imitate and relate to. This is important because non-whites need models they can identify with. They need a non-white administrator who has had similar problems and conflicts.

A second point about the present administration must be made. When a non-white youth comes into contact with administration officials, he is subtly told that he is inferior. He sees white people giving orders and running the school.

From this realization, comes the mistaken idea that there are no non-white people who can run institutions, who can successfully carry out large assignments.

The overall effect of this idea is the stifling of initiative, the decrease and bringing to ahalt of positive dreams and desires. The same effect comes from the non-white student's contact with the faculty. A non-white sitting under a 99% white faculty is subtly being told that only white people can teach him the things he needs to know.

May 6, 1968, Letter to President Odegaard.

A third point must also be made. The faculty are products of a racist-society. Faculty trained in the twenties and thirties came up through an educational system based on the assumption of non-white inferiority. Consciously and/or unconsciously the faculty transmits their racism to black and white students.

One way in which they transmit racism is their ignorance. A professor in Classics, enthused over the wonders of Rome, in many cases is unaware of the great achievements of African Universities such as the University of Timbuktu. This university was a magnet for scholars and philosophers while Europeans were running around in caves.

A professor in Contemporary Literature praising the works of Hemingway or Faulkner, would do well to consider the beauty and power of a Richard Wright or a Claude McKay.

Omissions, distortions, and out-right lies produce students that feel all the great ideas came from whites, and came from the West. As we indicated earlier, the white student believes in the lie of his superiority, and the black student in the lie of his inferiority.

A fourth aspect the Black Student Union feels strongly about is the University admission policies. We've been told that the University does not "discriminate" and that they take all students who are Qualified. We realize that standards are necessary if the University is to produce well-trained people, but we also realize that the present elementary and secondary educational system stifles the desire and creativity necessary for achievement.

The majority of non-white students who pass through the present educational system do not:

(1) gain a knowledge of their past
(2) get encouragement from the faculty and administration.

For example, a non-white student is taught only the achievements of white, he learns about Lincoln (a racist), George Washington (a slaveowner), etc.

When we see these things clearly, we realize that the educational system from kindergarten to graduate school must be changed.

The Black Student Union feels that a good starting place for change is at the university level.

Although the administration, faculty, and admission policies have been racist in effect, the Black Student

2

Union feels the University should be given a chance to change, to prove its "good intentions." As long as we feel the University is making an honest effort to change, the Black Student Union will cooperate and work closely with the University.

However, when the University begins to make phony excuses and racist needed changes, we will be forced to look at the University as an enemy to black people, and act accordingly. In short there will be political consequences for politcal mistakes.

With this last point in mind, the Black Student Union submits the following demands:

(1) All decisions, plans, and programs affecting the lives of black students, must be made in consultation with the Black Student Union. This demand reflects our feeling that whites for too long have controlled the lives of non-whites.
We reject this control, instead we will define what our best interests are, and act accordingly.

(2) The Black Student Union should be given the financial resources and aids necessary to recruit and tutor non-white students. Specifically, the Black Student Union wants to recruit: (1) 300 Afro-American, (2) 200 American Indian, and (3) 100 Mexican students by September.
Quality education is possible through an interaction of diverse groups, classes, and races. Out of a student population of 30,000, there are about 200 Afro-Americans, about 20 American Indians, and about 10 Mexican-Americans.
The present admission policies are slanted toward white, middle-class, Western ideals, and the Black Student Union feels that the University should take these other ideals into consideration their admission procedures.
(3) We demand that a Black Studies Planning Committee be set up under the direction and control of the Black Student Union. The function of this Committee would be to develop a Black Studies Curriculum that objectively studies the culture and life of non-white Americans.

We make this demand because we feel that a white, middle-class education cannot and has not met the needs of non-white students.
At this point, as American Indian interested in studying the limits of great Indians like Sitting Bull and Crazy-Horse has to go outside the school structure to get an objective view. Afro-American members of the Black Student Union have had to go outside the school structure to learn about black heroes like Frederick Douglas, W.B. Debois, and Malcolm X.

3

One effect of going outside the normal educational channels at the University has been to place an extra strain on black students interested in learning more about their culture. We feel that it is up to the University to re-examine its curriculum and provide courses that meet the needs of non-white students.

(4) We want to work closely with the administration and faculty to recruit black teachers and administrators. One positive effect from recruiting black teachers and administrators is that we will have models to imitate, and learn from.

5) We want black representatives on the music faculty. Specifically, we would like to see Joe Brazil and Byron Polls hired. The black man has made significant contributions to music (i.e. jazz and spirituals), yet there are no black teachers on the music faculty.

The five demands above are legitaimate and worthwhile, and we hope you will consider them carefully. In view of the seriousness of these demands, and the need for the University to change, we have set a five day deadline for a reply from you.

We have set this time limit because the University in the past has moved too slowly, has avoided facing key issues squarely.

Sincerely,

Black Student Union

The Black Student Union had allies in wanting to achieve this goal of recruiting more non-white students. Although at the time it seemed like increasing the number of Afro-Americans, American Indians, and Chicanos by a total of 600 was a relatively large number, Arval Morris, chair of the Faculty Council on Community Services and a law professor, believed the number should be higher. Morris thought that, based on the proportion of these groups' population in the area, 750 Black students and 1,500 minority students should be enrolled in the fall of 1968.

The letter submitted to President Odegaard stipulated that he had five days to respond. "Evasive," "too talkative," and "not facing issues squarely" were words and phrases the BSU used to describe Odegaard's tactics heretofore.

Shortly after the submission of this unprecedented letter at UW, a group comprising about 10 percent of the faculty issued a press release stating they supported changing the curriculum to include Black Studies and the hiring of more Black professors.

President Odegaard responded in four days, although the letter was addressed to Dan Keith who had by that time resigned his position as BSU president. The full text of President Odegaard's letter appeared in *The Daily*. This was probably done for two reasons: to counteract the BSU letter from being made public and to document that the administration had indeed responded. Odegaard stated that much of his response had been discussed in a meeting held on April 30, 1968, before BSU's letter was submitted to the administration. He indicated that he supported the BSU demands and suggested ideas regarding how they could be achieved.

With respect to consultation with the BSU regarding the first demand, Odegaard requested assistance in establishing a mechanism for seeking advice and a list of names and contact information for designated consultants.

Odegaard pledged to call a meeting with Frank Byrdwell, a counselor who had been hired in January to work with minority students, to address the recruitment of minority students. Odegaard also wanted to include the BSU, the Faculty Senate Council on Academic Standards, the Board of Admissions, the Board of Advising, the Office of Financial Aid, the Associated Students of the University of Washington (ASUW), the Graduate and Professional Student Senate (GPSS), and selected schools and colleges that were already recruiting Black students. However, no mention was made regarding the implementation of a tutoring program once these students were enrolled. Neither did he commit to providing financial resources and other aid.

Regarding the third demand, Odegaard agreed with the establishment of a Black Studies Planning Committee and acknowledged that "studies of culture and life-style of non-white Americans was an appropriate and needed part of the University curriculum" and pledged to ask for a meeting with the Arts and Sciences Dean and Curriculum Committee.

In terms of hiring more Black teachers and administrators, Odegaard welcomed recommendations from the BSU of names and credentials of prospects that could be forwarded to the appropriate departments and agencies. He stated, "I am sure you know that the deans and other administrative directors have been and are seeking to increase the number of qualified black persons on the University faculty and staff" (Odegaard, 1968a, Box 68). The BSU leadership was skeptical that a good faith effort was being put forth. After all, they thought, how many times has one heard the statement "we tried, but have been unable to find qualified applicants?"

With respect to the fifth and final demand, Odegaard stated that "Conversations have already been held between the black musicians named . . . concerning the incorporation within the school of ways of presenting music by black men" (Odegaard, 1968a, Box 68,). The BSU later found out that there was no serious effort to hire the two musicians, but instead it amounted to offering one or two concerts. For BSU leadership and the body in general, the upshot was that the administration was not opposed to the idea, but its approach held no sense of urgency—exactly opposite to the BSU members' position, which was to get it done now!

The BSU leadership responded to Odegaard's answer in a position paper written on May 17, 1968. The paper noted that meetings between Black students and members of the Black community with President Odegaard had been ongoing for almost a year and the results were "We agree in principle. But. . ." The University's response was perceived as stall tactics. Also, the BSU felt that referring action to various departments and units placed an undue burden on students who were already spending too much time essentially educating the faculty rather than the other way around.

In the meantime, following a meeting with members of the BSU on May 13, Odegaard met with the Board of Deans on May 15, and shared how he thought the situation with BSU should be addressed. He stated, "The black student problem must be dealt with sympathetically and ways must be found to communicate with the rational constructive element [sic] who want to move in our society in a dignified, humane, sensible way, but who face the problem of fitting into a culture which is mostly white." He went on to say, "We have not paid much attention to the dignity of the black movement; we know we have erred and have been slow and have often looked at things through white spectacles" (Odegaard, 1968b).

Meanwhile, in a follow up to the letter of May 6, Brisker demanded that the University make available $50,000 to begin recruiting students for fall quarter. President Odegaard was hesitant to commit to this request citing there was no immediate source of funding. He stated that it would take time. In the interim, the BSU leadership went beyond the confines of the institution in their efforts to make known the situation of Black students on campus and the demands were later presented to Governor Dan Evans at Husky stadium while he was attending the ROTC Governor's Day event. Brisker was accompanied by Miller, chair of the Seattle chapter of SNCC, and Aaron Dixon, captain of the Seattle chapter of the Black Panther Party. The BSU tactics were aggressive and relentless, reflecting the signature personality and leadership style of its president, E.J. Brisker. For Brisker, this approach to getting things done was cultivated during the years he spent as a field worker in SNCC. Brisker, Gossett, Miller, and Demmings, as well as others, were students of revolutionary theory and practice. Being courageous, fearless, and relentless fueled their

Miller, E.J. Brisker, and Aaron Dixon marched to Husky Stadium to present funding demands to Governor Dan Evans while he was attending an ROTC Governor's Day event. (Evans, back to the camera, E.J. Brisker, center; Aaron Dixon, right).

aggressiveness. Channeling the rallying call of revolutionaries of the day, the BSU chose to "seize the time." In reflecting on those times, Brisker made a poignant observation. He said, "People were under the impression that BSU was a rebel-rousing group with no true sense of direction, but we were an intellectual group that acted with purpose."

On May 19, 1968, President Odegaard stated efforts were underway to recruit and provide tutoring for admissions using special consideration. He specifically spoke of "Special recruiting and tutorial arrangements." He also stated that the University was seeking to employ more Negroes (Cour, 1968b; Dunphy, 1968).

Faculty members who supported the BSU's aims submitted a letter to Odegaard the morning of May 20. They included Arval Morris, Simon Ottenburg, and James Goodman. Their letter strongly suggested that immediate action be taken.

Impatient with the snail-like pace of the administration, and after a few days of meetings, demonstrations, and protests, the BSU body came together and using participatory democracy voted to stage a sit-in at President Odegaard's office. Reflecting on this moment, Eddie Demmings stated, "Our thinking was words were not enough; it's just that simple. We gave them words, now we are going to give them action. We gonna shut this thing down to let them know we are serious, and we expect our demands to be met" (Hinckley, 2007). The group considered occupying the office on May 19, 1968 (Malcolm X's birthday); however, that day came on a Sunday. So, they thought—on what day would the occupation have the greatest effect? It was agreed that the next best alternative would be Monday when it was thought that Governor Dan Evans would be meeting with the UW president and his executive staff. The plan was to hold this august group hostage until the demands were met.

"People were under the impression that BSU was a rebel-rousing group with no true sense of direction, but we were an intellectual group that acted with purpose."

—E. J. Brisker, 2016

At around 5 p.m., a group of 60 to 150 individuals—the actual number is disputed—marched up to the third floor of the administration building where the meeting of the Faculty Senate Executive Committee was in session, in what is known as the Regents Room, adjoining the president's office. Governor Evans was not in attendance. Undaunted, the leaders of the contingent, interrupted the meeting attended by President Odegaard and members of the Faculty Senate Executive Committee. E.J. Brisker, Carl Miller, Larry Gossett, Eddie Demmings, and Jimmy Garrett reiterated the demands the BSU had sent two weeks earlier. Garrett was present as a consultant from San Francisco State College because of his standing as an SNCC organizer, the co-founder of the first BSU, the Western Regional Director of Black Student Unions, and the Black Panther Party Minister of Education.

Soon afterwards, UW police locked down the building. At least two protesters managed to gain access to the third floor of the administration building by using a rope to scale an outside wall and enter through an open window, a very risky maneuver indeed. These wall-scalers were later identified as Bobby Morgan (SNCC) and Eddie Walker (BSU). They were late for the revolution! Eddie Walker said it was because he had been out in the community recruiting folks to participate in the sit-in.

According to minutes taken at the meeting by Oliver V. Nelson, secretary of the Faculty Senate, President Odegaard asked, appearing visibly annoyed, "Do you have a spokesperson?" E.J. Brisker replied, "Everybody is a spokesman." He stated, "We don't want to move until we get what we want." A pledge of $50,000 and the employment of recruiters were given as reasons for not leaving until those concessions were made. Although not one of the five demands, Brisker also mentioned to the group that he had tried to get a Black representative on the Board of Regents for at least a year. Odegaard acknowledged that the issues raised by the group were legitimate and admitted that more should be done to address them. One faculty member brought up the question of a budget. Brisker stated that a budget had been drawn up and that it included hiring Jimmy Garrett as a Black Studies consultant. With regard to admission, Brisker argued that the standards for admission should be changed, but graduation standards should remain as they were. He also spoke about implementing a two- or three-week orientation in which tutoring would be provided by members of the UW's Graduate and Professional Student Senate (GPSS).

Regarding curricular changes, Brisker insisted that the BSU should be able to hire and fire teachers. Odegaard countered that the faculty must have control and authority. However, it was agreed that Garrett would be consulted. Odegaard emphasized that in matters of admission and curricular changes, the faculty had a say. He criticized the BSU for not following through on a request made earlier when he had asked for names of various BSU members to assign to committees. Brisker provided a list of members off the top of his head for the Black Studies, Liaison, and Recruiting committees.

Charles Evans questioned whether the BSU should choose the recruiters. Brisker's retort was that the candidates were chosen based on their familiarity with the people targeted for recruitment, including living with them. He further stated, "We already know who is qualified." Two American Indians, one Mexican American, and two Blacks were identified. Odegaard stated that recruiting had to be worked out with faculty. Garrett, speaking like the warden in the movie *Cool Hand Luke*, countered "It is a failure to communicate." He clarified his intent by saying, "These are people from our organization to work with your people" (Evans, 1968a).

At a moment during the dialogue, Charles Evans extended an invitation to E.J. Brisker to meet with and speak to members of the Faculty Senate as a representative of the Liaison Committee. Evans referred to Brisker as a very eloquent spokesman. At that point, President Odegaard pleaded with the BSU to recognize that on the points they had raised it would take time. He further stated he had already been working on these same issues for the previous five years. Garrett replied that these reports would not have the information students need. He further told Odegaard, "You have a good speech, but it took a year to do nothing."

Odegaard felt that to sit-in further was not necessary and asked the group to withdraw from the offices and building, and to know that he and the Faculty Senate Executive Committee would continue to work on the students' behalf. But no mention about the $50,000 pledge was made.

After adjournment Chairman Evans, President Odegaard, and five committee members retired to an inner office. They were joined by Vice Presidents Thieme, Waldo, and Anderson, UW Police Chief Kanz and Secretary Nelson. Remaining behind with the students were seven professors, one of whom was Arval Morris. Moments later, BSU members took over

Bobby Morgan being hoisted to third floor of occupied Administration Building, 1968.

the president's outer office and barred the door. From that point on the sit-in literally became an occupation. Negotiations ensued between a group led by Attorney General Wilson, Chairman Evans, and Vice President Thieme (Evans' group), and Professor Morris who remained with the BSU group. James Goodman, Professor of Social Work and an adviser to the BSU at the time, also participated in the negotiations, serving as a facilitator. Some of the members helped Brisker, Gossett, Miller, Halley, and others to craft a statement which Dr. Odegaard would sign. Chief negotiators were Professors Morton David, and Evans in the Evans group, and Brisker, Miller, and Arval Morris in the BSU group.

The issue of control over funding and programs was a sticking point. As Evans' noted, with no resolution in sight, the administration representatives moved to request that the occupiers vacate the premises in 15 minutes. Before the time was up, a revised text was submitted to the administration and was accepted and signed by members of the Executive Committee and President Odegaard with a couple of minor revisions. The statement endorsed by the 12 members of the Executive Committee and accepted by the BSU reads as follows:

We, the below listed members of the Executive Committee of the Senate, acting individually, heard the demands of the Black Student Union wherein members of the Black Student Union requested the University to find ways to fund an expanded recruitment of minority-group students with the aid of minority-group students: and an expanded Black Studies program in the University curriculum, but did not demand authority and control over the programs. We believe that the Senate of the University of Washington, and President Charles E. Odegaard, should pledge themselves at the next Senate meeting to continue to take steps necessary to secure the

Left: BSU founder Verlaine Miller leaves the sit-in when it becomes an occupation. Right: Raphael Angelo Fortier reading *Time* magazine and Chester Northington reading revolutionary material, *The Wretched of the Earth* by Franz Fanon, while awaiting outcome of negotiations between BSU and administration.

funds from private or public sources and to implement the above demands, recognizing throughout that the responsibility of the University is to maintain its authority and control over its program, and that it must operate through its existing, or its newly created channels.

There was also a supplementary statement by President Charles Odegaard, Charles A. Evans, and Morton M. David, chair of the Faculty Senate Committee on Academic Standards.

It read: "We are signing this statement because it is a restatement of the positions which have already been taken and indicated in previous communications."

Worthy of note is that two professors did not sign the agreement. Also, of note is that there was only one female member on the Faculty Senate Executive Committee.

Although the estimated size of the group of BSU members and their supporters varied between 60 and 150, the BSU participants totaled only about 20 individuals. Where did the remainder of the protesters come from? Besides Blacks who were middle and high school students, the others were members of the Seattle chapter of SNCC (who were not UW students), Black Panther Party members, "Street Brothers" (Black men who used their wit and ingenuity to survive on the streets of the inner city), and a dozen or so white students. "Regardless of their lifestyle, they respected Black Powerites, and that's how they saw these as cats in the community, and from the community," said Gossett. Among the white students was Robby Stern who was president of Students for a Democratic Society (SDS). What follows is Stern's account.

The story of our participation in the sit-in was somewhat controversial with my SDS comrades. The BSU leadership determined that they would keep the plans for the sit-in secret from their SDS allies (and everybody else) to take advantage of the element of surprise to occupy the office.

According to Stern, he was unaware that the sit-in was going to happen that Monday, but he was asked to meet at the administration building to provide support for the struggle to bring more African Americans onto the UW campus as students. He stated:

The agreement to the students' demands is read to E.J. Brisker as
Kathleen Halley and Carl Miller look on.

When the BSU and other allies from the Black community, including
members of the Black Panthers, moved into the building, four of the SDS
members, including me, decided to join them while other SDS members,
who at the time were angry that we had not been told the plan, decided
to remain outside in a supportive capacity. The four white students who
went in were, besides me, Susan Stern, Skip Demuth, and Leslie Mullen.

Stern went on to say,

The leadership of the BSU, Larry Gossett, Carl Miller, and E.J. Brisker
were welcoming of our presence and we remained, despite the threat of
police action and what proved to be an unfriendly gathering of non-SDS
students outside, until the negotiations were completed, and we all left
together. The SDS members who remained outside were supportive of those
on the inside and countered the hostile students gathered outside.

In retrospect, Larry Gossett said, ". . . the role of white students that we
worked at, week by week throughout the months of March, April, and early
May, to educate, [and] politicize, proved quite advantageous to us."

When asked why he chose to support the BSU efforts, Stern explained his motivation to become involved in the BSU movement as follows:

When the civil rights movement and specifically the sit-in movement began, it had an enormous impact on my life from the time I was 18. The injustice of what was going on in our country and the leadership and bravery and sacrifice of the young people involved in the struggle was so admirable. Being a student, I had the privilege of being able to read and understand the role of racism in our country and how it also related to the role the US plays throughout the world. The struggle for racial and economic justice and desire to make democracy real for all people in our country was fundamental to the tenets of SDS and its founding document.

Backing by the SDS, the Vietnam Committee, and Black and White Concern (a study group that would become a strong supporter of BSU efforts) did not go unnoticed. Eddie Demmings said it best: "We had tremendous, tremendous support from the white students, and we could not have done what we did without that support" (Hinckley, 2007).

This support by white students was cultivated in several ways through the efforts of the BSU members, especially the leadership. According to Carl Miller, chair of the Seattle chapter of SNCC at the time, Stokely Carmichael gave specific instructions such as, "encouraging local involvement in electoral politics and garnering support from Democratic Party regulars and from the campus Young Democrats and Young Socialists, encouraging favorable coverage and use of mainstream press radio and TV, and not being afraid of accepting endorsements and direct support from 'old left' groups, i.e., the Freedom Socialists Party (FSP), the Freedom Workers Party (FWP), the Socialist Workers' Party (SWP), the Revolutionary Communist Party (RCP), and other 'old-leftists' groups."

In addition, Larry Gossett offered the following point: "The Black Student Union on this campus was unique in that we had experience interfacing with whites in the overwhelmingly white environment that existed here in the Greater Seattle area. And all of us had had a political education with Harry Chang and other really progressive internationalist teachers, progressive revolutionary intellectuals, Marxist intellectuals that talked to us about the importance of multiracial unity."

Another form of cultivation was participation in the "soul search" sessions that took place weekly in Husky Hollow, in the basement of the HUB. The purpose of the sessions led by Dr. Simon Ottenburg of the anthropology department was a "search for identity." After a few sessions, E.J. Brisker asserted that the University was racist. This assertion piqued the interest of two groups with mostly white participants, including the study group Black and White Concern. Miller also added the name of another group, called Friends of the BSU, as supporters. Gossett further shared that "We just talked about the objective historical reality of our experience here in Seattle and in Washington State and in Cali [California] that led us to organize a Black Power organization on this campus that we called the Black Student Union, and why it was needed. And we encouraged them to ask questions of us."

Other means of garnering white students' support included leaflets, rallies, and forums. E.J. Brisker recalled passing out leaflets containing the five BSU demands to white students as they entered buildings on their way to their classes. Garry Owens recalled receiving invitations from various professors to speak to their classes about the Black student movement. The large forums attracted hundreds of mostly white students who listened attentively and demonstrated strong support. Thus, one can conclude that the campaign put forth by the BSU leadership was effective and enduring.

During the almost four-hour sit-in and occupation it was reported that 74 helmeted police were lurking behind a nearby building (Walker, 1980). But President Odegaard wanted to avoid a situation similar to

Many white students supported the efforts of the BSU.

what happened at Columbia University, and Professor Chapman concurred. Worthy of note is that Governor Dan Evans was also against the idea of bringing in the police to remove the occupiers, according to E.J. Brisker, who had a conversation with the governor years later.

The Columbia University incident that Odegaard wanted to avoid occurred on April 30, 1968, when the Columbia University administration called in 1,000 police officers to remove protesters from campus buildings occupied by student protesters. Police kicked and beat protesters, injuring more than 100. More than 700 protesters were arrested. Students responded by going on strike, essentially shutting down the University for the rest of the semester.

According to Don Hannula of *The Seattle Times*, looking out of the window at the large group of police from the third floor of the administration building, Jesus Crowder was determined to stay the course. He said, "We had cast our fate to move on with our demands" (p. 1). The decision by Odegaard to avoid bringing in the police probably was a wise move because matters could have escalated to unintended consequences, considering the potential for a clash between the police and some occupiers, including the Black Panther Party members.

One of the participants said, "I was not apprehensive about the sit-in. I felt we had to make a stand in regard to recruitment of students of color and have studies that reflected the history and interest of students of color" (C. Adkins, 2017).

Toward the end of the sit-in/occupation, some students became apprehensive upon hearing that the police would be storming the premises to remove them from the building and the likelihood of a confrontation. Fear got the best of them, and they left.

Those at the scene of the sit-in/occupation were ecstatic upon hearing that the administration agreed to the demands. "We left the administration building in triumph," exclaimed Eddie Demmings. "We felt like we had made our point. . . We were on the road to getting what we wanted."

On the following day, Odegaard wrote a letter to a group of 35 prominent businessmen, including chairmen and presidents of the top companies and banks in the area, as well as newspaper publishers, thanking them for inviting him to a luncheon on the day the sit-in took place and sharing with them what transpired when he returned to campus for a meeting with members of the

Eddie Demmings (left) and Gordan DeWitty (right, who is blind)
speak to the press after the sit-in.

E.J. Brisker speaks to press at conclusion of the sit-in.

Executive Committee of the Faculty Senate. He described the composition of the group that crashed the meeting as mostly black, "but there were an Indian or two and a Mexican." He assured the luncheon attendees that any language that implied control other than by the University was rejected. To affirm his assertion, a copy of the agreement was attached to the letter. He also wrote about addressing the issues that prevented the attainment of the "American dream" for all citizens. (A blind copy of the letter was forwarded to the Board of Regents, whose names can be found in Appendix D.)

Following up on Dr. Evans' invitation, E.J. Brisker, accompanied by Larry Gossett and Carl Miller, delivered the keynote address to the Faculty Senate on May 23, 1968. According to the May 24, 1968, *The Daily*, it was worthy of note that he was only the second student to do so. In his speech, Brisker requested three things:

- *Support for recruitment of non-white students*
- *Development of remedial and tutorial programs that would aid newly admitted students' transition to university life*
- *Development of a Black Studies curriculum*

Regarding the Black Studies curriculum, one would think that the purpose in its broadest sense would be to enable Black students and others to learn about the history and culture of Black people. However, in his speech to the Faculty Senate, Brisker stated a more inclusive purpose, calling for "a Black Studies Curriculum which would enable white and non-white students to learn about the cultures and lifestyles of such groups as Afro-American, Mexican American and Indian American peoples" (Steward, 1968). This inclusivity is indicative of the influence that the Native and Chicano members of the BSU had in crafting the demands.

Brisker's speech received resounding applause. Members of the Faculty Senate Executive Committee signed a resolution to support the establishment of Black Studies and recruitment programs. As reported in *The Daily*, it was the opinion of Morton David, chair of the Faculty Council on Academic Standards, that the Faculty Senate's interest helped the outcome.

Professor David went on to say, "The BSU has presented its demands not merely as questions for interesting discussion and debate, but as matters of survival." In his report, David recommended that funds be made available

---

The BSU transformative citizens recognized and unapologetically challenged blatant contradictions, cared enough to disregard the possibility of negative consequences, boldly acted to change the landscape of the University, and insisted that the institution become more inclusive in its curricular offerings.

---

for the recruitment and tutoring of non-white students and that the tutoring begin as soon as possible. An excerpt in the report read:

> *"The Council supports increased efforts to recruit Black faculty and administrators, recognizing among other considerations that successful performance of black students at the University depends to a degree upon the presence of models to learn from and identify with. It also recommended that the core of the Black Studies curriculum be established by the following September"* (A list of the first recruiters, 1968-70, can be found in Appendix D).

How can one aptly describe those activists referred to as the BSU and their supporters? The answer might be gleaned from a talk given by UW professor James Banks, the Kerry and Linda Killinger Endowed Chair in Diversity Studies and a renowned expert on multicultural education. Banks was the Samuel E. Kelly Distinguished Lecture series keynote at the UW in 2018. He describes three types of citizens: denied (unprivileged), recognized (privileged), and transformative (change agents). For the third group, Banks identified three key characteristics—they know; they care; they act. The BSU transformative citizens recognized and unapologetically challenged blatant contradictions, cared enough to disregard the possibility of negative consequences, boldly acted to change the landscape of the University, and insisted that the institution become more inclusive in its curricular offerings.

President Odegaard's Role and the Aftermath

A multitude of factors led to what turned out to be not only historic, but transformative. Unbeknownst to those students of color who began to realize something was not right, change actually began more than nine years prior to the sit-in. On February 3, 1959, a year after being recruited from the University of Michigan to serve as the 19th president of the University of Washington, Charles Odegaard issued a policy memorandum that read in part, "The University of Washington, as an institution established and maintained by the people of the state, affords equal opportunity, without regards to race, creed, color, to all persons, whether students, teachers, or members of administrative and services staffs" (Manning, 1968, p. 14). This statement was indicative of the president's intentions to lead a university that would be open to the entire citizenry of the state.

Four years later President Odegaard came to the realization that these were mere words when, at the 1963 Commencement, he and members of the Board of Regents noticed that Black students were visibly absent among the graduating class. He surmised that it was likely the case at other universities around the country. He called it a national tragedy and urged the faculty to take steps to remedy this tragedy.

To address this invisibility, Odegaard established a Committee on Special Educational Programs with Dr. Eugene Elliot serving as chairman. Professor Elliot was later appointed Director of Special Educational Programs. One strategy was to consider bringing Black children on campus visits in hopes of arousing their interest in college. However, there was no evidence that the University reached out to Black students at the UW who could have played an integral role in getting more prospective students interested in attending the UW.

In anticipation of students entering the University perhaps less prepared than regularly admissible students, Odegaard also introduced the idea of creating a four-week refresher program for entering freshmen to improve their chances of successfully navigating the University.

Regarding employment, most of the Black hires at UW were semi-skilled and service workers. In fact, there was only one Black faculty member, and he was a visiting professor. To remedy the dearth of skilled workers, the UW advertised with agencies that could get the word out to potential minority candidates. But the University failed miserably when it came to hiring Black faculty. After a couple of years of minimal progress, Odegaard went to the Faculty Senate on May 27, 1965, imploring the body to support the objectives of the Special Educational Program in finding ways to remedy the "social tragedy" in American society. He realized that to change matters, an attitudinal shift, i.e., a conversion of hearts in faculty, would be necessary. He made his first attempt to affect such a shift while delivering his report. An excerpt from that report further drives home this assertion:

> *It is to this conversion of human hearts that I hope we in universities can make a special contribution. For those who suffer racial discrimination in our society are in a real sense separated brethren, parted from our culture even though they are within it, persons deprived of many skills and ways characteristic of our culture which, if acquired, would enable them to perform more often respected and prestigious roles and would make them more fully partners in our society. The ground still to be covered after segregationist barriers are removed can be covered in large part only through the availability of educational and employment opportunities to the Negro and his use of them. If we can help them help themselves, they will help us too; and the brotherhood of man will be more widely recognized by men themselves out of that respect for one another which cannot be bought or forced, which can only be given freely by one man to another* (Odegaard, 1965).

Two years later, President Odegaard returned to the Faculty Senate to provide a status report. He spoke of improved financial aid opportunities and efforts to create a welcoming environment. He spoke of the first Black woman to be elected to the ASUW Board of Control. Hundreds of UW students became tutors in the Central District (inner city) public schools. Odegaard (naively) felt that this effort would translate into more minority students enrolling at the University. Considering the students who were being tutored were struggling academically, not to mention the notion that these students' low academic performance was attributable to all the ramifications of poverty, segregation, and racial isolation, it was highly unlikely that they would be interested in attending the UW. A dead giveaway to this naiveté was the fact that even though there were a few Black students enrolled at the UW between 1965 and 1967, there was no mention of any of them serving as tutors. Having Black students from the UW serve as tutors would have sent a strong message to tutees to strive to emulate their tutors and realize that they too could be students at UW, thus increasing the likelihood the desire to enroll upon graduation.

Another strategy was to encourage faculty to become involved in the Black community to help promote goodwill. While faculty involvement in the inner city might show a small segment of the community that the University cared, it is unlikely that having faculty work on issues of urbanization, poverty, and welfare in the community would pique the interest of minority students to pursue a college education.

As for increasing the number of Blacks in the faculty ranks, the number went from zero to five, mainly because of the efforts of deans and faculty in education, medicine, nursing, and social work. There was no mention of an appreciable increase in non-academic staff, particularly in the skilled sector.

One nominally positive outcome shared by Odegaard with members of the Senate was that the UW College of Arts and Sciences had secured funds from the Department of Education to establish an Upward Bound program, which would prepare low-income and first-generation high school students for college. Thirty-seven students were brought to campus, and from that group, 14 Black students had enrolled in fall of 1967, including the future Black Student Union founding members: Richard Brown, Jesus Crowder, Marcie Hall, and Carmelita Laducer.

Perhaps the most poignant explanation for why the sit-in agreement was reached in record time—no other known occupation ended in such short span of time—can be found in a presentation given before the Seattle Community Council at Mt. Zion church. The *Seattle Post-Intelligencer* reported that Odegaard said "he feels the BSU objectives were appropriate," and he admitted that efforts by the University to recruit Black students were inadequate. He further admitted that "although UW had programs to find solutions to black student problems, they were moving very slowly" (Glover, 1968). In essence, the occupation of the president's office served as a catalyst to act definitively and with a sense of urgency.

The fact that President Odegaard signed off on the agreement and, thus, approved an avenue for a successful outcome was of paramount importance. However, many members of the BSU leadership felt he was still evasive and

Students, press, and officials crowd Brisker as he leaves with an agreement.

appeared unwilling to work out an agreement. Besides, based on his comment about concessions or capitulation, it is likely that the impasse would have continued without resolution if not for the BSU action.

It was fortuitous that the BSU demands resonated with the faculty members present at the sit-in who worked intentionally and purposefully to broker an agreement between the students and the barricaded group. It was clear that the faculty "got it," and I am convinced they allayed any reservations President Odegaard may have had. It is this group and the Faculty Senate that should be duly recognized for their efforts. Without them, along with the political savvy of the BSU leadership, the outcome may have been markedly different. Furthermore, it is important to recognize the efforts of Michael Rosen of the ACLU who worked out a compromise whereby no student was suspended or expelled, and no one was arrested, nor was prosecution pursued despite two figurines, two decorative masks, and a picture were never recovered.

This series of actions is considered without question to be responsible for changing the face of diversity and inclusion at the University of Washington forever. Although viewed as one of the greatest feats in the history of activism at the UW, because it happened in the northwest corner of America, it received little notice outside of the confines of Seattle. Surely, had there been arrests and injuries, there would have been national coverage. And if that had happened, it is highly unlikely that the administration, departments, faculty, staff, and business community would have worked in concert to support the establishment of an enduring program.

Apparently, it was a defining moment for President Odegaard as well. In his autobiography, he devoted a full chapter detailing the BSU efforts to increase the participation of minority and disadvantaged white students at the University and the addition of courses in Black Studies. The chapter was titled "A Season of Discontent and the Establishment of a Black Studies Program." E.J. Brisker was the only student whose name was mentioned, and the full text of Brisker's presentation to the Faculty Senate was also included. President Odegaard credits Brisker's reasoned approach with being responsible for facilitating communication between students and faculty, fostering a cooperative spirit. As a result, the Black Studies Program was created and Chicano, American Indian, and Asian American Studies followed. "It was the genesis of profound change" (Hinckley, 2007).

In a black notebook that is now archived in UW Libraries Special Collections, Dr. Charles Evans kept track of many different things. One was the names of Black faculty, of which there were 12 in 1968 and an additional six in 1969, with the caveat that the list was incomplete. Their departmental affiliations included chemistry, oral biology, preventive medicine, social work, psychiatry, education, English, psychiatric nursing, history, urology/microbiology, and anthropology. Three of the 18 listed were women.

It seems clear that the increase in positions held by minority faculty, administrators, and staff at the University of Washington during those years was a direct result of the pathway paved by the efforts of the Black Student Union of 1968 and its supporters. Although some will insist that their achievements are attributable to self-achievement alone, others will acknowledge the giants upon whose shoulders they stand.

STUDENT CASES

VERLAINE KEITH-MILLER. Verlaine Keith was the second youngest of four siblings and grew up in Holly Park, one of Seattle's public housing projects. She attended Sharples Junior High School (now Aki Kurose) and Cleveland High School. A junior high friend, Suzanne Petersen-Sanderson, recalled that Verlaine said she always wanted to be a bullfighter. According to Verlaine, she was popular in high school and held a position in student government.

In 1966, along with classmates Eddie Demmings and Eddie Walker, she enrolled at the University of Washington. She commuted to school accompanied by an older brother, William Daniel Keith, and his friend, Larry Gossett, who as time progressed became increasingly politicized and radicalized. Although Larry constantly spoke to her about issues of concern to Black people, his words fell on seemingly deaf ears until one day, according to her, "I had an epiphany and embraced being Black." She subsequently became an activist and a founding member of the BSU serving as its secretary. In 1968, she participated in the sit-in and occupation of President Charles Odegaard's office. She said, "I remember Odegaard turning bright red when the BSU crashed the meeting" (Hinckley, 2007). During the sit-in she became apprehensive when she saw police cars through the window, but her best friend, Kathy Halley, assured her that they would support each other through it all.

In hindsight, Verlaine said, "I thought Odegaard was really an honorable man and that he seemed open to the changes that were happening." She also thought Dr. Charles Evans was committed to change. Regarding the positive gains that came about because of the BSU's actions, she said, "We can really feel proud of what we did and what our priorities were. It was really about changing the world for the better" (Hinckley, 2007). In June 1968, Verlaine, E.J. Brisker, and Larry Gossett accepted the Sidney Gerber Award for outstanding accomplishments in the field of civil rights. On August 1, 1970, she married fellow founding BSU member, Carl Miller, hence the name Keith-Miller.

Verlaine earned a bachelor's degree in Black Studies—the major that the 1968 BSU fought for—in 1973 and earned a JD from the UW School of Law in 1980. She went on to serve as an assistant attorney general for the Washington State Office of the Attorney General and then established a private organization where she represented plaintiffs. Her last job before retirement in 2015 was as an industrial appeal judge for the Washington State Board of Appeals.

Worthy of note is she, along with other 1968 BSU founding members, received the Charles E. Odegaard Award for unwavering commitment to educational

Dr. Abby Franklin presents Verlaine Keith-Miller, Larry Gossett, and E.J. Brisker with the Gerber Award on June 7, 1968, in honor of the BSU's work to stop racial injustice.

opportunity and diversity at the University in 2008. And in 2017, she was a panelist with other UW alumni civil rights leaders who discussed the legacy of the occupation of the UW president's office and the state of the UW's ongoing commitment to equity and justice for all. Verlaine Keith-Miller passed on October 18, 2018.

KATHLEEN RUSSELL TYLER. Kathleen Russell Tyler came to the UW after attending Seattle University (SU) for a year. As a student at Seattle University, she had followed the news about the beginning of the UW's Black Student Union and wanted to help start a BSU at her university. However, there were very few Black students at SU and efforts to start a BSU there were not fruitful. So, in her words, "I transferred to the UW . . . and my story begins."

According to Kathleen:

> It is important to note that I was not the daughter of a wealthy or even middle-class household. I was born in Everett, Washington, but was placed in foster care in Seattle, supervised by Catholic Charities, when I was about 9 years old. Through Catholic Charities I attended Catholic schools including Immaculate Conception High School. After leaving foster care upon high school graduation, I worked and lived independently for a year. A high school friend encouraged me to apply to college, and so I did. I was fortunate to obtain Social Security financial benefits as result of my father having served in the military during war time. My biological aunt (Alpha Coffee) had schooled me on my entitlement to that benefit. I was also fortunate and grateful to have received a full tuition scholarship from the Seattle Urban League.

> So, while I was largely alone, I did receive some encouragement and help along the way in my early adulthood and was able to organize the basic financial support I would need for college. Many, if not most, children or students in need do not have this level of support.

> My interest and motivation for membership in the BSU, a motivation shared by all BSU members at that time I believe, was to seek the integration of more minority students into the University and to influence the University to add minority administrators and teaching staff.

> I am told that I was an active and vocal member of the BSU. I do not remember many details except that the small BSU office was a place where I spent significant time and where I was often busy. I do recall that I had recommended that an incoming EOP class would benefit from an orientation program and helped organize the initial program.

During those years, our country was involved in the war in Vietnam. There was an explosion of anti-war and anti-government student activity throughout the country and at the UW. While some of the BSU members participated in anti-war demonstration, our organizational focus was concerned with making higher education more available to minority students in the Seattle area. Why? We wanted greater opportunity to participate in our society; we wanted inclusion, not exclusion; we wanted integration, not segregation. In my opinion, the BSU efforts were a success. The EOP program exists to this day, and it has grown.

I had visited New York City once while at the UW and just loved the energy and diversity of the people. I felt I needed to live in a more diversified community and that in a city such as NYC I would find more opportunity. This [New York] is now home.

I had a few jobs in the for-profit and not-for-profit, educational sector after arriving in New York. My most significant job change was joining NYC government. Working for a huge organization such as NYC government has given me the opportunity for exposure to various careers and upward mobility under that umbrella. I worked as a civil service examiner (writing and administering exams), a contracts director of a major Medicaid funded home health program (directing the solicitation and administration of contracted services, rate setting, and negotiations), and as budget director for more than one City agency. My final position, from which I retired, was Deputy Commissioner for Budget Administration for the NYC Human Resources Administration.

I am proud to have worked for NYC Government and I enjoy living in NYC. My UW and BSU experiences, my BSU lifelong friends, and my current family propelled me forward and for that I am grateful.

CARL MILLER. As Carl Miller wrote in response to questions about his life, he was the "eldest of seven children and grew up with his siblings sheltered and lived in public housing projects in Philadelphia, PA, his father's hometown" (C. Miller, 2016). According to Carl, his father, Arthur Miller was a WWII army veteran who served in a segregated labor brigade. His father "traced the family ancestry through oral history back through Barbados to an island off the coast of West Africa." Carl said that despite familial love, "life was relatively difficult growing up in the rougher parts of the City of Brotherly Love," and he lost a few teeth defending his younger sister against a neighbor bigger than he was.

Carl described himself as "a nerdy kid, churchy, an avid reader, science clubber, and Boy Scout leader." He further stated, "I sang in school glee clubs and choirs. I was on TV twice dancing at the Atlantic City Steel Peer integrated version of American Bandstand." He was also in a club that organized weekend bus outings to Coney Island, New York, and other alternative activities as a way to stay out of the neighborhood street gangs. Carl said his first glimmer of real hope for higher education came from a counselor at a Y-teen program who touted scholarship offers at St. Olaf College in Minnesota (C. Miller, 2020).

Carl noted that even as a child, he read widely, starting with *The Scout Manual*, *Boy's Life*, comic books, *Readers Digest*, *Time*, *Life*, *Look*, and *MAD* magazines. He read three white daily newspapers and several black weeklies, *Ebony*, and *Jet* magazines. Once his reading interest could not be fulfilled by the public housing project library, he said he was given permission to visit the white branch library. There he sought books on Black people but found them "terrible." Said Carl, "I filled the void with Conan Doyle, Agatha Christie, and Robert Heinlein." In his high school library, he found one book by a Black author filed in the science section. It was titled *Invisible Man* by Ralph Ellison. According to Carl, he was confused when the subject did not actually disappear. However, he added, on those pages one summer, through Ellison's brilliant storytelling, he found unexpected but solid clues that would help to forge his own identity (C. Miller, 2016).

After high school graduation in 1963, Carl enlisted in the army for the GI bill. Carl reported that he was patriotic enough, but he enlisted mostly for the opportunity to travel and to get himself and his family out of his "impoverished, opportunity-less, street-gang- and crime-ridden North Philadelphia neighborhood. Carl contends, "If I'd stayed in Philly without further education, my career choices were busboy or junkie. College was way out of reach, but the military was a relatively easy way out." While in the army, Carl studied Spanish, Japanese, Judo, and read dental textbooks. He always wanted to become a dentist (C. Miller, 2016).

When asked about the state of his political consciousness before coming to Seattle, Carl's response was:

> Television coverage of the Civil Rights demonstrations and two books truly changed my life—Before the Mayflower *and* The Autobiography of Malcolm X. *I read both in single nights and then set out to read everything in the Black canon. History, fiction, essays, everything. I couldn't get enough. Thank goodness for the Yesler branch of the Seattle Public Library and for Langston Hughes, Richard Wright, James Baldwin, Howard Zinn, Herbert Aptheker, Gunnar Myrdal, and Melville Herskovits.*
>
> *I was greatly influenced by the lynching of Emmett Till, the Little Rock school integration fight, radio news talk about de facto and de jure*

*public school segregation, the Montgomery Bus Boycotts, the Woolworth
sit-ins, the Freedom Riders, Malcolm X, the Congress of Racial Equality
(CORE), the Southern Christian Leadership Conference (SCLC), and the
Birmingham Church Bombings* (C. Miller, 2016).

Carl left the army in 1966 and took a skilled labor job at Boeing. But he quit
to attend Seattle Community College on the GI Bill of Rights, "so that a friendly
coworker from Kentucky, a white man living in his car with his family wouldn't be laid-
off" (C. Miller, 2016). In 1967, Carl became a founding member and chairperson of
the Seattle Chapter of the Student Nonviolent Coordinating Committee.

In 1968, at the urging of Larry Gossett, Carl and E.J. enrolled at the
University of Washington where they, along with others, founded the BSU. Carl
was one of the leaders who met with President Odegaard and other members
of his administration to discuss the need to change the face of diversity at UW.
And when these discussions appeared to be going nowhere, he helped lead
the contingent that occupied the president's office that same year. Before that
occupation took place, he, Brisker, Gossett, and Elmer Dixon were instrumental
in the establishment of the Black Panther Party for Self Defense. Regarding
the results of those efforts, Carl remembered, "We stood on the shoulders of
silent giants, including most of the few dozen minority students already present
on campus. For those thinking of following the same path, keep in mind that
definite goals and patient organizing are the keys to success" (C. Miller, 2020).

In 1974, Carl earned a Bachelor of Arts degree in history from the UW. He
completed two years of post-graduate work at the UW School of Law but left before
earning a law degree. After leaving law school Carl worked for some time at the UW
OMA as a Student Services Counselor and Minority Recruitment Coordinator.

Carl credits his mother, Tecumseh-a EsterBell Herd Miller who, through her
unrelenting urging about being responsible, made certain he and his siblings
would all graduate from high school. Carl said that it is totally to his mother's
credit that four of his seven siblings went on to earn bachelor's degrees, three
went on to graduate schools, and one is a physician assistant.

In 1980, Carl relocated to California where he went on to work in what he
described as "a very fulfilling career" in California state service, first as an
Employment Program Representative/ Disabled Veterans Outreach Program
Specialist (DVOP) at the Employment Development Department field offices
in Oakland, Berkeley, and Richmond, California. In 1988, Carl went to work
for the California Department of Social Services first as a Licensing Program
Analyst, then as a regional trainer, and finally as a statewide Senior Care
Program Trainer. He retired from state service in 2012. Four years after

retirement he became a member of the American Society of Composers, Authors, and Publishers (ASCAP). Carl is a multi-instrument musician, a music publisher, composer, and arranger. He currently owns joint copyrights to over 1,254 music recordings.

For the thousands of minority students at UW who went on to earn degrees, including dental degrees, Carl Miller helped pave the way.

KATHLEEN "NAFASI" HALLEY. Kathleen Halley, one of two children, was born and raised in the heart of the Seattle Central District. Her mother was an elementary school teacher and her father worked as a longshoreman. Her parents were one of Seattle's pioneer Black families arriving in 1936 from Kansas before migration of Blacks from the south had begun. Both Kathleen and her brother, Floyd, attended Horace Mann Elementary, Washington Junior High, and Garfield High School, all neighborhood schools. Her parents' views on race relations led to an early development of political consciousness. This 10th grader and her best friend Leathia Stallworth appeared on a radio show and spoke about the struggle of Black people in Seattle and across the nation. The talk focused on discrimination. Kathleen remembered that other classmates and the teacher were very impressed with the scope of their knowledge.

After high school graduation, Kathleen enrolled at Western Washington State College (later Western Washington University) in Bellingham, Washington. She did well, but there were only a small number of Black students at Western. So, she transferred in her sophomore year to Wilberforce University (affiliated with the AME church), an old private historically Black college located in Ohio. It was 90 percent Black. She joined the Black student organization and got involved in the Black struggle in the area. Her college enrollment was short lived. She was suspended for violating curfew—late getting back because she was participating in a demonstration at Central State University where the National Guard had been called in to break it up.

Kathleen returned to Seattle and got involved with the local chapter of SNCC. In winter 1968, she enrolled at UW just in time to help establish the BSU. According to Larry Gossett, "Kathleen was a very hard-working activist in the BSU. She went to meetings with professors to discuss why Black Studies should be established at the university, gave talks to UW classes about the Black student movement on campus, spoke to high school Black Student Union groups, researched Black history to share with Black students, recruited Black high school students to participate in the sit-in, and participated in study groups." Gossett also shared that Kathleen was very impressed with E.J. Brisker's intellectual brilliance and valued the close relationship she forged with Verlaine Keith-Miller (Gossett, 2020).

That spring from April 6th through 8th, Kathleen, Aaron Dixon, E.J. Brisker, Larry Gossett, Carl Miller, and other Black Student Union members traveled to a conference at San Francisco State College. The highlight of the conference was a speech given by Bobby Seale, chairman of the Black Panther Party. According to Gossett, "The Black youth from Seattle were really inspired by Bobby's words calling for Black Power and revolutionary change. We all went and fell in love, and us all—at least brothers and sisters from Seattle—fell in love with the Black Panther Party." They spoke with him about the possibility of establishing a chapter in Seattle. Seale agreed to consider the proposal and invited them to attend the funeral of a fallen Panther, Bobby Hutton, who was killed (reportedly in an ambush) by the Oakland police. Kathleen remembered, "That funeral impacted me deeply."

Just over a week after the conference, Seale visited Seattle, gave his stamp of approval to establish a chapter of the Party in Seattle, and appointed Aaron Dixon captain. Kathleen was a member of the chapter which was comprised of one third women. Dixon gave her the name "Nafasi" (one of the meanings in English means "highly ranked"). She remembered getting along with all the male activists and leaders in the organization. She helped lead the organization at doing certain kinds of research, speaking at rallies, and developing models for organizing the community. Kathleen said, "Black women were a sustaining force in church and the party" (Gossett, 2020).

Kathleen graduated from the University in 1972 with a degree in political science and two years later graduated with a master's degree in social work from the UW. She worked in family services in Seattle for about eight years before moving to Washington, DC, to work as a legislative assistant in the office of congressman, Mike Lowry. Her duties included writing policy, giving talks, and meeting with constituents from Washington State. According to Larry Gossett, Kathleen enjoyed her time on the hill.

For more than 20 years, Kathleen served as a social worker in a county just outside of Washington, DC, working with youth and their families from a wide variety of backgrounds. She said, "I am fortunate to be in a profession that gives me the opportunity to work with children and their families from all over the world,"—the words of a true servant of the people.

EDDIE DEMMINGS. One of the founding members of the UW BSU, Eddie Demmings was raised in the Beacon Hill area of Seattle. He was a classmate of Verlaine Keith-Miller from kindergarten on. Having grown up in Seattle, Eddie's "impression of Seattle was that it was liberal, tolerant, and racially diverse despite geographic anomalies like the predominantly Black Central Area and the white north Seattle."

Eddie's best friend at Cleveland High School was Eddie Walker. In Demming's words, "We were inchoate Intellectuals, reading Franz Fanon, Jean-Paul Sartre, Albert Camus, Franz Kafka in our spare time! At the same time, I joined with Verlaine on the school debate team. She was uncomfortably self-conscious, but that trait belied her fierce determination."

Eddie continued:

> In the 50s and 60s, I was aware of the struggle in the South: the sit-ins, church bombings, police dogs, attempts to desegregate the schools, marches, rallies, etc., but naively thought these issues had little or no bearing on Seattle in the Pacific Northwest.
>
> In our senior year, a boycott was announced to oppose the severe racial segregation of the Seattle public schools. I had no inclination to go because my sole focus was to get good enough grades to be accepted into college (the UW is the only college to which I applied). My mother, like every other strong Black woman, had a different opinion and only her opinion counted. I joined the boycott, not at her "urging" but her order. The boycott was a good experience. The students participating reflected the diversity of Seattle, including some whites. That was my first ever political experience.

Eddie was accepted at the UW and worked as a riveter at Boeing over the summer to earn enough money to pay for school. But when he arrived on the UW campus, he "went into virtual shock." As he explained:

> How could a public university with more than 30,000 students be almost completely white? This shock persisted through all of my first year and detrimentally affected me mentally and physically, thus, leading to my desire to bring about change. A year later, we founded the Black Student Union (BSU) inspired by the civil rights movement, Malcolm X, the Panthers, Black writers, and all else happening in the country. We were determined to fundamentally change the UW. Together, with other people of color and a surprising number of white students in support of our cause, we marched forward. Beyond what was achieved on the UW campus, I was profoundly transformed. I became a self-conscious citizen of the world. Committed to being in solidarity with those who fought against oppression and exploitation wherever it existed (E. Demmings, 2020).

Later, Eddie was approached by the National Conference of Black Lawyers ("the legal arm of the Black revolution"), which recruited Eddie to apply to Rutgers Law School in Newark, New Jersey. According to Eddie, Rutgers had an affirmative action program since 1968, and he "entered the school under its auspices in 1978." He noted:

> *During my first year, conservative professors argued that the program
> had to be dismantled because of the Supreme Court Bakke decision.
> Would you believe it? I found myself back on the picket line to preserve the
> program. We won! The program was expanded rather eliminated.*

In law school, Eddie faced a decision of whether to be a civil rights or a union
attorney, spending two years interning at a law firm that specialized in unions.
He said:

> *It did not take long to learn how little the legal profession, in all
> sectors, was committed to hiring minority attorneys. I saw that the union
> firms were not hiring people of color. There was a plethora of excuses for
> not hiring minorities, even though NYC had hundreds of thousands of union
> members, many of whom were people of color.*
>
> *Nonetheless, I was hired by AFSCME, DC 37, right out of law school.
> The legal department had one Black lawyer, but he was a year away from
> retiring. When he left there did not seem to be much incentive to hire other
> minority attorneys despite frequent turnovers.*

Over the years, Eddie moved up the ladder from staff attorney to Senior
Assistant General Counsel, Associate General Counsel, and General Counsel. As
he advanced in his career, he noted that:

> *I made sure other people of color were hired, Puerto Rican, Honduran,
> Guyanese, Taiwanese, Indian, Jamaican, and so on. Moreover, all, but one,
> were women. I proudly consider this my legacy at the union. My every
> step in later years was informed and guided by our collective and historic
> experience at the University of Washington.*

Founding BSU Members and Officers

The BSU at UW was founded after a visit by a group of Black students to a Black Youth conference in Los Angeles, California, during Thanksgiving weekend, 1967.*

The inaugural BSU officers were William Daniel Keith, President; Emanuel James (E.J.) Brisker, Vice President; Eddie Demmings, Minister of Education; and Eddie Walker, Minister of Arts and Culture.

Founding members of the BSU included:

William Daniel Keith
Emanuel James (E.J.) Brisker
Larry Gossett
Carl Miller
Verlaine Keith (-Miller)
Eddie Demmings
Eddie Walker
Kathleen "Nafasi" Halley
Marcie Hall (Colville Tribe)
Carmelita Laducer (Colville Tribe)
Lee Leavy
Richard Brown
Jesus Crowder (Chicano)
William (Billy) M. Jackson
Leathia Stallworth
Gordon DeWitty
Aaron Dixon
Garry Owens
Thomas McAllister
Charlotte Moore McAllister
Lyn Ware
Frances Johnson
Anita Connell
Meredith Matthews
Patsy Mose
Pauline Alley (now known as Royal Alley-Barnes)
Patricia Yates
Paul Fletcher
William Stinson
Emile Pitre

It is interesting to note the influence of the Black Panther Party (BPP) in the latter two officer titles. Eddie Demmings later stated that he was very impressed with the Black Panther Party (BPP) even though it was a community-oriented group. At least five of the founding members of the UW's BSU were also Black Panthers: Tony Buford, Aaron Dixon, Kathy "Nafasi" Halley, Billy Jackson, and Garry Owen.

*Contrary to what was stated in one account, it was not founded after a visit to Oakland, CA, in the spring of 1968. Rather, it was the Seattle chapter of the Black Panther Party that was founded after that visit (Walker, 1980).

Students (left to right) Jose Correa, Antonio Salazar, Eron Maltos, and Jesus Lemos posed for a photo holding a United Farm Workers flag when *The Daily* ran an article about the UMAS (United Mexican American Students) organization, the forerunner to MEChA. The Aztec eagle represented dignity.

CHAPTER 2

1968–1977: Foundation Building and Exponential Growth

With the embryonic stage of the evolutionary journey complete, the second leg of the journey bears the resemblance to that of a quantum leap.

—Emile Pitre, 2020

Following the approval of the BSU proposal by the Faculty Senate, attention now turned to recruitment, which was funded by businesses and the private sector. On June 3, 1968, Bill Hilliard, a returning UW student, former football player, and Garfield High School graduate, was hired to coordinate the recruitment of minority and economically disadvantaged students to attend the University. Although he worked closely with Dr. J. Robert Long, director of New Student Services, Hilliard was given authority to approve student applications. He hired eight UW students to help with the effort: six were Black, two were American Indians and all, but one, were founding members of the BSU. The first student recruiters hired were Frances Johnson (Tacoma), Eddie Demmings (Seattle), Lyn Ware (Renton), Patricia Honeysuckle (Seattle), Paul Fletcher (Pasco), Thomas McAllister (Seattle), Marcie Hall (Toppenish), and Carmen Laducer (Toppenish).

Students were recruited from Tri-Cities, Yakima Valley, Spokane, Tacoma, Bremerton, Makah Indian Reservation, State Multiservice Center, and East Madison YMCA. As a result, 257 students were admitted to the University; roughly 13% were Chicana and 86% were Black. Hilliard described the outreach process:

> We set up at grocery stores: Safeway, Tradewell, and so forth. We talked to parents and handed out applications to the parents, because students really didn't come shopping with their parents very often back then. We traveled to Tacoma and all the way down to Vancouver, Washington. . . . We got some students out of Portland as well in the first group. I think it was somewhere around the 12th or 13th of August when we got our first tally, and at that point we had about 310 students with completed applications in just a little over two months.

Recruitment of Black students was not limited to undergraduates. Several graduate students were hired as recruiters: Nadine Anderson (Psychology), Clark Butler (Classics), Yvonne Jones (Chemistry), and Winston Williams

(Microbiology). Of the 381 students accepted, 260 (68%) registered, with 57% coming from high school and 43% college transfers (including from both two-year and four-year institutions).

Next came the issue of securing funds to support students once they were admitted. Dr. Eugene Elliot, special assistant to the president for Special Education Programs, brought in Bill Baker, director of financial aid, to provide resources. The resources came in the form of Educational Opportunity grants, loans, and summer employment. Funds were also solicited from foundations and businesses. In addition, faculty and staff were asked to contribute one hour of their pay to a fund that would be used to support tuition, textbooks, and fees, as well as living expenses for an estimated 300 students scheduled to enter school in the fall.

In his infinite wisdom, President Odegaard chose an individual who had broad and in-depth knowledge of the issues to implement the pending program, as well as would have the vote of confidence of the faculty, office of admissions, office of student financial aid, and the BSU collective. His choice was Dr. Charles A. Evans, former chair of the Faculty Senate and professor of microbiology in the School of Medicine. Evans replaced Dr. Eugene Elliot to serve as special assistant to the president and director of the Special Education Program (SEP) on September 6, 1968. (The Evans Papers, UW Libraries Special Collections, 2598-001, -003, and -004.)

Dr. Charles Evans

Odegaard's rationale was that the time had come to consolidate all previous efforts under the stewardship of one person. Charles Evans knew better than anybody the history of what led to the decision to establish such a program, understood the urgent need for immediate implementation, and had the ability to muster support from key faculty members who would join him on a path of uncharted territory. The main challenge at hand was to determine what strategies would be required to support students who, in many cases, were admitted based on their potential to succeed rather than on their academic credentials. The mean GPA of those students entering directly from high school and from college was below 2.00. The GPAs ranged between 0.00 and 3.38, with students entering with a GED assigned as a 0.00 GPA.

Programming to support the newly recruited students entering the institution at various levels of academic preparedness would require offering classes and activities to help them prepare for the academic rigors of the University and transition into college life in advance. An orientation program was implemented three weeks before the start of fall quarter. Refresher and review courses in English, reading, and mathematics were designed and taught by Professors Irmscher, Sebesta, and Monk, respectively. A course in study habits and methods was also offered. In the evenings, BSU members, including Eddie Walker and Eddie Demmings, addressed the students and introduced them to members of the Black community. There were 300 participants at an estimated cost of $25,000.

According to Charles Evans' notebook and papers, 122 students lived in Lander Hall during orientation without encountering hostility, much to their surprise. Over 90% of the SEP students lived in Lander Hall. Books, housing, and food were paid for by contributions from businesses and the University Fund for Disadvantaged Students. Part of SEP students' tuition was paid from more than $76,000 in funds contributed by almost 1,300 faculty and staff via payroll deductions.

Evans reported that courses were needed to bring some students up to speed before enrolling in regular university courses. Faculty who had a sense for what was needed, and cared enough to see to it that the SEP students had every chance to be successful, chimed in. English 101 was developed by Professors William Irmscher and Jean Hundley. Math 100 was developed by Professor Steve Monk. Social Science 150; Afro-American History 132; Humanities 101, Study of Literature of Black Authors; and Philosophy 113, Philosophy of Racial Conflict courses were also offered.

Evans appointed Bill Hilliard as assistant director, and Jerline Ware as coordinator of the tutoring office. Willie Winston of the Graduate and Professional Student Senate arranged for the more than 400 graduate students and faculty volunteers to provide tutorial assistance. Thus, the journey began.

According to Evans, in 1968, autumn quarter enrollment at the UW included more than 465 Blacks, 100 American Indians, and 90 Mexican Americans, including students in the Special Education Program and students who were non-SEP. Though none were recruited, 830 Asian students were enrolled as well. Ethnic information was ascertained by having students fill out a form (Census Card) requesting them to self-identify with an ethnic group. All but 75 complied.

There were growing pains at the beginning of the program due to the lack of dedicated counselors. Graduate students from the School of Social Work provided that service but, according to Bill Hilliard, they did not do a very good job because their graduate school obligations made them unavailable when students most needed them. Professional advisers were added to the staff to remedy this situation.

Hilliard and others visited programs at other institutions—for example, Michigan State, Berkeley, and UCLA—to find out what could be learned and adapted for the SEP. At the California schools there was conflict between Blacks and Hispanics, so nothing useful was gained by visiting those campuses.

Evans relied on enrollment numbers, attrition rates, and grades earned to monitor the progress of the program. In his report to the Faculty Senate in October 1968, he urged the members to bear in mind that "Success is not to be measured by ordinary criteria. As with any pioneering educational program, the success of the early years will be found not only in the achievement of students present at that time, but equally in the progressive improvement in the program as experience is gained in successive years" (Evans, 1968a, Box 1).

So how did these Special Education Program students fare in this new environment? An analysis of grades earned by those SEP students who entered UW in fall 1968 with a GPA of 2.0 or less was conducted by the UW's Institutional Research Office. The findings revealed that students who entered with higher high school GPAs (upper third of their classes) achieved cumulative GPAs that were higher by 0.56 grade points than those who entered with lower high school GPAs (lower third). Furthermore, the students entering with higher GPAs, earned more credits than did those who entered with lower high school GPAs.

What were other educational outcomes? At the end of spring quarter 1969, 27 SEP students were dropped due to low scholarship (i.e., their cumulative GPAs were below 2.0). For the SEP class that started fall 1968, 49% were enrolled in fall 1969. This group was composed of two-thirds transfers and one-third high school entrants. When BSU leaders were crafting the original demands, they did not foresee that the new recruits would need academic counseling in addition to tutoring. Thus, the $50,000 agreed to was insufficient. Even with a skeleton staff (director, assistant director, tutorial coordinator, clerical staff, tutors, and graduate students serving as counselors), the cost for running the program came to $125,000 for the first academic year.

After the first year, the program made concrete changes.

- *New recruitment emphasized prospective students who demonstrated the potential to be successful in a college setting even though their high school and community college grades did not meet the general admission criteria.*
- *The tutoring program transitioned from relying solely on volunteers to a combination of paid and volunteer tutors.*
- *Recruitment and admission goals were justified based on the proportion of minority groups residing in the various counties in the state from which the general student body came.*
- *Goal attainment was evaluated and strategies for improvement were designed and implemented.*

The program decided to use a three-tier admission system that ranged from regularly admissible (Group I), to alternatively admissible (Group II), to inadmissible with potential based on reading and writing tests (Group III), for minority and economically disadvantaged students. Reading and writing tests were established by the Department of English.

Student involvement in the decision-making process became an integral part of the program early on. An SEP Student Board was established in 1969. It was composed of three students each from BSU, AISA (American Indian Student Association), ACE (Asian Coalition for Equality), and MEChA (Movimiento Estudiantil Chicano de Aztlan).

SEP First Student Board Members

Members included Eddie Demmings, Wade Hill, Larry Merculieff, Lloyd Pinkham, Edna Paisano, Norma Berona, Felicita Franco, Delores Harris, and Jose Correa. Pinkham was chair and Harris was secretary. Worthy of note is that UMAS (United Mexican American Students) changed its name to MEChA in October of 1969.

Describing his role while serving in SEP, Hilliard spoke of other challenges he faced. One was particularly unforgettable. He vividly recalled his first meeting with the BSU. Some members demanded that he contribute 10% of his salary to the organization along with other demands. Hilliard exclaimed, "No, you go to the University. You get your money from them. You're not getting any money from me.... Not a dime!" He said he was told, "You need to tithe." Hilliard said, "What? Do you all realize that I've got a wife and two children, and you want my money?" He later provided funds for a student scholarship every year thereafter.

Bill Hilliard

Asian Inclusion

For the first year of SEP's establishment, Asian students were not targeted for recruitment and inclusion. Anthony Ogilvie, a UW alumnus, took exception to this exclusion following his brother's denial of admission by the University, even though he came from a background of poverty. The issue was called to the attention of the Asian Coalition for Equality (ACE), which sought an explanation from Dr. Evans.

According to Larry Matsuda, the explanation was that Asians were overrepresented. Finding this response unacceptable, ACE, Carl Miller, and Richard Brown confronted Dr. Evans on July 11, 1969. They were supported by members of the Asian community and BSU members including Larry Gossett, as well as ACE students Larry Matsuda, Anthony Ogilvie, and Woody Wong. They demanded that Filipinos and needy "Orientals" be recruited and become participants in the Special Education Program.

According to Larry Matsuda, the list of demands included:

To commit the SEP program to the formation of a recruiting committee for Filipino and needy Oriental students

- *To recruit Filipino and needy Oriental students*
- *To change the SEP brochure to include Filipino and needy Asian students*
- *To name Asian recruiters for the summer*
- *To ensure that the addition of Asians will not exclude students from other minority races*
- *To hire a Filipino or Oriental counselor as the need warrants*
- *To open the SEP Admissions Committee membership to Filipino and/ or Oriental descent*

Asian students demand inclusion, 1969.

Here is how Dr. Matsuda described the function of ACE:

That's what the Asian Coalition did [support the movement of other groups]. It coalesced around issues. If there was a labor issue we coalesced with any number of groups in protest, and then we would kind of go away, and for another issue we'd coalesce with different groups. For this we asked that they come and coalesce with us, and show up, so that we looked like we were bigger than we were which, you know, that's the old strategy.

Others who were present during the confrontation with Dr. Evans on July 11, 1969, included Ruthann Kurose, Roland Kurose, Andres Tangalin, Sonny Tangalin (principal of Franklin High School at one time), John Eng, and Joe Okimoto, a physician.

Dr. Evans was given 10 days to respond. He agreed to all the demands, with the caveat to demand number six. Hiring counselors would be based on whether funds could be secured. Funds were secured within five days.

SEP hired Larry Matsuda, Anthony Ogilvie, Teri Escobar, and Ruthann Kurose to recruit Filipinos and needy Asians. Matsuda, in reflection later, asserted:

But because of what we did, Tony and I, we got the Asians legitimatized into the EOP. So, we did actually have a division, we did actually have recruiters, and since then I would say thousands of Asian American kids have gone through there. I would say that I think that's a tremendous legacy in the sense that we were able to get kids in who wouldn't normally have gotten in. And who got in and then graduated and contributed to the community. One person who comes right to mind; I don't know if you know Al Sugiyama. He, in turn, started the Center for Career Alternatives, which helped thousands of people get jobs. Not only Asians but all kinds of folks get jobs and training. So, there's this kind of legacy.

SEP 2.0

In 1969, the Department of English, led by Professor Irmscher, designed the reading and writing test that students coded "Group III" were required to take for admission consideration (UW Office of Minority Affairs, Box 31). In 1970, the English 101–104 series was offered. Although remedial in nature, these courses brought EOP students up to speed. According to Larry

The Sugiyama Legacy

The Sugiyama legacy lives on not only in folklore and in the students whom he helped, but also in a Seattle city street being named in his honor. What follows is an excerpt from an article written about the occasion.

Alan Sugiyama, Celebration 2016.

The City Council passed Resolution 31827 today to honor the legacy of community activist Alan "Al" Sugiyama. 15th Avenue South between South Nevada Street and South Columbian Way will have an honorary designation of 'Alan Sugiyama Way.

It went on to say:

Sugiyama founded the Asian Family Affair *newspaper in Seattle in 1972. In 1989, Sugiyama was the first Asian American elected to the Seattle School Board where he served two terms, advocated for educational equity, and honorably served as President of the Seattle School Board. Sugiyama established the Center for Career Alternatives in 1979, an organization that provided free education, employment and career training for disadvantaged adults and youths in King and Snohomish counties. He later served as executive director of the Executive Development Institute.* (Council honors activist, 2018)

During Sugiyama's tenure at the Center for Career Alternatives, the program served more than 30,000 people. He served as executive director for 30 years. Also worthy of note is that Sugiyama was a 1974 EOP Recognition Award recipient, as well as the Charles Odegaard Award recipient in 2007.

Matsuda, "Professor Irmscher was a strong supporter, and real tough scholar, so I don't think anyone would want to challenge him for anything. He was well respected."

In addition to the English composition courses, the Mathematics Department, led by Professor Steve Monk, created the Math 100–103 series.

Unlike other remedial courses, EOP English and Math did not charge extra fees, and students received credit for the courses that counted toward graduation.

During that same period, a Policy Advisory Board was appointed by President Odegaard to provide guidance to administrators of the Special Education Program. The Board was composed of 12 faculty, eight students, and one non-academic staff member. An Academic Council was also established. It was composed of seven faculty, four staff, Sam Kelly as a consultant, Herman McKinney from the graduate school, and Carver Gayton from UW athletics, as well as students from BSU, the United Mexican American Students group (UMAS), ACE, and the American Indian Student Association (AISA), who were invited to observe and participate in the discussion.

President Odegaard appointed a Special Education Admissions Committee in preparation for the 1969–1970 recruiting cycle. It was comprised of Professor Charles Evans; Professor Virgil Harder, chair, Board of Admissions; Harold Adams, director, Officer of Admissions; and William Baker, Financial Aid.

During the 1969–1970 school year, recruiting was expanded with an ethnic-specific focus. Norma Berona, Felicita Franco, Domingo Nemesio, and Kip Tokuda were hired as Asian recruiters. Irene Castilleja, Gilbert Garcia, Eron Maltos, Jesus Lemos, Floyd Sandoval, and Tomas Sandoval from UMAS served as Chicano recruiters. Edna Paisano and Lloyd Pinkham were the American Indian recruiters. Darcy Drew was hired as the recruiter for economically disadvantaged white students.

According to Evans' notes, this expanded effort led to an increased enrollment of SEP students as well as minority students in general: 322 SEP students enrolled for fall quarter 1969, and another 71 enrolled in winter quarter 1970, with females representing 35% and 39% of each group, respectively. In all, 472 students were admitted to the University. At the end of two years, enrollment had doubled, and the budget tripled, but the high attrition rate of about 50% was still a challenge.

After two-years, Charles Evans decided to return to his role as chair of the Department of Microbiology. He took it upon himself to find his successor. The logical choice was Sam Kelly, who had served as a consultant during Evans' tenure. Kelly was a special assistant to the president of Shoreline Community College and director of Minority Affairs there. This relationship led to Kelly being recommended for director of SEP. The first leg of the evolutionary journey was completed.

"Dr. Sam" Kelly Builds the Foundation for the Office of Minority Affairs

Sam Kelly, a retired US Army lieutenant colonel, taught Black history at Shoreline. This provided a connection with faculty, although not at the depth and breadth that Professor Charles Evans had enjoyed. Kelly also brought his experience dealing with individuals in the upper level of the organizational

Increased Enrollment Figures

Distribution of students by category
Group I: 72 students
Group II: 309 students
Group III: 91 students

Fall quarter 1969 ethnic composition
150 American Indian
553 Black
987 Oriental
147 Spanish Surname
an increase from 1968 for each group

1969–1971 SEP biennial budget: $357,400 for salaries and wages; an additional $311,000 (over 50% in loans) secured for student financial support

Staffing: a director, two assistant directors, a personnel counselor, clerical staff, a half-time tutorial office coordinator, a tutorial office clerical staff member, an academic counselor, a special counselor, 75% of a Black Studies and special adviser costs, 33% of a special adviser, and clerical staff

(Evans, 1968b)

Samuel E. Kelly

hierarchy. Once offered the position, Kelly did not immediately agree to accept it. Experience taught him to avoid a middle level position; after all, he was projected to become a general had he remained in the military. Instead, he requested that the UW position be elevated to Vice President for Minority Affairs. At that level he would report directly to the president and would avoid having to rely on a vice president or dean to make the case for the needs and goals of the program. President Odegaard agreed to a vice president level appointment, a decision that profoundly affected the program's course of history.

With the embryonic stage of the evolutionary journey complete, the second leg of the journey bears the resemblance to that of a quantum leap. It was during this phase that a foundational infrastructure was set up. On June 1, 1970, Samuel E. Kelly assumed the role of vice president for the new Office of Minority Affairs (OMA). This appointment marked the first time a major university had named a vice president for minority affairs in the country.

The Special Education Program, of which the Office of Minority Affairs was the parent organization, was renamed the Educational Opportunity Program (EOP). This move not only minimized the probability of a stigma being associated with the name, but EOP more accurately described the unit's purpose and intent. Kelly's rationale for the name change was to avoid confusion with the Special Education Department in the College of Education.

This explains the reason for the name change; however, it does not explain the choice of the new description. When Bill Hilliard was asked in an interview about the rationale for calling the program EOP, he replied that "nationally, the programs were called Educational Opportunity Programs. So, he [Sam] adopted that immediately." The name Educational Opportunity Program was coined by Bill Somerville, the first director of EOP at Cal Berkeley. Educational Opportunity Programs in California were implemented as early as 1966 at Berkeley and UC Santa Barbara, as well as across New York's state university system in 1967. There were also Educational Opportunity Programs at Seton Hall, the University of Colorado, Oregon State University, and California State University schools.

The OMA organizational structure crystallized into a multifaceted operation. Kelly appointed Hilliard to the position of assistant vice president for student services. One year later he became Kelly's top assistant, supervising all staff including the directors of the four student divisions and the tutorial office (initially). Kelly's other choice for assistant vice president was Jim Collins, who was responsible for administration and financial services. One facet of OMA's organizational structure were semi-autonomous ethnic student divisions and an economically disadvantaged (white) division. These were responsible for recruitment, admission processing, financial aid, housing, and personal and academic advising. According to a brief prepared for the Second Annual Conference on Special Emerging Programs in Higher Education:

The rationale for organizing along ethnic lines, as opposed to a centrally organized, integrated group, is that this arrangement would best assure the cultural identity of each minority group while at the same time permit the five groups to work together, with the strongest possible voice and force, under the aegis of the Vice President for Minority Affairs. Working under the same guidelines for admissions, recruiting and counseling, each division could make best use of its awareness of the cultural, social, and economic circumstances of its minority community in recruiting and counseling—which included academic, financial aid, and personal counseling.

To supervise each ethnic student division, Kelly hired individuals who demonstrated strong leadership qualities, had the respect of students and their communities, and came from a history of activism. (See Appendix D for a list of the first supervisors.) He appointed Emmett Oliver, who had participated in Native American protests at San Quentin, to supervise the American Indian Division. (Emmett Oliver's son, Marvin Oliver—a gifted artist and sculptor—taught in the American Indian Studies Department for 40 years. In 2018, his grandson, Owen Oliver, also enrolled in the EOP). In addition, Kelly appointed Filipino community activist Mike Castillano to supervise the Asian and Poverty Divisions of the new OMA; Larry Gossett, a BSU founder, to lead the Black Division; and Sam Martinez, who was active with the United Farm Workers, as the supervisor of the Chicano Student Division.

Interestingly, despite knowing that Larry Gossett had not earned his bachelor's degree and had been to jail three times for sit-ins and protests, Sam Kelly, with Bill Hilliard's recommendation, chose Gossett to be the supervisor of the Black Student Division. Insightful, Kelly saw in Gossett strong leadership characteristics that were independent of educational attainment. It is not surprising that a retired lieutenant colonel would be very adept at recognizing such traits. Moreover, it is also likely that Kelly realized that Gossett's appointment would be accepted by Black students, as well as the Black community, without question. Ironically, six advisers with master's degrees would be reporting to Gossett. Gossett held the position for four years before taking a position as the director of the Central Area Motivation Program (CAMP).

In 1974, the Asian and Poverty Student Division was reorganized into the Asian Student Division, directed by Michael Castillano, and the Economically Disadvantaged Student Division, supervised by Judy Carr. "Some OMA staff fought against the decision to create this white student division. However, Kelly insisted, stating, 'We can't turn our backs on the poor white students who also don't have a chance'." Besides, Kelly was well aware the minority students who occupied President Charles Odegaard's office in the spring of 1968 had insisted that white students from poverty backgrounds be included in the program.

Another facet of the structure Kelly focused on was academic support services. These were expanded to encompass not just tutoring, but also

40th Street Instructional Center

reading, writing, and math study skills workshops supported by graduate students experienced in teaching introductory level courses in their respective departments. In 1971, the Reading Study Skills Center (J. Nathan Ward, director) was established to complement the efforts of the existing OMA Tutorial Center (Alexis Martinez, director) to address the less than adequate study skills with which EOP students entered the University. The tutorial office morphed into a tutorial center in 1972.

To house the two centers, Kelly secured a building across the street from the newly built Ethnic Cultural Center that would also serve as a home for an ethnic cultural theater. The Reading Study Skills Center offered workshops in math, writing, reading, and vocabulary building. This space also made it possible to eventually create discipline-specific drop-in centers, thus avoiding the cost inefficiency of scheduling one-on-one tutoring sessions. Larry Matsuda, employed in the OMA at the time, worked in tandem with J. Nathan Ward, founding director, in launching the Reading Study Skills Center. The Department of Mathematics also played an integral role in operationalizing the workshop component.

Although there was convincing evidence the Reading Study Skills Center would improve EOP students' chances of successfully matriculating at the UW, funding was not readily available. So how would Sam Kelly keep this fledging program afloat? Earlier that year, Kelly persuaded UW Athletics to donate revenue from the eleventh football game to the OMA budget. His effort was aided by the newly established Friends of the Educational Opportunity Program (FEOP), a group of supporters focused on raising private support for the EOP (see Appendix B for a list of founding members). According to Bill Hilliard:

> *The universities' West Coast teams were going to expand from 10 games a year to 11. At the time, Sam had been working with UW football coach Jim Owens to try to bring about some smoothing out of the ruffled feathers that had happened there during the Harvey Blanks era, and the demonstrations and so forth. [Harvey Blanks was a star running back who was kicked off the football team for his political activism.] So anyway, when they talked about expanding the game—of course Sam said, "Well, can we help to promote it? Is there something we can do to get in on some of this money that you all are going to raise from this eleventh football game?" Of course, Jim Owens was willing to do whatever he could to try to help smooth over things, because he wanted to remain as head football coach.*

The co-sponsorship by FEOP and Intercollegiate Athletics garnered $150,000 between 1971 and 1974. Securing these funds from the eleventh football game, Kelly was able keep the new program operational until a more stable funding stream was found.

The first annual EOP Scholarship Fund Drive was launched in 1971 to shore up the Scholarship Fund.

Other responsibilities of this newly formed group were "involvement in supporting student activities and communicating to the community EOP's goals and objectives" (*Friends of EOP*, 1972, UW Office of Minority Affairs, Box 54). In 1973, the Friends group began to sponsor an annual event celebrating the academic achievement of EOP students, and recognizing an individual from the campus community, or public or private sector, playing an integral role in supporting diversity efforts at the UW.

In his first annual report, Kelly had this to say about the group:

Friends of the Educational Opportunity Program (FEOP)

Kelly soon realized that to secure more students who qualified for the EOP, it was imperative that college was made more affordable (Office of Minority Affairs & Diversity historical records). Besides staff and faculty contributions via payroll deductions and funds from public agencies, private businesses, and individual contributors, a community group was founded in 1972 and named Friends of the Educational Opportunity Program (FEOP). FEOP Board members came from the private and public sectors. Their goal was to serve as a fundraising arm of the OMA, to serve as community advisors, and to raise private funds to support economically disadvantaged students.

The idea for the group was the brainstorm of Mrs. Dalwyn Knight and Dr. Kelly. The inaugural Board was composed of 25 members: 11 women, 14 men, 10 Blacks, and one Chicano. Also included in this group was Dr. Charles Evans; the *Seattle Post-Intelligencer*'s publisher Dan Starr; the first Black Regent, Dr. Robert Flennaugh; the only two Black architects in the state, C.R. Merriwether and Benjamin F. McAdoo, who had designed the newly created Ethnic Cultural Center; and one banker.

The Friends of EOP have been increasingly important in providing information to the majority community about EOP and in obtaining funds and other resources from the larger population. . . The President of the Friends of EOP (Mrs. Dalwyn Knight) and the Board of Directors gave countless hours of careful attention to the details for fund-raising and community education (UW Office of Minority Affairs, Box 1, p. 17).

Additionally, "The UW Alumni Association demonstrated its support for the EOP by publishing an article on the fundraising efforts of the Friends of the EOP in *The Washington Alumnus*" (February 1972, p. 4). The article helped to publicize the existence of the EOP and the FEOP, the need for scholarships, and the students who would receive them. Perhaps unspoken was the fact that some readers might doubt that the students were qualified, so the article also noted: "Of the thousand EOP students last spring, nearly 80% were in good academic standing with a grade point average of at least 2.63. Twenty-two percent had grade point averages above 3.0, 11% above 3.5" (p.4).

Along with the fundraising support the Friends provided, the EOP relied heavily on the Friends to help students resolve social problems. These included having a file of names on hand of volunteers who could provide emergency housing, transportation, dental, and other needs of the students.

An additional facet of Kelly's new organizational structure was implementing a social and cultural support system through the establishment of the Ethnic Cultural Center (ECC) and Ethnic Cultural Theater (ECT), the first center of its kind in the nation to have a multi-ethnic focus. According to a story in *The Daily*, the purpose of the ECC was "to act as a unit responsive to the academic, cultural and social needs of not only the University's minority students but also their own communities along with the majority community."

The benefits and rationale for having an ethnic cultural center on campus was that minority achievement would be enhanced through opportunities for EOP students to engage in cultural and social activities in a safe environment; a space considered by many to be a home away from home. To house this essential and relevant program, the vice president secured the site and the funds—approved by the Board of Regents—to build the facility. This accomplishment is a testament not only to Kelly's gift for persuasion, but also to Odegaard's and the Board of Regents' commitment to ensure that the program would be afforded every opportunity to succeed.

Ethnic Cultural Center site opened for business in the fall of 1972, following a ribbon-cutting ceremony attended by both Odegaard and Kelly. Roy Flores became the first director of the ECC and ECT. Besides student organization offices, staff offices, and a library, four ethnic specific rooms (American Indian, Asian, Black, and Chicano) were available for multiple purposes.

Murals were painted in three of the rooms. At the time, it was said that there was no interest in having a mural in the Asian Room until 1985. The American Indian Room mural was installed, but then removed and would not be painted again until 1985.

Realizing the role students played in creating SEP and the need for continued consultation with the Black Student Union, Kelly established a Student Advisory Board in 1971. This facilitated two-way communication between students and the OMA administration. The Board was composed of three student representatives from each ethnic student division to provide advice to the vice president for minority affairs on issues that were of concern

Ethnic Cultural Center Ribbon Cutting Ceremony, 1972.

to their constituents. This also allowed them to share with their constituents the OMA VP's position on relevant issues.

Building on what was begun under Charles Evans' leadership, Kelly garnered the support of key departments. This led to the development of introductory courses in English, biology, mathematics, and physics to provide a knowledge and academic skill-building bridge to regular university courses for EOP students. Of note was securing the involvement of Dr. Leonie Piternick, a biology professor. Piternick developed a course in learning the biological sciences. She also conducted workshops at the Reading Study Skills Center. Not only was she selfless in her support for EOP students, but she was also philanthropic, donating the $1,000 prize she received for winning the UW's Distinguished Teaching Award to the EOP Scholarship fund. She also was instrumental in persuading her colleague in physics, Professor Lillian McDermott, to develop a three-quarter physics sequence to help prepare EOP students for the physical sciences prerequisites.

Kelly also expanded and intensified recruitment of minority graduate and professional students. He saw the need not just to recruit, enroll, retain, and graduate minority and disadvantaged students with undergraduate degrees, but also the need to support minority and disadvantaged graduate and professional students. He brokered a deal with the dean of the graduate school, Joseph McCarthy, whereby the assistant dean of the graduate minority student division, Herman McKinney, would also serve as a special assistant to the vice president for minority affairs. Kelly later created a similar dual report arrangement with the director of Minority Health Sciences, Luther Strong.

These accomplishments notwithstanding, Kelly felt that minority graduate and professional students' completion rates were declining. He was highly critical of the various departments for the lack of support for minority graduate and professional students and questioned whether it was fair and equitable. He was also critical of the scarcity of minority faculty at the institution.

Recruitment Challenges

One would think that the opportunity for more minorities to attend college would be welcomed by high school staff throughout the state. While OMA Student Division supervisors developed amiable relations with some high school counselors, this was not universal. The recruitment staff, which consisted of work-study college students and one or two counselors, encountered resistance at some of the target high schools. For these challenges, and for prospective students who were not in school, recruiters visited community agencies, migrant worker fields, and prisons, as well as contacted recently discharged veterans and sought referrals from the State Employment Security.

Kelly was successful in persuading the University administration to allow OMA to administer the admission process for EOP students with input from a Policy Advisory Board. This move created a two-tier admissions system which lasted 27 years. As a result, all applications stamped EOP were forwarded to the EOP Admissions office. An EOP Admission Committee was established to determine student eligibility for enrollment in the program. A more formal version of the system established during Charles Evans', tenure was instituted.

Admissions categories were divided into three groups. Group I students entered with high school/college GPAs of 2.5 or better, had no core deficiencies. Group II included those students admitted with GPAs ranging between 2.49 and 2.0 and one high school core deficiency. Group III students with a GPAs below 2.0 and two or more high school core deficiencies and were required to pass a reading and writing test.

It is important to point out that applications stamped EOP, as well as the applications of other underrepresented minority students (Black, American Indian, and Mexican American) who applied through regular admission procedures, were all forwarded to EOP admissions (Washburn, 2015). It should come as no surprise that this divergent group, even with support services in place, would not earn grades comparable to the regularly admissible students in general. The GPA differential between EOP students and the all-UW student body was -0.4 grade points, and the good-standing gap was -11 percentage points. Needless to say, there were general concerns about the status of undergraduate minority students' academic performance and retention rates.

What was surprising was the lower-than-expected percentage of students admitted through the EOP who actually enrolled. One would assume that once minority and disadvantaged students who had been historically denied the opportunity to attend the University were given the opportunity to enroll, they would not hesitate to enroll once accepted. However, just over two-thirds actually did enroll.

Three Admission Categories

A core deficiency meant that the student was lacking the minimum number of high school credits in one of the specified subject areas, such as English, math, social studies, world languages, sciences, and others.

Group I students entered with high school/college GPAs of 2.5 or better, had no core deficiencies. They were deemed regularly admissible as they met the University's admission standards for all students, not only EOP students.

Group II included those students admitted with GPAs ranging between 2.49 and 2.0 and one high school core deficiency.

Group III students were student with GPAs below 2.0 and two or more high school core deficiencies. They would have been deemed inadmissible according to the University's regular admission standards. For Group III applicants to be admitted, they were required to pass a reading and writing test.

(UW Office of Minority Affairs, Box 1)

Another surprising revelation was that the proportion of EOP males attending the University was greater than that of females by a substantial margin, 61% vs. 39%, unlike the proportion that exists today where females dominate.

Unlike the Educational Opportunity Programs at the California institutions, some EOP admits at UW came from out of state. In fact, in 1970, Arthur "T" Boy Ross, a brother of the famous Supremes' lead singer Diana Ross, and Linus Griffin, the son of a Motown executive, transferred from Morehouse College and participated in EOP orientation. These students, along with Samuel L. Jackson and others, were expelled from the historically Black Morehouse College for locking board members in a building.

Once students were enrolled at the UW, OMA conducted an orientation program designed to familiarize them with campus and the role that EOP would play in their academic lives. They were introduced to college lecture scenarios and afforded the opportunity to review and learn new study skills. Students also participated in social events that encouraged inter-ethnic group interactions.

With Sam Kelly at the helm, the staff grew to 48 people after just one year. Fifteen were counselors. However, it was difficult to retain staff. The turnover rate hovered around 50%. The main reason given for this exodus was better pay and opportunities for advancement at the UW or in the private sector. Other reasons may have been that overqualified staff (with advanced degrees and years of experience) were being hired, or that those who were hired were not committed to the cause of helping program participants succeed. In terms of staffing demographics: 46% were women, 24% Black, 25% Asian, 24% white, 15% Chicano, and 12% American Indian. During this period, there were charges of discrimination by the Chicano Student Division in areas of employment and internal allocation of funds for recruitment and other support services.

Kelly continued to expand OMA's reach. Upward Bound, a pre-college program funded by the Department of Education that prepared minority and other disadvantaged students with potential to enter the University, was brought in under the aegis of the Office of Minority Affairs in 1972. It had been previously run by a faculty member in the College of Arts and Sciences.

Kelly was also a risk taker and highly skilled in the realm of persuasion. He convinced President Odegaard to consider a proposal to establish a prison education program on campus, which would be called the Resident Release

Project. This recruitment program was the first of its kind in America. Carl Miller broached the idea to Bill Hilliard, who was the conduit to Kelly. According to Hilliard, he had to convince Sam Kelly that it was Hilliard and Kelly's idea. It started with two male students, Willie Ryalls and Armando Mendoza, who were living in a halfway house in Seattle's Central District (30th and Jackson), a historically Black neighborhood. Ryalls and Mendoza argued that the commute time could be better spent studying if they were closer to campus. Establishing a program on campus was proposed to Kelly by their parole officer. Without trepidation, Kelly retorted, "I don't know why not." However, Kelly had already taken steps before approaching Odegaard to garner support for the idea from a group of judges, probation and parole officers, and select community activists whom he invited to his home on a weekend. Karen Morell, who at the time was a consultant in OMA, described it this way:

Sam miraculously—I don't know that anybody else could ever have done this—but he sat down and got Charles Odegaard to sign off on this and say this was something the University should do. Sam went as high as he could to get that kind of approval, as Sam knew how to do that better than anybody.

Following the compelling case made by Kelly to President Odegaard, the Resident Release Project was established in 1972. Participants were housed in McMahon Hall, a relatively new dormitory on campus. The selection of participants was administered by a UW faculty advisory committee chaired by Charles Z. Smith. Smith was a professor and associate dean of UW Law School. He also served on the area's first Black lawyer to serve as a municipal court judge in Seattle.

Later, the program became co-educational with the addition of women from Purdy, a state prison for women. The selection of this dormitory in the heart of campus was highly criticized and disapproval was further exacerbated when two of the participants became pregnant not long after joining this group. According to Hilliard, "Those were some difficult times, trying to negotiate that."

Participants were fully integrated into the OMA family of programs. Armando Mendoza, one of the first project participants, was chosen as its first director, reporting to Mike Castillano then director of the Asian and Poverty

Student Division. Karen Morell played an integral role in writing proposals for grants and conducting research related to the Resident Release Project. On average two participants were recognized annually for their academic achievement at the EOP Celebration Dinners. At least two became tutors at the Instructional Center.

The first EOP-sponsored banquet, Celebration '73, was held on April 27, 1973. According to the program minutes, its purpose was to honor the "tremendous personal commitment" of President Charles Odegaard and his wife Betty to the EOP; Sam Kelly and the EOP staff for their outstanding achievements in building the program; the University community for its consistent financial support and personal educational services; the individual efforts of students in the program; and "the impressive community backing reflected in our growing body of Friends," said Dalwyn Knight, president of the FEOP Board. Governor Dan Evans gave the principal address, and President Odegaard was honored with the creation of the Charles E. Odegaard Award. The award would be given in 1974 to honor an individual from the community or the University "for sustained and continued support of the Educational Opportunity Program at the University of Washington." The event was held in the Central District at a night club called the Heritage House. Making a cameo appearance at the event was Joe Frazier, former heavyweight boxing champion at the time.

The 1973 celebration was the first that honored the achievement of OMA students, including Resident Release Project participants. Eleven EOP students were so honored. The banquet allowed the EOP to be introduced to people in the community who may not have understood its purpose and progress. The event was such a success that

Student Recognition at Celebration '73

The first EOP-sponsored banquet, Celebration '73, was held on April 27, 1973. It was the first celebration honoring the achievements of OMA students, including Resident Release Project participants. The honorees were: Enrique Morales, Daisy Brooks, Silme Domingo, Norma Calderon, Rod Kawakami, Judy Charles, Haywood Evans, Michael Dixon, Rick Rosales, and Resident Release Project participants Manny Carvalho, Jr., and Al Raymond.

the FEOP Board decided it should become an annual event.

In 1975, a special sculpture for the award, titled "Unity," was created by noted sculptor and UW faculty member George Tsutakawa and donated by Ann Hauberg and Ray Merriwether, members of the FEOP Board.

Being one of the finest minority student programs in the country afforded OMA the opportunity to host a conference held November 7–9, 1974, entitled "Tomorrow's Imperative Today: Multi-Ethnic

President Charles E. Odegaard, 1973.

Programs." Larry Matsuda helped with the logistics for the conference. At the time Matsuda was working as a staff assistant and was completing coursework for his master's and PhD degrees in the College of Education. Appreciatively, Matsuda stated, "So EOP was an EOP [educational opportunity] for me, too."

Impressed with OMA's achievements in access, low attrition, and substantial graduation outcomes, the UW Board of Regents issued Policy Statement 11 on June 13, 1975. The statement expressed support of the admission of minority and disadvantage students as well as women using an alternative admission method. It stated:

> *The Board of Regents considers it to be one of the highest educational priorities of the University to provide special educational opportunities to persons from minority groups which have been historically denied access to higher levels of higher education, and to women in those professional and academic fields where they have been traditionally grossly underrepresented (and directs) the Office of Minority Affairs to continue to recruit minorities and provide such special educational opportunities as it deems necessary in order that more persons from underrepresented minority groups may qualify for admissions into graduate and professional schools.*

When Policy Statement 11 was issued, Dr. Robert Flennaugh was president of the board, the youngest ever to serve at the time, and the first

Black regent. He served from 1970 to 1977 and was a charter member of the FEOP Board. Also worthy of note is that he was the first Black student to graduate from the UW School of Dentistry and was the drum major for the UW marching band in 1961, one of the years when the football team went to the Rose Bowl.

The Charles E. Odegaard Award 1974–2021

Emile Pitre, 2020	Ron Moore, 1995
Marvin Oliver, 2019	Bernie Whitebear, 1994
Ricardo S. Martinez, 2018	Ron Sims, 1993
Joanne and Bruce Harrell, 2017	Sandra Madrid, 1992
Richard A. Jones, 2016	Ken Jacobsen, 1991
Colleen Fukui-Sketchley, 2015	Herman D. Lujan, 1990
Denny Hurtado, 2014	J. Ray Bowen, 1989
Rogelio Riojas, 2013	Frank Byrdwell, 1988
Gertrude Peoples, 2012	Andrew V. Smith, 1987
Assunta Ng, 2011	Phyllis Kenney, 1986
Nelson Del Rio, 2010	Norman Rice, 1985
W. Ron Allen, 2009	Nancy Weber, 1984
1968 Black Student Union, 2008	William Irmscher, 1983
Alan T. Sugiyama, 2007	Mark Cooper, 1982
Charles Mitchell, 2006	Millie Russell, 1981
Mike McGavick, 2005	Minoru Masuda, 1980
Jeff and Susan Brotman, 2004	Toby Burton, 1979
Herman McKinney, 2003	Vivian Kelly, 1978
Constance L. Proctor, 2002	Sam and Joyce Kelly, 1977
Ernest Dunston, 2001	Leonie Piternick, 1976
Vivian Lee, 2000	Larry Gossett, 1975
Albert Black, 1999	Dalwyn Knight, 1974
Bill Hilliard, 1998	
Andy Reynolds,1997	*Due to the COVID-19 pandemic,
Hubert G. Locke, 1996	no recipient was selected for 2021.

Bill Baker Joins OMA

A driven individual, Sam Kelly was highly motivated to be successful in his role as OMA vice president. Accordingly, he made a conscious effort to hire highly competent people. Bill Baker was one of those people. As early as 1967, President Odegaard enlisted the services of Bill Baker, director of financial aid, to facilitate financial support for Black enrollees who were former Upward Bound students. Here is what Hilliard said about Baker:

Bill Baker was as skilled at getting money into the University of Washington for scholarships as anybody I had ever seen before. He knew Featherstone Reid. Featherstone Reid was the top aide to Magnuson [US Senator from Washington 1944–1981] in DC. He and "Feather" were like combinations, Featherstone Reid being Magnuson's chief staff person for these issues, funding, and so on. Bill Baker got basically all the money he needed and could justify over the years when he was the head of the financial aid office. It was Jim Collins who told Sam [Kelly], when he [Collins] was getting ready to resign and leave, he said, "If you can get Bill Baker to come up here and take my job, you're going to have a genius in terms of money, handling money, raising money, and so forth.

Hilliard went on to say, "So Sam recruited Bill Baker, and he took over Jim Collins' job." Collins had been assistant vice president for minority affairs until 1972. Hilliard continued:

Bill was just a genius in getting money; getting work study money, getting regular scholarship funds at a certain level—because when we started the program, all of a sudden, we got all these poor people, much poorer than regular university students. So, we broke the bank within the first two years of financial aid, because we had all these needier students, and the neediest got the money. Bill had to come up with another whole set of money for these other students, basically white students that had been getting all this financial aid money prior to EOP happening. . . That was a hell of an achievement because there's only so much money to be allocated nationwide for scholarship funds. Bill Baker had an in with Feather Reid and Maggie's office, and he was able to pretty much accomplish whatever he needed to get money for the majority of the students that were needy.

His heart was always in the right place. I've never seen a guy get to work
at 6:30, 7:30 in the morning, and he's there at 6:30 and 7:30 at night, and
his hair's hanging down off his head and he's sweating and, you know, his
tie is half down and he's still working just like he was at eight o'clock in the
morning and it's seven o'clock at night. I've never seen a harder working guy.

In addition to his financial roles, Bill Baker also filled in as interim vice president several times when the position was temporarily vacant. Raul Anaya, a long-time academic counselor in OMA, added to the praise others have expressed: "I think Bill Baker was kind of like the rudder, or the stalwart, in the sense that he had that institutional history and memory to maybe inform and advise some of these VPs that followed to make them a quick study.

As Larry Matusda put it, "Bill Baker, truly one of the unsung heroes during the early years of OMA and beyond. With Baker on the team, Kelly was able to make the case for providing needed support for minority undergraduate and graduate students, which at the time was designated as EOP as well, which in turn led to enhanced graduation outcomes for EOP students, thus leading to an even more favorable view of the efforts of minority affairs."

Sam Kelly realized early on that he needed to have in place in-depth accountability measures. He felt compelled to be proactive in addressing the challenge of defending the legitimacy of the program. Not only did he require annual reports from all ethnic division and unit directors, but he also submitted annual reports to the University president and the Board of Regents. Included in these reports were enrollment numbers, number of degree earners, attrition data, and cumulative GPA data, all used to monitor program effectiveness. Challenges were highlighted, and Kelly recommended the steps to be taken to elicit improvement in program operations.

Studies were conducted to determine predictability of academic success. One such study showed that program participants outperformed expectancy based on their test scores. Another study was conducted by then-doctoral student Larry Matsuda to identify predictors of success for those EOP students who were inadmissible (Group III) but were allowed to enroll if they passed a reading and writing test. The most salient finding was that if students could successfully complete nine credits or more their first quarter, they would likely persist. Matsuda concluded: ". . . it seems like initial success is the best predictor of continued success. It had nothing to do with whether you went to church, who you hung around with, what your high school GPA was because they were all low GPAs anyway, whether you had a high school diploma or not. It had nothing to do with any of that. It had to do with whether you were successful your first quarter, and you could write your ticket if you were."

All Was Not Well in Camelot

Sam Kelly enjoyed what was considered analogous to a quasi-extended honeymoon that lasted nearly four years, from 1970 to 1974. All of that was about to change. As mentioned earlier, there were charges of discriminations against the Chicano Student Division in areas of employment as well as internal allocation of funds for recruitment and other support services. The Chicano student leadership met with President Odegaard and shared that OMA was not taking their concerns seriously. "The meeting focused mainly on increased staff to support high-risk rural Chicano students," said Enrique Morales, who was a MEChA student leader at the time. "Recruitment of students was equally an issue and, I believe, later led to the hiring of a full-time recruiter after Sam left."

The director of the Chicano Division left in frustration over being unable to expand the services and reach of the Division," Morales said in retrospect. "The students were primarily MECHISTAS as they are the ones who historically held UW and OMA&D accountable."The students suggested that the office should be split into Brown Affairs and Black Affairs. It should be noted that enrollment of Chicano students in EOP increased by 85% between

---

". . . it seems like initial success is the best predictor of continued success. It had nothing to do with whether you went to church, who you hung around with, what your high school GPA was because they were all low GPAs anyway, whether you had a high school diploma or not. It had nothing to do with any of that. It had to do with whether you were successful your first quarter, and you could write your ticket if you were."

—Matsuda, 2016

---

the time Kelly took office and the time he left in 1976. In fact, enrollment of Chicano students in EOP did not increase after Kelly left office, but instead declined by nearly 6% between 1976 and 1980.

Another issue of concern was the lack of Chicano faculty at the University. Kelly, too, was critical of the dearth of minority faculty at the institution. Tensions escalated when the Political Science Department refused to hire a Chicano faculty member. On May 13, 1974, a group of nearly 100 students occupied the office of the Dean of Arts and Sciences (George Beckmann) to protest a decision by the chairman of the Department of Political Science not to hire Carlos Muñoz, Jr., despite a majority vote of the department's faculty in favor of hiring him. Muñoz, a professor at UC Irvine, had chaired the first Chicano Studies department in the country at Cal State Los Angeles. During the protest, Beckmann's office was trashed, and he was temporarily held hostage. Beckmann was generally considered not to be friendly to the Office of Minority Affairs and its programs because of severe budget constraints and a strong effort to get rid of EOP Group III admits during his tenure.

Following the incident, there was a call for legal action against the director of the Chicano Student Division, Juan Sanchez, and an adviser in the Black Student Division, John Gilmore. Kelly sided with his staff, whom he had sent over to prevent matters from getting out of hand. On top of that, Kelly accused the chair of the department of being an institutional racist. Some members of the University community in turn accused Kelly of instigating the protest. This resulted in a chasm between OMA and those who sided with the Political Science Department. Nonetheless, Kelly showed demonstrable support for his staff and a strong commitment to social justice.

Did this good deed not go unpunished? A year later, Kelly fired Sanchez for insubordination and apparent blatant disrespect. Students protested the decision and directed their anger toward Kelly. Twenty-nine Chicano faculty and staff resigned over this and other matters. According to Kelly, in his autobiography, some members of the BSU, along with others, called him a sellout because he was unable to broker a successful outcome.

Speaking of Sanchez, Bill Hilliard was not very complimentary:

Anyway, he [Juan Sanchez] came in and before long they were agitating because they wanted the vice president for minority affairs to be Hispanic, kind of like [what] they were doing down there in California. A "Me

Reflections on Bill Baker

Karen Morell had nothing but praise for Baker as well. In her words:

He did extremely well, as far as I know, at all times in working with the Board of Regents. Talk about another person that loved the core mission of the university, education. Bill, being an avid reader, loved sitting down and talking to students, loved being able to make some kind of a situation work so that a student could get financial aid, and if any student was getting desperate for money the word was out there: go see Bill Baker. If anybody can make it work for you, Bill will make it work. Bill would set aside everything else he was doing in order to get that student that loan or that grant or whatever it was. So that value, again, on the individual was so great.

There was one time I remember Sam saying, "I don't know if OMA could be here if Bill Baker wasn't," because he took care of the budget in Sam's era so well. Having come out of Financial Aid, he was probably the only one in the office that really understood how to handle the fiscal side of the beginnings of OMA. He also knew that you needed data. Sam knew you did, too, so he would give it to him to do. . . . Bill Baker's role really was to shore up the nuts-and-bolts administrative work and make OMA look professional to the rest of the University, and to look as if it were an office with real fiscal integrity and policies that were in accordance with the University.

Adrienne Chan, a counselor who worked at OMA for more than 30 years, had this to say about Baker:

Actually, I think that oftentimes in the office, people underappreciated Bill. Bill did a lot, I thought, especially when it came to the Celebration. He wrote a lot of the narratives honoring the students. He was always in the background, but he didn't mind being there. That's one thing about it. He was Caucasian, but I think he had a conscience, a social justice conscience, and he didn't mind being in the background. Oftentimes people would say things, but I really think that in his heart he wanted to promote justice and he did it his way.

Jim Morley, who served as an executive staff assistant working with Bill Baker for several years in the early 1970s, shared his memories:

As far as Bill Baker is concerned, I think that Bill at one point had been the director of financial aid, so he knew a great deal about financial aid, grants, and student loans, and where to get money. He was great for getting students through all the twists and turns and all the things that you needed to do. He was a very strong advocate for the program, and he worked very closely with Sam Kelly. They worked closely with—I think it was [John] Hogness at that time—the president of the University. I think they were pretty effective, all things considered. I know that Bill had a lifelong commitment to the students. Even the kids that he had helped get financial aid years ago would drop by and thank him. I thought very highly of him; I think he worked very hard to make the program a success.

Too" program. Anyway, this particular guy, I guess he headed up the demonstration in the Arts and Sciences dean's office. The demonstration over in the Arts and Sciences building was only part of it and then of course that picture was on the front page of The Daily *with him sitting up there with his hat on, smoking a cigar, with his feet up on the dean's desk. Anyway, it was a mess.*

Regarding the groups that opposed Sam Kelly and called for his resignation, it was ironic that the Black Student leadership (according to Kelly) was among them, considering enrollment of Black students in EOP was the highest in 1974, increasing more than six-fold during the 1967–1968 enrollment period. That level would not be reached again until the fall of 2017.

One might also wonder why any group would revolt against Kelly, who had structured the organization so that it emphasized ethnic-specific services to the students and represented the interests of that particular community. The

ASUW members (left to right) James Cantu, Francisco Irigon, Isaac Alexander, and Larry Bizzell, 1972

answer may lie in the operative phrase "interests of that particular community." All is well and good as long as there was not a situation whereby an ethnic-specific group felt the need to coalesce around an issue that was germane only to that group. When that happens, the ethnic student division can easily become a political force of resistance disrupting the stability of the entire organization.

What was striking about this period is that students, staff, faculty, and community groups did not hesitate to offer opinions on various issues including hiring, firing, and policy decisions. Calls for the resignation of administrators was commonplace. What did not happen was the call for removal of staff. Nor was there a demand that students receive support to ensure their successful navigation through the University, which would lead to the ultimate goal of degree attainment.

Eventually, Kelly opted to remove himself. On September 26, 1975, he announced that he intended to resign as vice president effective July 1, 1976. Kelly felt he did not have the same support from President Hogness that he had enjoyed with President Charles Odegaard. Once this realization had sunk in, he decided that he could not be effective as a vice president, so he tendered his resignation.

At the October FEOP Board meeting, he expressed his appreciation for the important role of the Board and announced his plans for the future. First, he wanted to assure the Board that he had not been forced out by President Hogness. Second, he viewed his experience as vice president for Minority

Affairs "as one of the most exhilarating experiences of his life." Third, he shared that he had accepted a half-time appointment as Special Assistant to President Hogness beginning after July 1, 1976. Fourth, he stated that "he could not visualize his successor coming in and not wanting the Friends of EOP's continued support." Dr. Kelly stated that President Hogness assured Kelly his successor would be hired at the vice-presidential level.

Considering all the positive things Kelly did to create a foundation and build one of the finest such programs in the country, along with the fact that some detractors wanted to see it fail, it defies logic that issues with one group would prompt his resignation at an ostensible untimely juncture—a fork in the road. According to Isaac Alexander, the first EOP and Black student to serve as ASUW vice president, "One thing Sam always would say, if he believed that he didn't have the support of the students, then he would leave."

Kelly spoke at the Celebration '75 banquet for the last time as the OMA VP. In his message, he acknowledged and expressed appreciation for the support that EOP had received from UW presidents Odegaard and Hogness, Governor Evans, faculty, staff, "numerous friends in the legislature, and from many very good friends indeed in the business and civic community." He added that, "Much of this support has come during controversy, during times when non-commitment or skepticism would have been easy." Indeed, 1975 was such a year, with challenges to the program from state funding cuts and from an increasingly conservative political climate nationally and in the state.

What also is notable is that some minority groups supported each other, but not all did. The Asian, American Indian, and economically disadvantaged white student groups seemed to avoid taking political stances for the most part, especially during the Kelly era. During the controversy involving the firing of the supervisor of the Chicano Student Division, these groups combined represented 45% of the EOP enrollment. Nonetheless, lack of opposition from these groups, coupled with support from other interest groups, were not enough for Kelly to stay the course and leave on a positive note ensuring that the tutorial center and the reading/study skills center would be adequately funded. Significantly, there is no evidence that President Hogness encouraged Kelly to stay on. Could there have been a notion that a change in OMA leadership may quell the unrest that continued to foment?

Once the decision was made to resign, Kelly delivered a number of farewell speeches. On December 17, 1975, Kelly gave a speech at the Administrative Council of high-ranking UW governance people. The speech was a "valedictory" summary of the good, the bad, and the needs for the future. He spoke about the Chicano protests and had words of advice. One piece of advice was never to favor one minority group over another in the hopes of quieting a protest, because "I can guarantee you that you will stir up animosities and resentments among the other groups that will haunt you for a long time!"

He also shared thoughts on EOP reorganization. He said that organizing EOP along ethnic or racial lines had seemed necessary and helpful at the beginning, but "the unhappy and wasteful events of last spring" had caused him to reconsider. He said, "It may now be possible to continue to progress, and to reduce the factionalism that organization along ethnic lines helps to preserve, by reorganizing the office according to function."

During the same year that Kelly addressed the Administrative Council, he posited the following futuristic remark: "We can't know how the story of the Educational Opportunity Program will turn out. I am certain that when we look back 20 years from now, and with better historical perspective, we will have reasons to be grateful for our determination of a first-rate program." He further stated, "I deeply hope that if someone is moved to write a history in the year 2000, he or she will look back at the 1970s as an enlightened time when a great university, confronted with deep and serious problems of social justice, demonstrated this by opting for a period of painful and difficult change, rather than for a vain defense of business as usual."

In 2016, almost two decades beyond the turn of the century, I was so moved to begin writing the history of OMA&D with the support of administrative and program leaders, and the cooperation of many people who care about the students.

"Sam was way ahead of his time," recalled Enrique Morales. "The one thing about Sam, you know, whether you agreed with him or not, you always knew he was going to go to the wall for the people. No half-ways, he was going to go to the wall."

About Kelly's tenure as VP, longtime staff member Raul Anaya said:

"[He was] very persuasive, and as a VP he was positioned to work with the cabinet and the president to get things done. So, he met that challenge of us becoming integrated and respected on campus, from the academic perspective

and the student support perspective, all of that. The community saw that the University was at least making an effort to have a representative, a URM (underrepresented minority) person, who has lived the life and experienced it personally, so that he could talk from experience as to what the needs were."

Dr. Karen Morell, a special assistant to Kelly for almost his entire tenure at OMA offered this illuminating description about Kelly's effectiveness:

It was Saturday night [at the Kelly home], and Charles Odegaard was there, [Governor] Dan Evans was there, Jim Ryan [vice president for finance and budgeting] and several of the vice presidents were there, and they were schmoozing, and by the time it was all done what Sam needed to have happen had happened, and we could move on. I mean, he did that. He was a genius at it.

One of the things that for me, still looking back, is really important is the way in which Sam especially, but a few others too, were leaders who were really passionate about supporting the individual lives of these students in OMA. It wasn't just a program, and you needed to dump X amount of money in it, and you needed this kind of supervision and all that stuff.

It was an incredible opportunity to sit in Sam's office and overhear the phone calls or the meetings whether it was with [UW President Charles] Odegaard or the regents or, you know, Jim Ryan, [vice president for planning and budgeting], and I began to find out how things worked. So, it was stunning to be able to do that, and with someone like Sam, to see all the different ways he found to persuade people to do what he thought needed to be done.

During Dr. Kelly's tenure at UW, OMA grew exponentially. Staffing went from 10 people to 57 (a 470% increase). The budget went from $357,000 to more than $2.3 million (Kelly & Taylor, 2010). In addition, the EOP enrollment grew from 882 to 2,633 (a nearly 200% increase), and a total of 912 EOP students had graduated from the University by the end of Kelly's tenure.

Despite a few hiccups along the journey, many of the programs established while Dr. Kelly was at the helm have endured with some modification over the five decades. It is important to bear in mind that the journey is not always smooth despite the good intentions of travelers along the way. Many obstacles may loom over the horizon.

Sam Kelly at a MEChA meeting, circa 1971.

Reflections on Sam Kelly

What did those with whom he worked have to say about Dr. Samuel E. Kelly?

Larry Matsuda described him eloquently:

> He became doctor later, but he was colonel first. There was a lot of "military" about him. The way he dressed, the way his expectations were. So, he was always upright, and he was always a man of principle. He wasn't afraid to stand up and say something. I know that in any organization where we've got a leadership role there are people who are trying to undercut you all the time, and he just played past it because he knew that what he was doing was important for kids, or students, and that was one of his organizing themes.
>
> Although he did have a doctorate, he was more the warrior. He was the warrior king, and we all knew it. What he did was,

in terms of his staff, we felt as if we were part of a movement. We were part of his unit, his team, and we knew what needed to be done and we did it. He held us accountable, too, but that's good. The other thing that stands out in my mind is he knew that he would have to expand his base. He worked with a woman named Dalwyn Knight and they started the Friends of EOP. Dalwyn Knight is very much like her name, like high society. He [Kelly] had a lot of charisma.

Adie Chan, who spent much of her professional career as a counselor in the Asian Division, said of Dr. Kelly:

He was a role model. He was very insightful. He got along with everyone. Even though he was barking at everyone, he got along with everyone too. I think Dr. Kelly really set the tone. I didn't realize it was Dr. Kelly who made the insistence on a VP position, but that's key. That's key because the other programs headed by directors can easily be eliminated or become very small in the United States, in the colleges like UC Berkeley. Directors run programs that are vulnerable to the whim of budget cuts, and oftentimes those programs are the first thing that go. And that means that issues for minority students go down the drain.

Jim Morley, former Instructional Center (IC) writing instructor, recalled Kelly's military career as important. He noted:

He had been in the military. I think he was a career man in the military, and he didn't broach any nonsense from just about anybody. He was a strong advocate. I think people respected him. They might not have agreed with him, but they weren't going to tangle with him. So yes, I think Sam got it all started. He was the one who laid the foundation, and some of the people we had after him I didn't think too highly of. I think Sam Kelly set the bar. I respected him because he was tough, and he did the right thing. He had high expectations and that was fine.

It is important to bear in mind that the journey is not always smooth despite the good intentions of travelers along the way. Many obstacles may loom over the horizon.

—Emile Pitre

Searching for a Successor

The third leg of the journey began with much anticipation and optimism. From a list of more than 300 candidates, the UW administration selected an academic (mathematician) from Drexel University to take the helm. Dr. Ewaugh Finney Fields received a dual appointment in OMA and the College of Education in 1976.

The honeymoon period for the new vice president was short-lived. Things did not go well when the UW leadership proposed to reorganize the ethnic student divisions along functional lines rather than by ethnicity. The rationale for the proposed change was budgetary constraints, and the need to eliminate duplication of services. Reorganization should prioritize academics that would better prepare EOP students for engineering and health sciences majors, as well as graduate and professional school. To achieve these goals, it would require a better funding model for the academic support units, which were disproportionately funded compared to those of the ethnic student divisions. When it came to advocating for the OMA biennial budget, some staff felt that it was not a priority for President Hogness.

Focusing on academics, as well as streamlining the budget, led to the merger of the two academic support units, the Reading/Study Skills Center and the Tutorial Center, renamed the Instructional Center (IC). To further strengthen the academic component of OMA, Dr. Fields was instrumental in upgrading the instructors to professional staff status. This professionalization resulted in a sizable boost in both salary and morale for the instructors.

During her short tenure, Fields made another significant contribution. Conversations between Fields and the faculty in the College of Engineering led to the creation of the Minority Introduction to Engineering Summer Bridge Program. The program attracted promising minority students from across the state. The science and math components were developed by a Reading/Study Skills Center instructor, Dr. Norihiko (Nori) Mihara.

Staff and students from two ethnic student divisions (American Indian and Chicano) strongly objected to the notion of dissolving the units. The Black Student Division, on the other hand, was in total support of the proposed change. A controversy ensued and was played out in the student newspaper, *The Daily*. Mike Castillano, assistant vice president for supportive services, also supported the change. Furthermore, according to archival documents, both President Hogness and Kelly supported the idea of reorganizing along functional lines. It was also recommended by the EOP Policy Advisory Board. Thus, the new vice president inherited the mandate for reorganization. Fields argued that more emphasis needed to be placed on funding the Tutorial and Reading Study Skills centers to improve the academic performance of EOP students. She was concerned that far too many EOP students were not being admitted to graduate and professional programs because of inadequate academic assistance.

The Asian Student Association came out in opposition almost two months after the reorganization was first proposed. The ethnic/community side argued that recruitment and retention would suffer as a result of decentralization. American Indian students felt that only staff from the American Indian Division could provide the services unique to their needs. Faced with internal challenges and apparent philosophical differences between Fields and the UW president, Fields resigned from the vice presidency and the leadership went through yet another transition in less than a year.

Following Dr. Fields' resignation, President Hogness named an ad hoc committee to evaluate the Educational Opportunity Program. Hubert Locke, the assistant vice provost for academic affairs, was named committee chair. The task force looked at the question of whether ethnic divisions were the most efficient use of resources and at the other internal problems that had been experienced. The positive side of the division approach was the enhanced ethnic identity and maximum rapport that could be achieved with the students served. In other words, students preferred to work with advisers who looked like them.

One might surmise that with such turmoil in OMA, leaving a position vacant at this level might lead to a dismantling of the program. When information was leaked that the ad hoc committee was entertaining proposals ranging from creating a unit with both professional and peer counselors outside of the ethnic student divisions, to replacing most of the counseling duties with those of UW departmental advisers, OMA staff and members of the community concluded the administration was considering replacing the position of vice president, possibly with that of a director. It was widely believed that the intent behind implementing this model was to transfer the savings to the tutorial center. To further exacerbate concerns, President Hogness did not say whether Fields would be replaced.

One of the conclusions reached by the ad hoc committee was that tutorial and study skills resources were woefully inadequate, and that the two units (counseling center and tutorial/reading-study skills center) should develop a closer working relationship with the ethnic student division staff.

Other recommendations included the following:

- *The student advisory board should be expanded to include faculty from the American Ethnic Studies Department*
- *Some of the staff should be assigned duties that are not ethnic specific*
- *Graduate student teaching assistants should be assigned to work at the tutorial/study skills center*
- *Students who appear to have a good chance of achieving academic success should be recruited*
- *Contracts should specify areas of deficiency and staff expectations for students participating in support programs* (UW Office of Minority Affairs, Box 25)

In its final statement, the ad hoc committee asserted it shared the conviction that EOP was vitally important to the mission of the University and merited continued support. The task force also recommended that OMA be retained with the vice president position remaining intact. With this, the third leg of the evolutionary journey ended.

Outcomes

Substantially positive outcomes were realized over the first decade of this evolutionary journey despite the untimely departures of two vice presidents in just over one year and what might be construed as an uncertain future of OMA. Staffing and enrollment of program participants both increased five-fold; the budget grew from $350,000 to nearly $2.3M; and 1,157 EOP students had earned bachelor's degrees. While OMA began tracking EOP degree earners by ethnicity in 1970, the University did not begin tracking in this manner until 1975. Out of this group of degree earners emerged alumni who went on to distinguish themselves in public service, education, law, business, healthcare, and the arts.

STUDENT CASES

ANTONIO SALAZAR. Although the eight minority recruiters who were hired after the sit-in visited various locations in eastern Washington, Kennewick was not one of them. So, how did Antonio Salazar end up at UW? While working at a summer job, according to Salazar, he was thinking "either [he was] going to enlist in the Army or go to Columbia Basin Junior College." However, these options changed when his supervisor, Ralph Button, encouraged him to consider attending the University of Washington. If interested, Button said he could facilitate the process including securing financial aid. Antonio was admitted into the Special Education Program (SEP). "Biggest break ever for me as I was the son of a farm worker family and never thought I would go to college as I knew that I could not afford it," wrote Salazar.

Salazar, along with more than 30 Chicano students, began their studies at UW in the fall of 1968. Soon after the quarter began, Salazar and a few other students founded a chapter of United Mexican American Students (UMAS). According to Salazar, he, Erasmo Gamboa, and other Chicano activists later established MEChA (Movimiento Estudiantil Chicanos de Aztlan) on the UW campus and "helped recruit Tomas Ybarra-Frausto to become the first Chicano Studies professor." Salazar served as the UMAS and MEChA photographer and chronicled the activities and demonstrations from 1968 to 1972. According to Salazar, he was taught by an older photographer who shot much of the United Farm Workers (UFW) activities.

While at UW, Salazar also served on the newly established Student Advisory Board. It is important to note that Salazar's endeavors were not only limited to the UW campus. In 1971, he operated the first bilingual bookmobile out of the Mid-Columbia library in Kennewick, Washington, promoting literacy in labor camps throughout eastern Washington. He and other Chicanos from the 1968 cohort, such as Eron Maltos, Jesus Lemos, Jose Correa, Roberto Trevino, and Gilbert Garcia, were also involved in the United Farm Workers movement.

In 1972, Antonio Salazar graduated with a BA in Latin American Studies. He went on to attend the UW School of Law. He was the classmate of Leroy McCullough, an SEP alumnus who became a King County municipal judge, as well as Richard Jones, half-brother of Quincy Jones. Richard became a United States District Judge for Western Washington in Seattle. Salazar graduated from UW with a JD in 1975. He also had fond memories of attending Georgetown Law School for a year.

As Salazar reported, upon completing law school, he "went to work for United Farm Workers in Calexico in the legal office to support organizing efforts."

"[My] first appearances as an attorney were in California on behalf of UFW." Salazar practiced law for 35 years. During that period, he stated [he] "wrote many articles on the practice of law, giving presentations before the annual meeting of the Washington State Bar Association, Continuing Legal Education seminars, and to many Chicano/Latino groups." He also practiced immigration, criminal, civil, and civil rights law with a substantial appellate practice." In one of his most notable cases, Salazar was one of three attorneys representing La Raza Lawyer's Association as amicus. The case "involved farm workers in the state of Washington (Macias v. Department of Labor & Industries), which led to a Supreme Court decision [that] reversed lower court decisions and gave farm workers the same worker's compensation coverage as everyone else, from day one" wrote Salazar. He further stated, "This was a very significant decision as it impacted a whole industry of workers."

Examples of other cases that he litigated included Filipino Alaskan canning industry workers, taco truck vendors, a Mexican asylum seeker, and a stop and search case of a Latino that was a violation of the defendant's 4th Amendment rights, to name a few.

According to Salazar, the impact of his photography came to the forefront almost 50 years later with the opening (2019) of the Sea Mar Museum of Chicano/a and Latino/a Culture in Seattle where between 40 and 50 of his images are housed. Another compilation of his photographic images appears in his Chicanismo collection at University of California, Santa Barbara. Continuing to give back to the community, Salazar volunteered every Saturday morning for three years at a legal clinic housed in Serve the People Community Health Center, a free medical clinic in Santa Ana, California. At the time of this writing, Salazar was working with a Colombian immigrant who was a writer/activist in Colombia to establish a new website for Latinos on political/other issues. "I am always learning," said Salazar.

ROGELIO RIOJAS. Two of the notable EOP alumni for the 1968 to 1977 decade were appointed to the UW Board of Regents by the governor of Washington State. One of them, Rogelio Riojas, was the first Latino to be appointed to this august board. For Riojas, the possibility of attending the University of Washington was highly unlikely considering his early years and family background. During his first 15 years, he, his parents, and 11 siblings lived a peripatetic life as migrant farmworkers. Between April and November, the family would move from Texas to the Yakima Valley (Washington), the Skagit Valley (Washington), California, and sometimes to Arizona, before returning to Texas, harvesting sugar beets, various fruits, and cotton along the way. It was the only viable means this family of 14 had for survival. When it came time for high school, Riojas' family settled in Othello, Washington. There, unlike his seven older siblings, he graduated from high school.

According to Riojas, his intentions were to attend Columbia Basin Community College because he did not believe there was any chance of his attending the University of Washington. However, all that changed when he was introduced to Chicano student recruiters and staff who informed him and four other Chicano high school graduates that attending UW could become a reality. Impressed with the recruiters' presentation (he specifically mentioned recruiters Floyd Sandoval, Eron Maltos, and Tomas Sandoval), Riojas applied to the UW and was accepted through the Special Education Program (SEP). At the UW, Rogelio received advising and tutoring support from the SEP staff and volunteers. Rogelio went on to earn a bachelor's degree in four years. He later earned a master's degree and credits the University of Washington for being responsible for the emergence of a professional Latino community in the state of Washington.

Riojas went on to become the president and CEO of Sea Mar, a multi-million-dollar health and human services non-profit organization, one of the largest in the nation. Riojas was appointed to the UW Board of Regents in 2013 and served on that Board till 2019.

Not forgetting from whence he came, Riojas gives back to the community not only through personal contributions but also through Sea Mar, which provides UW graduates with internships, scholarships, and career opportunities at its medical and dental clinics (The power of giving back, 2009-10). For 25 years, his agency has been awarding scholarships to Latino students. Currently, 200 students receive $1,000 scholarships annually.

FAUSTINO RIOJAS. Perhaps inspired by Riojas, his older brother Faustino Riojas decided to attend the UW at the age of 35. He had been a high school dropout but earned an associate degree at a community college. He entered the UW through the EOP, earned a BA in Biology in 1985, and went on to earn an MD from the UW Medical School in 1990. He has been practicing medicine in the state for more than 25 years. In addition, Riojas has three children who are EOP alumni, one of whom serves on the FEOP Board of Trustees.

Notable EOP Alumni from the Early Years

While the attrition rate of students who entered the UW through the alternative (special) admissions process was relatively high, a considerable number (more than 60) earned degrees within five years. A few went on to earn advanced degrees, e.g., masters, law, and doctoral degrees. One earned a Doctor of Chiropractic degree. During their undergraduate studies, a few took up the mantle of activism. One of them was Antonio Salazar, a 1968 graduate of Kennewick High School whose story appears in the previous "Student Cases" section.

Erasmo Gamboa, '70, '73, '85, PhD (UW)
Joseph S. Gauff, Jr, '71, '73, MBA (UW), '79, PhD (UW)
Wilson Edward Reed, '71, MA (University at Albany, SUNY), PhD
    (Northern Arizona University)
Mylon Winn, '71, '75, MA (UW), '81, PhD (UW)
Emilio V. Aguayo, '72, MA (Oregon State)
Donald Felder, '72, PhD (Union Institute)
Sidney Gallegos, '72, '76, DDS (UW)
Richard Harr, '72, MD (UW)
Richard L. Haynes, '72, DC (Palmer College of Chiropractic)
LeRoy McCullough, '72, '74, JD (UW)
Norman Rice, '72, '74, MPA (UW)
Ramon Rodriguez, '72 (UW)
Daniel DeSiga, '73 (UW)
Annie Galarosa, '73, MEd (Western Washington University)
Theodore Olivarez, '72, Certificates, Training & Development and
    Project Management (Portland State)
Rogelio Riojas, '73, '75, '77 MHA (UW)
Lynn D. French, '74 MHA (UW), JD (Seattle University)
Ruthann Kurose, '74 (UW)
Ricardo Martinez, '75, '80, JD (UW)
Allan L. Bergano, '75, '81, DDS (UW)
Isaac Alexander, '75, '76, MA (UW)
Deloria Jones, '75 (UW)
Lillian Trevino, '75, PA (UW)
David Della, '76, (UW)
Phyllis Hursey, '76, MD (Howard)
Joanne Harrell, '77, '98, MBA (UW)
Steve Pool, '77 (UW)
Barbara Earl Thomas, '77, MFA (UW)

The third vice president, Dr. Herman Lujan, pushes for changes and meets resistance.

CHaPTer 3

1978–1987: A Decade of Turbulence and Change

Students, staff, and community members vehemently opposed such changes, especially testing and residency requirements. Chicano and Asian (mostly Filipino) students and community members moved to occupy the building (Schmitz Hall) where OMA staff and administrators were housed. There was a call for a change in the policy, for the formation of a committee of student and community leaders that would be consulted concerning changes in minority program policies, for Lujan to resign, and for no reprisals for to those taking part in the demonstration.

—Guillen, 1980

With the departure of Ewaugh Fields from OMA, and Bill Baker's appointment as acting director, student protests subsided. However, the absence of controversy was short-lived. OMA hired a person who was not Chicano to serve as one of the counselors in the Chicano Student Division. It was the first time in the history of OMA that someone (Bernice Letoy Eike, a Sioux Indian and social worker) was hired to work in a student division whose ethnicity was different from her own. The rationale was that race could no longer be used in EOP hiring decisions, as ruled by the UW Human Rights office. Chicano students and their community vehemently objected and staged a sick-out. After seven days, the sick-out ended when the University administration reversed its decision. Raul Anaya, one of the counselors, was pleased with the decision. He considered this to be a "small victory" of which many more were needed. Eike remained in OMA serving as an American Indian adviser until her retirement in 2007.

Later that year, the Black Student Union objected to hires Bill Baker was involved in. In a confrontation with Baker about one hire at the Instructional Center, students alleged Baker with cronyism and told him they did not believe he should be chosen as the next vice president of OMA. Another was the appointment of a new director at the ECC. This was called into question once it was leaked that the search committee had recommended someone else for the position, even though the person chosen was American Indian, the first to be chosen for a leadership position outside of the American Indian Student Division.

One might surmise that with the ongoing controversies, and the fact that Bill Baker was not appointed interim vice president, it may have been a sign that President Hogness was contemplating demoting the position, especially since, at the time, President Hogness did not guarantee that Ewaugh Fields would be replaced. Thus, it comes as no surprise some minority communities feared the vice presidency of Minority Affairs would soon end. Their fears were allayed when the position for vice president was advertised. Two plausible reasons why the position was not abolished were because the ad hoc committee took a strong stance against abolishing the position and because of the steadfast support for OMA by the Board of Regents, including such members as Mary Gates, James R. Ellis, and Robert Flennaugh. The Board had adopted a favorable resolution on minority student admissions in 1975 and was highly unlikely to support an abolishment.

The third vice president for Minority Affairs, Dr. Herman Lujan, was appointed in 1978 after a year of interim leadership. The fourth leg of the journey was launched. Lujan, too, had notions of reorganizing. The first step was to create an academic advising unit. Implementation of Lujan's plan would require shifting staff from the ethnic divisions. Elaine Miller was appointed director of the new unit. Lujan felt that it was more important to emphasize academic survival. He was concerned about students flunking out and leaving the University with heavy debt. He also felt that more emphasis should be placed on study skills and tutoring.

He was also concerned about the attrition rate, which hovered around 40%. One strategy was to implement a summer bridge program lasting four to six weeks, designed to give the most underprepared EOP students an early start on preparing for the rigors of the University curriculum. It never came to fruition due to lack of funds. In 1995, however, a three-week program was successfully implemented.

Lujan also felt that the academic advising unit, coupled with increased academic support, would improve EOP students' chances of being admitted to graduate and professional schools. This strong emphasis on preparing students for graduate school was likely coming from Lujan's professorial bent with the intent of creating a more credible program in the eyes of the academicians, a concern minority communities would call elitist. Along the same line, Lujan proposed creating an EOP honors program. Lujan believed that making admissions more selective would further enhance credibility.

In addition, his plan was to add graduate students to the newly formed unit. This paradigm shift did not sit well with some student groups, especially Black students, or with staff. In fact, Myrtis Thomson, supervisor of the Black Student Division, resigned citing the lack of substantive data and definition of the problem. She also took issue with the fact that no input was solicited from staff other than Lujan's two assistant vice presidents. The Black Student Union president, Tricia Kinch, questioned whether there were data and studies to justify the need to make what was considered a major change.

This proposed change was also met with resistance from the Chicano Student Division. The most vocal opposition was from Jesus Rodriguez. It resulted in UW MEChA students occupying the Chicano Student Division of the OMA and organizing a sick-out to protest the proposed reorganization, which amounted in their minds to an attempt to create a separate admissions unit (Castaneda, n.d.). MEChA—Movimiento Estudiantil Chicanx de Aztlán, "Chicanx Student Movement of Aztlán" [the x being a gender-neutral inflection]—is an organization that seeks to promote Chicano unity and empowerment through political action.

Another change Lujan implemented during his first year was to establish an EOP Admissions Office to process the admissions applications received by each ethnic student division and to handle financial aid matters. Dr. Mira Sinco was named as the first director. Prior to this organizational restructuring, the ethnic student divisions were responsible for these functions.

Next came a policy change. The vice president proposed instituting significant changes in the admissions criteria in 1980, less than two years into his tenure.

In summary Lujan's, goals were:

- *To place greater emphasis on academic advising for those EOP students who had earned 45 or more credits and had no high school core deficiencies*
- *To increase the number of EOP students who graduated and would be eligible for admission to graduate school*
- *To establish an EOP Honors Program*
- *To lower the attrition rate and increase the graduation rate of EOP students*

To achieve these goals, Lujan felt applicants should meet what were called "stringent admissions criteria." One of the main reasons for this view was that between 1970 and 1980, of the 17,000 students who went through the program, only 17% had graduated. Lujan later admitted that the 17,000 number was likely inflated. It is likely that some of the same students were counted more than once.

Even so, 35 years later, Lujan still claimed that "something needed to be done because only 17% of EOP students were graduating." This low rate suggested that the reasons for attrition were primarily academic. However, opponents of the decision to invoke more stringent criteria argued that, based on the data analyzed by the Chicano Student Division Director Gary Trujillo, less than 5% of students who left the University did so due to a GPA of less than 2.0.

So, what led the vice president to believe low academic performance was the main reason for high attrition of EOP students, a claim also made by former vice president Ewaugh Fields? One possible explanation is that it was based on feedback from Instructional Center instructors who felt many EOP students were being admitted with little to no chance of graduating. Data showed that between 1976 and 1982, the cumulative GPA for EOP students ranged from 0.24 to 0.41 grade points lower than that of all UW students. In addition, the average attrition for EOP students was determined to be 54%. Knowledge of these data may have been part of the rationale that a more stringent admission requirement for EOP admissions was warranted.

The admissions policy proposed by Vice President Lujan was based on GPA, test scores, recommendations, interviews, ethnicity, and educational disadvantage. The program plan referred to regular EOP admits (2.5 GPA with one high school core deficiency) and special EOP admits (2.0 with more than one high school core deficiencies). Students, staff, and community members vehemently opposed such changes, especially testing and residency requirements. Chicano and Asian (mostly Filipino) students and community members moved to occupy the building (Schmitz Hall) where OMA staff and administrators were housed. There was a call for a change in the policy, for the formation of a committee of student and community leaders that would be consulted concerning changes in minority program policies, for Lujan to resign, and for no reprisals to those taking part in the demonstration.

The counter argument was that there were factors other than academics responsible for the high attrition rates. Jesus Rodriguez was spokesperson and organizer. Protesters met with Lujan in an attempt to have the policy reversed. When Lujan did not make a commitment, the following is Rodriguez's account of what the negotiators' reactions were: "Arriba, abajo, Lujan es un carajo." Translated, that means "Up down – i.e., any way you look at it – Lujan is a tyrant" (Lujan, 2015).

In response to criticism that he was placing the program in jeopardy, Lujan stated that he had been fighting in the trenches for EOP and that it was one of the most successful in the country. An example of fighting in the trenches is exemplified in a passage from Lujan's oral history interview: "I was able to convince Bill [Gerberding], bless his soul, to keep the Office of Minority Affairs open because there were some faculty who were wanting to get rid of it because of non-academicness." According to Lujan, President Gerberding did not capitulate but felt that Asians were not underrepresented and were earning GPAs that were relatively high. Lujan said that he made the case based on the virtues of excellence and inclusion using numbers.

Chicanos hold a heated meeting with Lujan over changes in the EOP admission policy.

Lujan struggles to find understanding and support with students around his admission policy direction.

Regarding numbers, the discontinuation of service to Asian and Pacific Island (API) EOP students would have constituted the denial of an annual enrollment of upwards of 300 Asian students since they could only enter the University as Group II and Group III EOP students. Surely this would have been a bone of contention for the Asian and Pacific Islander (API) community.

Initially, the protest was not officially endorsed by Black student groups. Malik Freeman, BSU president, stated that Black students wanted to study the situation further before taking any action. Later, more than 100 Black students agreed to join the protest. It is interesting to note that there were no mentions of American Indian students joining the protest. According to *The Seattle Times*, "Lujan had said that the new admissions policy was intended to weed out low achievers from the program, which Lujan contends had a high dropout rate." In a statement, President Gerberding gave assurance that he had no intentions of reducing the number of EOP students served by the office." In addition, he pledged a review of the administration and its admission policies.

Protesters claimed that Lujan retaliated against staff who criticized his policies. Gary Trujillo, supervisor of the Chicano Student Division was arrested and later suspended for participating in the demonstration. Also arrested were community leaders, such as Juan Bocanegra, Roberto Maestas, Jose Cervantes, Ricardo Aguirre, and Francisco Irigon, to name a few. All told, 25 OMA staff resigned. The protesters attributed the exodus to lack of support for the leadership and others cited Lujan's "harassment tactics." Lujan dismissed the idea that he was responsible for the exodus, saying that OMA was a "training ground" that prepared minority staff to be hired away by businesses outside of the University.

They burned me in effigy, as I recall, the next morning [in Red Square]. They had built this effigy of me; I must say it was a decent piece of work.

–Dr. Herman Lujan, 2015

Interestingly, the choice to resign in protest of administrative decisions on policies appeared to be the strategy of choice. It begs the question—with so many staff leaving at one time, did this exodus severely compromise the critical services to EOP students who were most at risk in terms of persistence and graduation? The answer lies in the fact that a core group of committed advisers remained on the job and that the academic support unit (the Instructional Center), as well as the ECC staff, did not become embroiled in these issues. Counselors continued to serve EOP student by temporarily moving their services elsewhere. Some moved their offices to the HUB and others moved their offices to the Ethnic Cultural Center. Business went on as usual at the Instructional Center and the Ethnic Cultural Center. And, since it was late spring quarter, the effect on recruitment was minimal except for substantially hampering the admission process.

In an effort to end the protest, members of the community, including Roberto Maestas, Diane Ochoa, Alfonso Simanio, Francisco Irigon, and Russell Fujiwara (and later Larry Gossett and Gary Trujillo) met with Lujan to engage in negotiations. The protest lasted for two weeks and resulted in 72 arrests (Task force named, 1980). The VP was burned in effigy. Here is Lujan's account of the incident:

They burned me in effigy, as I recall, the next morning [in Red Square]. They had built this effigy of me; I must say it was a decent piece of work. Anyway, they lit the fire, and I figured what the hell. I'm going to stay here and if they want to stay here with the fire I'm going to stay here with my eyes [and watch]. I came, wandered around, and that's the end of the story.

With all the turbulence and turmoil, one might wonder how OMA survived, especially with a US Supreme Court decision in 1978 ruling racial quotas were not permissible (the Bakke decision). The answer may lie in the fact that the Board of Regents did not waver. Following a review of the US Supreme Court's Bakke decision, which affected affirmative action programs based on race, the UW Board of Regents issued another policy statement on admissions. The Regents' statement emphasized that "an important and essential component of any educational program is the exchange of information and life experiences through a diverse student body, with representatives from all cultural backgrounds given the opportunity of participation." The Regents affirmed that "special attention must be paid to members of those constituencies traditionally underrepresented in all or segments of the educational programs of higher education, including those groups of minority and women applicants who have been the objects of past societal discrimination." The Regents' policy demonstrated strong institutional support for affirmative action.

Responding to claims that the University was attempting to get rid of OMA, UW President William Gerberding reiterated his commitment to the EOP and to minority admission to the University. Dr. Herman Lujan would be retained. Gerberding appointed a task force to review EOP admissions practices at the University. The task force was chaired by Judge Charles Z. Smith and was composed of community members, faculty, and students. The task force concluded that the admission criteria proposed by Lujan should be abandoned and recommended that a longitudinal study be conducted to determine the predictors of the academic success of EOP students and the role that financial aid plays in EOP students leaving the University. Select members of the student ad hoc committee argued that access should take precedence at that point in time. Then, once solidified, attention could turn to retention and graduation as long-term goals.

The [Board of] Regents' statement emphasized that "an important and essential component of any educational program is the exchange of information and life experiences through a diverse student body, with representatives from all cultural backgrounds given the opportunity of participation."

The end results were the abandonment of the admissions criteria. However, the idea of placement testing for EOP students was implemented. According to Nori Mihara, assistant to the vice president at the time, and later assistant vice president for academic services in OMA, the placement test was:

> *. . . one of the early ideas that Herman had in 1978 when he came to the University of Washington. In part, the idea was born out of the Skills Center. I was instrumental in that along with Ferd [Ferdinand] Dario and Eric Halsey. We concluded that EOP was admitting students without really knowing what their basic needs might be once they got here on the campus. We would then plug them into various classes having no idea if they were going to succeed. That was a very bad thing to do. The whole idea of the placement test was to streamline it so that we had a better sense of what the student's needs are like. That would provide for ostensibly better advising, taking different classes, controlling the credits that a student might take, making sure that they go to the Instructional Center for help as needed, and so on.*

> *I think that Herman wanted to strengthen the ties academically with the various academic units, to tie the academic teaching and instructional*

activities. Quantitatively, it was because we would see students at the Skills Center at that time with very weak math skills. The only way we could assess that was to administer an in-house test at that point to see what their needs were like, and then tailor the instruction as we tutored them or held group tutorials. That was the quantitative driver.

We also needed to assess writing and English skills. We had this program started by Professor William Irmscher in the English Department. He started the English 104, 105, and 106 series. We needed to know how to deal with that too, in the same way that we need now to have English tutors and instructors at the Skills Center or Instructional Center to help with those students.

In 1984, the Universal Placement test was implemented for all entering EOP students. By 1986, all state resident students admitted through EOP were required to take the Universal Placement Test (UPT) except those who had taken the Scholastic Aptitude Test (SAT), or the American College Test (ACT), or the Washington Pre-College Test. The results of the placement tests were used to determine the need for space in math and English remedial courses as well. Non-residents would be required to take either the SAT or ACT.

The upside was that the outcome of the protest was a victory for the demonstrators. Conversely, the downside was that it was a loss for both sides. OMA could no longer recruit and serve regularly admissible minority students. EOP became a special admit program. This change in the admissions policy negatively impacted both program participants as well as OMA. Regularly admissible students, especially underrepresented minority students, would lose the advising and academic support needed to improve their academic standing and increase their chances of gaining admissions to graduate and professional schools. The change in policy would also alter the

Dr. Herman Lujan with a Political Science graduate student, 1984.

ethnic make-up of EOP students, thus preventing the interaction of high-risk students with non-risk students, resulting in the loss of the educational achievement value inherent in such interactions.

The effect was that Group I enrollment went from 1,475 students in 1980 to 662 in 1983, a 55% decrease. However, Group I students who had enrolled prior to 1981 remained in OMA. Despite this setback, the program continued to evolve.

Considering one of the main goals of the new admission policy was to increase the pool of minority students who would be eligible for graduate and professional schools, it appeared this goal would now be unachievable. As a result, the UW Graduate School would be hard pressed to achieve its goal of increasing the enrollment of underrepresented minority students. Not accepting defeat, a group of administrators and faculty met to discuss the problem. The group included the assistant dean of the Minority Education unit of the Graduate School, Dr. Trevor Chandler, who reported dually to the dean and the VP of OMA (an arrangement brokered by Sam Kelly in 1971); the assistant vice president for academic services, Dr. Nori Mihara; College of Arts and Sciences assistant dean, Dr. Fred Campbell, and sociology professors Robert Crutchfield and George Bridges.

The group brainstormed and came up with a program called the Early Identification Program. The Early Identification Program (EIP) was designed to identify talented Black, Hispanic, and American Indian students and prepare them for graduate school by exposing them to the kinds of research activities they would likely experience in graduate school. Dr. Carlene Brown was the first graduate assistant hired by Dr. Chandler and the first stand-alone director. She described her primary duties as follows: "monitoring students' academic progress; designing and implementing workshops to encourage and motivate students to further their academic careers; providing mentoring relationships with faculty; advising on graduate school application packets; coordinating in-service presentations to university faculty and staff; developing program plans, goals and evaluation; establishing networks with other university faculty and staff throughout the country."

EOP and non-EOP underrepresented minority students (regularly admissible) were invited to participate. "We then again began serving Group 1 students in the graduate preparation aspect of it," said Enrique Morales, who at the time was coordinator of recruitment.

There were other ways that regularly admissible minority students could receive advising and academic support from OMA programs. Students who were first-generation and low-income were eligible to participate in the Special Services for Disadvantaged Students Program, which was established within OMA with a grant from the Department of Education. They were offered regular workshops and presentations and provided counseling and academic support regardless of EOP status. Thus, they were eligible to participate in EIP if selected. The Upward Bound and Educational Talent Search programs, both also funded by the Department of Education, provided a pipeline to the Special Services for Disadvantaged Students Program. While these programs mitigated the loss of Group I students, about two-thirds of these students lost the opportunity to be served by OMA programs and may have missed out on being admitted to such competitive majors as business, engineering, computer science, and nursing.

From the data provided in the EOP profile report (1976–1982) it was clear that the academic performance of EOP Group I students was comparable to the UW average. It is likely that this revelation made it difficult for OMA to justify continuing to serve this population. From 1971 to 1980, Group I students contributed significantly to the academic success of EOP students, regarding both cumulative GPA and degrees earned (58%).

It was clear that this policy of omission adversely affected the graduation outcome of EOP students in terms of rate and numbers of degrees earned. Not satisfied with these outcomes, the OMA Admissions Policy Committee recommended that OMA be allowed to admit cohorts that would be composed of a mix of predominantly Group I and II students.

The administration realized that a more proactive approach was needed to increase the pool of students who were aware of the opportunities that college could afford, and the sooner the better. In 1984, Enrique Morales, director of EOP Admissions and Recruitment, and Bill Baker, assistant vice president for support services, created a program modeled on the University of California, Irvine, partnership program. "Part of that effort is to start at the middle school, educating kids and their parents about what are the right course patterns to be taking to be prepared for the school of your choice. That made a significant difference," said Morales. It was called the Early Outreach Program, with Lette Hadgu serving as the first director.

On the opposite end of the academic preparedness spectrum, the OMA administration implemented a community college transition program to improve the chances of the most academically underprepared applicants to gain admission and successfully navigate the University.

When the dust settled, Lujan again introduced the idea of a major reorganizational plan. The argument against reorganization was the loss of autonomy and the political accountability of each group to their ethnic communities. The opponents of reorganization also feared that EOP would eventually be eliminated because, without ethnic specificity, there would be no need to maintain a minority program. The OMA administration countered that reorganization would improve efficiency and save division directors' jobs in light of an impending 7.5% budget cut. Despite opposition, after 12 years, the ethnic student divisions were dissolved.

In the newly reorganized structure, directors' positions were absorbed, and incumbents were placed in service roles. The supervisor of the Economically Disadvantaged student division became a counselor in the newly created counseling center.

Upon analysis of the data as part of my job in OMA, I discovered that the numbers being used to determine graduation rates were inflated and that the methodology was flawed. To properly determine graduation rates, separate cohorts must be tracked for four to six years. The proper approach would have been to identify students entering from high school (1972, 1973, and 1974), and after four, five, and six years, determine the percentage who had earned degrees. Comparison of these percentages to either a benchmark rate or the rates of the full UW student body would have indicated the gap to be closed. Once these outcomes were known, it should not stop there. The next step would be to determine what percentage of those students who left without a degree were on warning, on probation, dropped because of low grades, or were unable to earn enough credits to keep their financial aid. These outcomes would have provided a clearer picture of the challenges that the OMA administration and the students it served faced.

Even with this information in hand, student groups and their communities would likely not accept tightening the admission requirements as a solution. They argued that access to higher education should be the priority. The ASUW Board of Control's ad hoc Educational Opportunity Program investigatory committee made a similar argument, stating, "Exposure should be emphasized until an educational basis is established. . . . When it becomes more traditional for disadvantaged students to enter college, then the focus of the program should be shifted toward higher retention, and thus higher graduation rates" (Bulger, 1980, p. 3).

This notion supports the philosophy of one of the founders of the BSU, Eddie Demmings. His position was that "students who were not considering going to college, now had an opportunity to do so. Furthermore, what they learned while in college could benefit their career placement later in life." He further stated emphatically that, "it is better to have gone to college and not earned a degree than to not have gone to college at all." He considered a graduation rate of 35% to be a successful outcome for EOP students, given, as he said, their level of preparedness from high schools and the community colleges. Also supporting Demmings' argument is evidence which shows that students whose parents attended some college went to college and earned a degree at a higher rate than those whose parent did not attend college at all (Cataldi, E. F. et al., 2018).

It was also during this period when a "paradigm shift" occurred. Responding to the 1977 ad hoc committee's concerns over the allocation of resources to the Instructional Center (IC) instead of to ethnic student division counselors, and ignoring the counseling staff's claim that "holistic" counseling by full-time staff was more important than instructional support, the OMA administration felt that increasing professional and tutorial staffing, and academic support, took precedence. After all, there was an academic performance gap of about 0.4 grade points between the cumulative GPA of EOP students and that of all UW undergraduates. Only one in four EOP students graduated in five years, and fewer than one out of every three EOP students were graduating in six years. The attrition rate was as high as 54%.

It is important to note that in addition to low scholarship being a contributing factor to relatively high attrition and low graduation rates, other factors may have been involved. Some students earned fewer credits yearly and thus may have taken longer than six years to graduate. Also, EOP students may have dropped out for financial, family, or other reasons and returned to graduate years later. For these reasons, many institutional researchers feel that EOP students' graduation rates need to be tracked for longer than six years.

Nevertheless, it goes without saying that the outcomes that were tracked were of grave concern to Vice President Lujan.

In the fall of 1982, I was hired (after working as a senior analytical chemist in industry) to design and implement a much-needed chemistry program for the Instructional Center. The program was deemed essential if EOP students were to become more competitive for admissions to science and engineering majors as well as admissions to medical, dental, and pharmacy schools. Multiple benefits were realized in that those tutors who joined the team possessed knowledge and skills that allowed for much needed support in biochemistry and biology at minimal cost, and demand eventually led to an additional instructor's position in biology.

At the time, 1985 Admission Test Preparation was subsumed under EIP; however, soon afterwards, it became the responsibility of the Instructional Center.

Enrollment Challenges

Because of not being able to recruit regularly admissible (formerly designated as Group I) minority and disadvantaged students, it became quite difficult to maintain the previously enjoyed enrollment level. Group I enrollment showed a decline of 82%, but the precipitous drop was mitigated by a 66% increase in Group II and a substantial increase in Group III enrollment. In 1985, more than 300 fewer (10%) EOP students were enrolled compared to the 1981 enrollment figures, with Asian and Black students experiencing declines. The downward trend for Black EOP students began in 1975, declining by 40% by 1986. Even worse, the overall Black student undergraduate enrollment declined by 50% over the same period. Interestingly, Black students were the only group that experienced such a precipitous drop. Needless to say, the OMA leadership expressed concern and offered the following reasons for the decline:

- *An increase in recruitment competition not only by Black Colleges, but also other institutions within the state of Washington*
- *High unemployment of Black families made college unaffordable*
- *High achieving Black students avoided applying to UW because they did not wish to be associated with the EOP stigma*

Other possible reasons for the decline were offered by Vice President Lujan early on during his tenure. He believed prospective students chose to enroll in community colleges at a higher rate and, because of an improvement in the local and regional job market, others chose to work rather than go to college.

Other possible reasons:

- *The word reached Black communities that the UW was not a very welcoming environment*
- *A negative association of attending the University and not succeeding, and having to leave with high debt and nothing to show for it*
- *The belief that if they applied, they would not get in*

Upon analysis of the data, it was learned that indeed fewer Black students applied to the University. Between 1974 and 1985, the number of applications by Black students fluctuated between a high of 583 in 1974 to low of 371 in 1985, a 36% decline. Attrition and relatively low enrollment yield were also contributing factors. One plan to stem the downward trend was to aggressively recruit Blacks from the military bases in the state. Another strategy was to redouble recruitment of high school and community college prospects across the state.

What were the thin lines that OMA needed to walk? One was the expectation that the vice president is responsible for mediating issues that minority students may bring up with the UW administration. Failure to do so could cause loss of credibility for OMA with both the UW administration and students. Tim Washburn, UW registrar in the early years of the OMA, described another aspect of the problem:

The other issue that I recall was that there was concern that the athletic department might use OMA as a back door for the admission of athletes. So, the decision was made that a student who was a recruited athlete, or someone with an athletic scholarship, couldn't come in through OMA. They could use OMA services, but they could not be admitted through the EOP admission program.

Indeed, in 1983, a policy prohibiting the use of EOP Admissions to recruit athletes was established. Stagnation and decline in enrollment, or access without retention and graduation, are outcomes that can keep an OMA administrator up at night wondering if the program would survive.

Dr. Millie Russell working with a student, 2004.

The Representation Challenge

Once the reorganization plan was successfully implemented and the academic support unit was given a boost, where would Lujan turn his attention?

Sensing the need to have a Black presence at the administrative level of OMA as well as the Black professional community, Lujan appointed Dr. Millie Russell as special assistant to the vice president. Her primary role was to serve as a liaison to the Black community, Biology Program, and Health Sciences. In other words, she would serve as the "Connector" (a la the description in Malcolm Gladwell's book *The Tipping Point*). Millie Russell knew a lot of people; she was extremely friendly and could bring people from diverse backgrounds together with both common and divergent views. And people gravitated to her. At the time, Dr. Russell served concurrently as the director of the UW Biology Program Preprofessional Program for Minority students, where many EOP students who aspired to pursue careers in medicine, dentistry, pharmacy, and nursing were participants. In addition, she taught a biology class that was a precursor for introductory biology. It included an academic advising course sequence flow chart designed by the Instructional

Center staff to optimize students' performance in the prerequisites for biology and health sciences majors.

Speaking of Millie Russell, Lujan said:

She set in place something that I often had to remind new people about. They thought that being counselors, their job was to take a person, shut the door, and talk. But part of good counseling is exposing people to comparable environments that are important in the success plan you have for your organization. Any student and any staff member that understood that was way ahead in the game, and Millie knew that.

Bringing Dr. Russell on board the OMA flagship was one of the best personnel decisions made by VP Lujan. She recruited individuals who were not only highly qualified but also made long-term commitments to the OMA family of programs. One was convincing the Biology Department to hire an instructor, Dr. Leonie Piternick, to teach a preparatory course to introductory biology for EOP students. Another was facilitating my hiring as an Instructional Center instructor. As an indication of Lujan's strong commitment to providing instructional support for EOP students, a position vacated by an assistant vice president was used to make the hire, a decision that paid dividends to OMA for more than three decades. Another person attracted by Millie Russell came in as director and garnered more than $20 million dollars in federal grants. Yet another became the director of a federally funded program with an annual budget of over $5 million dollars.

Besides the connection with EOP students, Dr. Russell had ties to the fundraising arm of OMA. Beginning in 1978, she served on the Board of Trustees of the Friends of the Educational Opportunity Program and is the only board member to become a lifetime member. She was instrumental in recruiting many board members.

Just one year into Lujan's vice presidency, John Hogness resigned from the presidency. Lujan suggested to the FEOP Board the establishment of a new recognition award for the EOP student who achieved the highest cumulative GPA and that it be named the Hogness Achievement Award in honor of his constant support for EOP during his five-year tenure. The award still exists to this day, but the name was changed to the President's Achievement Award. The award was approved by the Board. Marion So, a pre-chemical engineering major, was the first recipient.

Beloved Mentor Millie Russell

Millie Russell was a mentor to many students and staff. While it was not possible to interview her for the oral history part of this project, many people who worked with her share their memories. She worked particularly closely with Lette Hadgu, who said of her: "Dr. Russell was also responsible for cultivating the Early Outreach Program into one of the finest after-school programs in the country, which was later elevated to exemplary status."

Dr. Millie Russell

When Hadgu was asked why she thought VP Lujan hired Millie, she replied:

> I don't know why Vice President Lujan did that. Nonetheless, I think he did the right thing by inviting Millie to join the Office of Minority Affairs. She had a lot to offer, and she did it with love and great commitment. Millie was connected not only to the University but also well connected to the Black community in particular, and the community in general. She was very resourceful and a fighter for justice and equality. She also cared deeply about the well-being of students, especially minority and disadvantaged ones. Herman Lujan might have realized her passion for helping and empowering students and others. I, myself, learned a lot from working with her.
>
> Dr. Russell enjoyed seeing others grow to their fullest potential, especially students. I believe Dr. Lujan might have seen Dr. Russell's vision and passion matching with those of the Office of Minority Affairs. Regardless of the underlying intentions, Dr. Lujan made a wise decision by inviting Millie as a special assistant to the vice president of OMA. Dr. Russell was able to better connect the African American community and the University of Washington, via the Office of Minority Affairs. Dr. Russell was loved by many and was a magnet to many good

things and people for the Office of Minority Affairs. . . . She was a voice for those who didn't have one. Millie's main focus was to see minority and disadvantaged young students better prepared for college, have equal access to higher education institutions, and succeed.

Another colleague stated:

When Millie's name is brought up in many circles, people talk about what she has done to impact the lives of many students since the 1970s, as well as the contributions she has made to the health care profession as a woman and a person of color. She had this network. She was inclusive. I think she is a good human being. But, when I say that, she's also a tiger. If you are not doing your job to help her students, she would talk to you. Millie later served as the OMA Ombudsperson, an intermediary to the University Ombudsperson. In the last years she was here, she served as the liaison to the Ombudsman on behalf of EOP students. Whenever issues came up, when students were having difficulties on campus, they would speak to Millie, and Millie would speak to the Ombudsman, and they would work it out, so the problems could get resolved (Mehary, 2016).

In 1981, she was chosen to receive the Charles E. Odegaard Award. In 2009, an endowed scholarship was named in Dr. Russell's honor. The scholarship would be awarded to an EOP student who was majoring in the sciences, and the recipient would be recognized as the Dr. Millie Russell Scholar at the annual EOP Scholarship Dinner, Celebration.

Reflections on Herman Lujan

When asked about the legacy of Dr. Herman Lujan, Steve Garcia said:

Herman Lujan

> Herm is a good man. He's got a big heart. He really cared about the students. He cared about the communities, but he also wanted to establish the program as an academic program, as a legitimately accepted academic program in the University of Washington. It's a major university and he wanted to make sure that we were one, successful in graduating students, and two, establishing its permanency. In those days, aside from the political pushbacks, we were always fighting to be relevant with the administration. We were always looked at as that little corner pocket over there in Schmitz Hall and would rather not be heard from. That's Herm's legacy. He established—and through all the political havoc that resulted from his emphasis on academics, not moving away from the community aspects of it, the access aspects, but strengthening the graduation rates particularly—really solidified the program and solidified his legacy.

Dr. Nori Mihara, former assistant vice president under Lujan stated:

> He wanted to have higher visibility in the academic circles on this campus . . . he was very instrumental in trying to work with the faculty, the academic side of the University. I think the one thing that Herman was very adamant about was ensuring the longevity of the Office of Minority Affairs. He was quite vocal at times with George Beckmann, who was provost, and the president, Bill Gerberding, about making sure the Office of Minority Affairs existed. That was the one thing. In those days, it was very easy for an office like this to get wiped off the board, especially at a time when a new vice president comes in.

Karen Morell, on the other hand, had a different take regarding Lujan. She said:

> The greatest difficulty with Herm, which I certainly personally experienced, was that you never knew what was really going on even in what it was you were supposed to be doing for him. You didn't know the undercurrents. Well, let's say the rug was frequently pulled out from under people.

Lujan also convinced the FEOP Board to establish an award to recognize an EOP student who had achieved the highest grade-point average from the lowest entering GPA (i.e., greatest academic progress) while overcoming major obstacles. The first recipient was Arturo Balderama, an education major.

In addition to everything else they did to support students on commencement day, the Friends of the Educational Opportunity Program sponsored a reception for EOP graduates.

Also, during 1978, Assistant Vice President for OMA Mike Castillano, recommended to a group of former graduates that an EOP Alumni Association be formed. It came to fruition with Cornell Archie, Linda Ramos, Jim Cantu, Sharon Maeda, and Ruthann Kurose serving as chair, co-chair, financial chair, communications, and career placement chairs, respectively. The alumni group participated in fund drives and organized ethnic-specific graduations. After five years the Association became inactive. Thirteen years later a group of Black students and selected staff resumed Black Graduation. Other ethnic groups soon followed suit. The celebrations are generally held during the week leading up to UW Commencement. These activities are communal celebrations and are not intended to supplant the general commencement exercises.

OMA Partnerships Forged during the Decade

The Office of Minority Affairs did not operate in silos or in a vacuum. Instead, the unit was proactive in seeking new opportunities to benefit EOP students. Nori Mihara recounted some of those partnerships:

OMA was much more directly involved with, for example, the College of Engineering, with their minority introduction bridge program, which ran in the summers. And the College of Engineering started what was called the MESA program, the Mathematics Engineering Sciences Achievement program. I was a part of that board. We made a pitch in Olympia and lobbied Governor Gary Locke, among others, to fund MESA statewide from the state budget.

MESA is now a program that functions under the auspices of the Office of Minority Affairs & Diversity.

Mihara continued:

Another involvement we had was with the Health Sciences. With Health Sciences, I guess it would be the Minority Scholars program or some such precursor to that. And that one came about because there was a grant that they received from the Howard Hughes Foundation. They funded some kind of minority student activities, preparing them for careers in medicine and dentistry. Milo Gibaldi [at the time dean of the School of Pharmacy] was very much involved with that.

I'm trying to think; did we have connections with others? Yes, there was, and I knew about it because I was from the physics department, and because I know Lillian McDermott, the professor. She was very much involved in physics education. She had programs that were designed for minority students, or at least her programs were adapted and asked minority students to enroll.

While there was a strong emphasis on partnerships with science and engineering programs, art and cultural programs were also important. Initially, murals at the Samuel E. Kelly Ethnic Cultural Center were painted on the walls of the Black Room and Chicano Room.

In the Black Room, two murals were painted by artist Eddie Ray Walker (1972), titled *Bearers of Culture* and *Bearers of Pain*.

The mural for the Chicano Room, *Somos Aztlan*, was painted by Emilio Aguayo. According to documents held in the ECC archives, it was the first to be created by a Chicano in the state of Washington.

Murals for the walls of American Indian and Asian rooms were created in 1985. Steve Garcia, then assistant to the vice president, said Lujan's staff

According to the artist, *Bearers of Culture* was inspired by the spirit, mind, and office labor of Black women. Walker stated in the 2007 documentary *In Pursuit of Social Justice*, "without them [Black women] we would be nothing."

Artist Walker also noted that *Bearers of Pain* represented "the struggle of the Black man in America once he came from Africa."

According to the artist, "the mural embodies the dawning of a new era for all Spanish-speaking people known as 'LA RAZA'."

The mural in the American Indian Room was titled *Reflections*. According to the artist, Michael Beasley, "the design is a symbolic reflection of students' time on campus."

was instrumental in the creation of these murals for the ethnic-specific rooms. OMA commissioned artists to do the work.

Garcia shared this story in reference to the Asian Room:

> *I don't know if you remember this, but when we put out a sort of an RFP [request for proposal] kind of thing, the person that got it, he put up a mural with Mao [Zedong, former Chairman of the Communist Party of China] on it. So, we ended up taking it down and we contracted with another person who put in the multiethnic, or I should say different cultures of the Asian community.*

Outcomes

Over the 1978–1987 decade, the budget increased by $1M. Gifts of nearly $610,000 were received and the first endowment, the Nancy Lawton Weber EOP Endowment, was established within OMA. Staff levels rose from 55 to 60. Underrepresented minority (URM) enrollment increased by 15%. EOP enrollment increased by almost 10%, despite the fact that regularly admissible minority students could no longer be recruited into EOP. The number of EOP

The mural in the Asian Pacific Islander Room, titled "Photo Montage," was painted in the fall of 1985. "The installation is a representation of achievement through adversity, sacrifice, and determination," said the artist, Jesse Reyes.

degree earners totaled 3,335, a three-fold increase over the previous decade. Retention rates of EOP students increased from 69% to 79%, and the average graduation rate increased from 24% to 34%. However, the graduation rate gap between EOP students and the UW student body remained prohibitively high (30 percentage points).

The graduation rate for entering transfer students, although less than half in size compared to entering freshmen, showed greater success. The graduation rates for these students went from 34% to 49% by the end of the decade (with a gap of 21 percentage points between them and the overall student body). With the much higher rate of success for transfer students, one would have thought that greater emphasis would have been placed on recruiting students from the community college system. Not doing so had to do with the policy of the University focusing more on students entering from high school than from two- and four-year institutions.

What is missing in the statistics provided above is the proportion of URM enrollment and degree earners that entered through the EOP. This figure is notable. On average, three out of every four URM enrollees were EOP during this decade and more than half (56%) of URM degree earners also were EOP—a strong indicator of the role played by OMA in changing the face of diversity on the UW campus. Also worthy of note is that 268 Resident Release Project participants earned degrees between 1972 and 1979, one of whom, Kenneth Von Cleve, went on to earn a PhD from the UW and became a clinical psychologist.

Toward the end of this decade, the EOP advising staff felt that in addition to annually highlighting students' accomplishments at Celebration, the outstanding accomplishments of first year EOP freshman and transfer students should also highlighted. Thus, the first EOP Student Recognition Ceremony was held near the end of spring quarter, 1986.

STUDENT CASES

NELSON DEL RIO. Were it not for the Educational Opportunity Program under the auspices of OMA, this future donor would not have been admitted to the University of Washington. Nelson Del Rio did not finish high school, but instead passed the General Educational Development (GED) test. A friend encouraged him to enroll at UW through the EOP. Once enrolled, Nelson excelled academically with the support of OMA. He was the recipient of the two highest EOP recognition awards in back-to-back years, with the latter being awarded to a graduating senior with the highest cumulative GPA. He graduated Magna Cum Laude. He went on to Harvard Law School and after graduating worked on Wall Street. Del Rio later co-founded a development company and became very successful.

Nelson never forgot the support and encouragement he received while an EOP student at UW. Initially, he donated funds to increase the monetary value of the President's Achievement Award, which he had received as a student. In 2003, he established an endowment named the Del Rio Global Citizens Endowment, which provides a scholarship for an EOP student to study abroad. His philanthropy did not end there. There is now a Del Rio Endowed Scholarship Fund in Environmental Studies in the College of the Environment supporting entering EOP-eligible students to promote real-world environmental research and problem-solving. Nelson Del Rio is not only giving back he is also paying forward. Thank you, Nelson Del Rio, for remembering from whence you came.

YENG BUN. Yeng Bun grew up in war-torn Cambodia during the rule of the brutal Khmer Rouge regime, known for killing more than a million people in sites known as Killing Fields. As a teenager, he was separated from his parents and was forced to work in labor camps. In the labor camp, one of his jobs was to collect waste to be used as fertilizer. Yeng dreamed of escaping these horrid conditions and coming to America.

That opportunity to leave the country finally came. He travelled on a bicycle with his two brothers for days until they finally crossed the border and arrived at a refugee camp in Thailand. After months in the camp, the opportunity to travel to America was granted. With two pairs of pants, a shirt, and two bags of rice (he thought he would never have rice again if he did not take it with him), the brothers headed for America and ended up in Seattle.

Yeng Bun's ultimate dream was to earn an education so that he would have a better life. He was 19 years old by the time of his arrival in the US and found out that he would need to graduate from high school before the age of 21. He enrolled at Ingraham High School and worked at a shop making donuts at night. Once he graduated, his desire was to attend the University of Washington. He was told that, with his grades, there was no way that would be possible and that his best bet was to either continue at the donut shop or learn a trade. That was unacceptable to Bun, so he continued to try to find a way to become a student at UW.

At last, he learned that there was a way to gain admittance. He was put in contact with Jerry Shigaki, Director of EOP Admissions, who facilitated a pathway to the University. Bun was overjoyed, but he wondered whether he could be successful on such a large campus. His adviser referred him to the Instructional Center where he received academic support in English and Mathematics. For Yeng Bun, the IC was where he found an environment conducive to learning challenging concepts and a staff (especially Ferdinand Dario) committed to supporting those students who sought help. After graduating in three years, Bun enrolled in graduate school in the Department of Applied Mathematics where he earned a PhD.

During this period, he met his future wife, Therese Mar. They later married and became the proud parents of three gifted children. Bun was one of the early employees at Zillow, Inc., which created an online marketplace for real estate. He served as a Principal Applied Scientist at Zillow, Inc., for more than 12 years.

Inspired by Yeng Bun's story, his wife, Therese, applied for a math position at the IC when the opportunity arose. Two of their sons also worked at the IC, serving as tutors. One of their sons is now an assistant professor of computer science at Boston University. The other son is now a UW graduate student in bioengineering. At the time of this writing, Therese served as the director of the IC and often talks about the center being a special place for her and her family. This is a prime example of the OMA family of programs that have touched the lives of two generations of a family who had its origin thousands of miles away.

Notable EOP Alumni from the Decade

It is noteworthy that a number of these alumni (by no means exhaustive) have distinguished themselves holding positions as professors, vice presidents, lawyers, medical administrators, directors/managers, businesspersons, architects, city council members, and philanthropists.

Nolan Cordell, '78, MD (Harvard)

Gary Kimura,'78, '82, '84, PhD (UW)

Maxine E. Liggins, '79, '85, MD (UW)

Blaine Tamaki, '79, JD (UW)

Norma Zavala,'80, '02, '07, EdD (UW)

Michael P. Anderson, '81, MS (Creighton)

Levi Christopher, '81 (UW)

Leonard Forsman, '81 (UW)

Marion So, '81, (UW)

Nathaniel "Nate" Miles, '82 (UW)

Rodney G. Moore, '82, JD (Santa Clara University School of Law)

Jacinta Titialii-Abbott, '82, '85, JD (UW)

Lydia Flora Barlow, '83, '88, MS (UW)

Rick Breseman, '83, MBA (UW)

Rafael Escribano, '83, MD (Harvard)

Judith Hightower, '83, JD (Seattle U)

Jerrie M. Simmons, '83, '97, JD (UW)

Nelson Del Rio, '84, Phi Beta Kappa, JD (Harvard)

Gary Holden, '84, Summa cum Laude, Phi Beta Kappa, PhD (Columbia)

Daniel Hopen, '84, JD (Seattle U)

Manuel A. Idrogo, '84,'88, MD (UW)

Mike Maglaya, '84.'86, MSW (UW)

Marsha McGough, '84, Magna Cum Laude, Phi Beta Kappa (UW)

Deirdre Raynor,'84, '89', '97, PhD (UW)

Alan Sugiyama, '84 (UW)

Kevin Ung, '84, MBA (UW)

Robin Beckham, '85 (UW)

Kimberly A. Bell, '85, MD (University of Wisconsin)

Yeng Bun, '85, PhD (UW)

Alex Estrada Rolluda,'85, '89 (UW)

Derrick Mar, '85 (UW)

Mutsuya Ii, '85, MSEE (UW)

Debra Earling, '86, MFA (Cornell)

Joe Finkbonner, '86, '91, MHA (UW)

Veronica Gallardo, '86, '98, EdD (Columbia)

Al Herron, '86, MSEE (Northwest Polytechnic University)

Karl Hoffman, '86, DDS (UW)

Marta Reyes Newhart, '86, MBA (Pepperdine)

Townsend Price-Spratlen, '86, '90, PhD (UW)

Bonnie Glenn, '87, JD (Seattle U)

Sherry Clark Petersen, '87, JD (Harvard Law School)

Debra O'Gara, '87, JD (Oregon), MPA (University of Alaska Southeast)

Stephen Torres, '87 MBA (UCLA)

Pow Wow celebration, April 2013.

CHAPTER 4

1988–1997: Movement toward Narrowing Education Outcome Gaps

After about two years of serving as the vice president, I remember one meeting that we had with the Board of Regents. They had asked me to make a presentation about OMA. I made the presentation and after the meeting they said, "Myron, we're going to close down your program." And I said, "Why?" They said, "Your retention rate is poor." And I said, "I know it's poor, but we are dealing with populations of students who are under prepared." So, this meeting led me to think, what can I really do to help change that statistic?"

—Myron Apilado, 2015

The next decade, and the fifth leg of OMA's evolutionary journey, began with the end of the Lujan era. Herman Lujan resigned from OMA to take a position in the UW provost's office as vice provost for academic affairs, then went on to serve as president of the University of Northern Colorado.

This decade also began with the State Higher Education Coordinating Board (HECB) establishing a new and stricter admission policy for all state colleges and universities, disallowing any core deficiencies from high school for prospective enrollees and marking the end of open admissions. To be admitted, students were required to meet a minimum admission index computed using an algorithm based on weighted high school grades and test scores. The algorithm predicted the probability of an applicant earning at least a C grade.

There was fear that the number of EOP enrollees would be reduced substantially. However, the worry was mitigated by what Tim Washburn called an "eloquent argument" made by outgoing Vice President Lujan. Lujan advocated for allowing an alternative admission path for a select number of applicants who did not meet the regular admission requirement. Thus, EOP enrollment was maintained at just above that of the 1988 level over the next five years and the overall enrollment of URM students (fueled by a 50% growth in Latino enrollment) increased by 17%. It was also around this time that the EOP Admissions Policy Committee issued a report stating the following: "Asian subgroups henceforth classified as underrepresented for EOP purposes shall include Filipino, Pacific Islander, and some Southeast Asian subgroups (e.g., Cambodian, Laotian)."

This decade started with great promise following the appointment of a vice president who was an accomplished academician and experienced administrator. Dr. Robert Pozos was a physiologist and co-director of the American Indian Education Program from the University of Minnesota, Duluth. The selection process was not void of controversy, however. The Asian community felt that a Japanese American applicant was overlooked, and there were complaints about the lack of minority faculty input. But optimism soon turned to disappointment when Pozos was asked to resign due to improprieties involving travel reimbursements made public via a leak to *The Daily* (Jewel, 1989). Despite this ostensible setback, the evolutionary momentum did not decelerate.

After 19 years of ethnic-specific advising, and despite the objection of the American Indian advisers, OMA adopted a multiethnic model enabling EOP students to benefit from a "wholistic" body of skills, knowledge, and experience over a broad spectrum. However, the American Indian advisers felt that such change would diminish the participation of American Indian students, would be counterproductive, and would lead to higher attrition rates. According to June Hairston, a longtime lead counselor in the EOP Counseling Center:

> *There was resistance to the multicultural concept, specifically by the Native American [counselors] for one, because they had a lot of privilege with their students. These privileges were more about creating community that they thought they were going to lose when we went into this multicultural role. They had their space, they had access to their advisers, and they had food, which was part of their culture. According to Letoy [Letoy Eike, a counselor for the Native American Student Division], kids would come and have peanut butter and jelly sandwiches and that might be their lunch for the day. They didn't want to lose that family and community support. So, they fought against coming together as a multicultural center.*

Mike Tulee (Yakama), who was a student in his second year at the UW, echoed his advisers' apprehension. In an interview years later, he stated: "I seem to recall there was a lot of inhibition from the students. They really felt that they were going to lose a cultural degree of strength in being able to go straight in to see a Native counselor. I was rather inhibited myself. I was unsure of how this would impact me knowing that I was still not clearly defined in my studies." The counter argument was that there still existed the option to request an ethnic-specific adviser. In the end, Tulee's concerns were allayed. He said, "But as time evolved, I found out that they all had strong understandings of where students of color were coming from."

During the period before the next VP was appointed, the office was placed administratively under Dr. Ernest Morris, vice president for student affairs, who would make all hiring and policy decisions with input from acting Vice

President Bill Baker, and Nori Mihara, assistant vice president for academic services. Business went on as usual with the appointment of new staff to positions that further stabilized key units within OMA. For example, I was appointed interim director of the Instructional Center to fill the void created by the incumbent director, Dr. Sandra Madrid, who had taken a position in the UW School of Law. Adelusa Judal was appointed permanent director of Special Services for Disadvantaged Students. In addition, a biology instructor and a lead academic counselor were also hired. It was also during this period that OMA advisers teamed up with the UW Alumni Association (UWAA) to establish a mentoring program to help entering EOP freshmen transition successfully from high school to college and continuing EOP students to prepare for careers beyond college.

OMA Grows and Matures: Educational Outcomes Improve and Private Support Increases

Continuing along this evolutionary journey (the sixth leg), Dr. Myron Apilado, a vice president from St. Martin's College in Lacey, Washington, was named the fifth Vice President for Minority Affairs in 1990. The position had survived for 22 years. Although there was not a lot of fanfare accompanying his appointment, it was clear early on that Apilado had strong support from UW President William Gerberding, Provost Laurel Wilkening, Vice President for Student Affairs Ernest Morris, and a few of the deans of schools and colleges. Unlike three of his predecessors, he did not assume both a faculty and an administrative position. In this way, he did not have to serve two masters and could focus on improving the educational outcomes of EOP students.

According to Apilado, the first thing that he did was read every document he could find about what had occurred before he came on board. The next step was to get out and speak with folks in the various communities. He also met with many campus administrators, faculty, and staff. Once this was done, having been told by a regent that the University should get rid of the program because students were not graduating, he did not make wholesale organizational changes. Instead, he focused on improving the educational outcomes of minority and disadvantaged students, particularly those served by the EOP. Unlike the previous decade, there was not a lot of staff turnover. Most of the program directors remained with OMA throughout his tenure,

Dr. Myron Apilado (center) with EOP students Willie Sahme, Lorne Murray, Cynthia Sim, and Aaron McCrary, 1999.

Apilado meeting with the 1990 Student Advisory Board.

which lasted into the next decade. Staff grew from 60 to 72 between 1988 and 1995.

Early in his tenure, Apilado determined that it would be best to establish endowments rather than rely on current-use funds to provide scholarships for EOP students. According to Enrique Morales, who worked in a variety of roles in OMA for more than three decades:

Much credit needs to be given to Myron Apilado because he is the person that moved us away from what we called—at that point they were called—immediate-use funds, all of our scholarships that came in. But we didn't have as much money back then. Myron said, "No, we need to start putting stuff away in perpetuity." So, he was creator of that whole [endowment] effort. . . . To this day I'll tip my hat off to him because I think that was a major step, and it will be there in perpetuity.

Apilado's vision was to provide scholarships to EOP students using the interest accrued from the principal. That way, there would always be funds available even in times when the yield from fundraising efforts might be less than desirable.

Responding to the call from Black student leaders for more financial help, Apilado's ambitious hope was to create an endowment of $6 million. Three endowments were established in 1990 followed by two in 1991, one of which was the Educational Opportunity Endowed Fund. This new EOP endowed fund had been a current-use scholarship fund since 1971. The Samuel E. Kelly Endowed Scholarship was established in 1993. All told, 11 endowments were established during Apilado's tenure. Those endowments had a total market value of $1,757,861 as of July 1, 2018 (37% of the value of the entire portfolio).

According to Apilado, however, one endowment got away:

I remember once in a meeting, I don't know if it was [UW Regent] Jerome Farris or [UW Regent] David Cohn, one of them wrote a check out for $85,000 and gave it to me. He liked me and what we were doing in OMA. I took the check. Later, Gerberding called me. He said, "Myron, what did you do with the check?" I said, "I'm going to put it away." He said, "You can't have that one." I said, "I can't have it?" I guess there was some other purpose he wanted to use the money for. I was always happy to *get donations and one of that size would have been super. He took it. He took it from me, but I still loved Gerberding. Gerberding said, "There will be others that will be coming your way."*

A few years later (1995), the William P. and Ruth Gerberding Endowed EOP Scholarship was established. The interest is now used to provide an annual scholarship to a student participant in the OMA&D EIP/McNair Program, which aims to prepare EOP students for graduate and professional school. Before the establishment of the endowment, Gerberding also made allocations for EIP Senior Project Scholarships and the Minority Scholarship Invitational Program, which was to be used to yield a higher proportion of high achieving URM students enrolling at UW.

Enrique Morales remembered that fundraising was needed for high-achieving students, not just those with high financial need. He said:

You know, we get a lot of applications from high achieving students and the one thing we knew is we couldn't compete on financial aid packages predominantly with some of the students, those that had offers from some of the universities with higher endowments or just more financial means. The feeling was that if we could attract them here based on the quality of our support services, if they could engage fully with our faculty, with our graduate preparation programs, and to the degree that we could fund them with our most prestigious scholarships, that we would have a much higher yield. . . We immediately showed results. Because remember, prior to right about that point, even the University went through a time where it felt it didn't need to recruit. [There was an assumption that] "We don't need to recruit, they come to us." Our position was quite different. We need to recruit them because every other college in the country is recruiting our students.

In addition to the endowment and other scholarship funds, OMA was successful in securing $600,000 in current-use funds to support the operations of the Early Scholars Outreach Program (ESOP).

Incentivized by criticism from a regent who threatened to get rid of the program, the OMA leadership made improving retention and graduation rates, as well as degree attainment, the primary focus. It did not take long for Apilado to realize that if retention and graduation rates were to improve, the IC would need to play a key role. Following in the tradition of the

The feeling was that if we could attract them [students] here based on the quality of our support services, if they could engage fully with our faculty, with our graduate preparation programs, and to the degree that we could fund them with our most prestigious scholarships, that we would have a much higher yield.

—Morales, 2015

third vice president, Herman Lujan, Apilado focused on the enhancement of the academic component. By increasing the salaries and number of the instructional staff, the IC could attract and retain dedicated and committed individuals who brought to the table a wide breadth of knowledge and the skills and abilities to impart that knowledge in such a manner that students' academic performance improved, and they were inspired to become lifelong learners. Funds were infused into the peer tutor budget, resulting in the center being able to attract a highly intelligent and motivated tutoring corps, which supplemented and complemented the efforts of the professional staff. These individuals, along with high-achieving IC users, served as models of success.

Beaming with pride, Apilado routinely brought regents and members of the FEOP board, and occasionally the president of the university, to observe tutoring and instruction in action. Visitors were impressed with what they saw. The demand for IC support by students was high, as evidenced by the fact that the place was bursting at the seams. Nonetheless, there was this burning question about which many visitors were curious. Does the popularity of the IC translate into students earning better grades? Is there a correlation between IC usage and grades earned? Several studies were conducted to answer these and other questions.

In 1995, one such study examined outcomes for selected math courses. A statistical analysis was done by an IC instructor and a graduate student referred by the Minority Graduate Education office. The goal was to determine whether there existed a correlation between IC workshop participation in selected math courses and grades earned. The findings verified that the correlation was positive (Moreno & Harmon, 1997). In the following year, a longitudinal study was conducted using data collected on IC usage and grades earned by students who enrolled in ten 100- and 200-level chemistry courses. Once again, the correlation was positive.

While EOP enrollment was not increasing appreciably during the first three years of Apilado's tenure, a steady state was being maintained, with the exception of Black enrollment which had been on the decline since 1974. However, this steady state was breached between 1993 and 1997 when EOP enrollment declined by 14.6% (See *Figure 1* in Chapter 6). Only Latino enrollment showed positive growth over that period.

One of the reasons for the overall decline in total EOP enrollment was a decline in enrollment of Asian students. Because their numbers were increasing in the general student body at a rapid rate, it became very difficult to justify recruiting this group into EOP when their proportion at UW was much greater than that of the general state population, especially considering a rising opposition to Affirmative Action.

Despite intense recruitment efforts, it appeared that the more restrictive enrollment policy had begun to take effect when it came to special admits (EOP students mainly) as the enrollment of URM students continued to grow, again except for Black students. The issue with Black student enrollment was revisited by the OMA leadership. When the new student enrollment data were analyzed over the 1993–1997 period, a significant decline was observed, especially among transfers between 1996 and 1997. (It should be noted that there was no documentation to show that the numbers were analyzed in this manner at the time.) The decline was attributed to lack of financial aid coupled with the increasing cost of college, a lower number of applicants meeting the HEC Board minimum requirements, and competition for students with Black colleges and other state institutions. Unlike all other ethnic group students, many Black students preferred to go away from home to college, especially to historically Black colleges and universities where they would be in the majority, rather than the minority, and they would be in an environment that was welcoming.

One long-term strategy implemented by OMA was to intensify outreach at the middle school level. This was made possible when funding was secured to expand the Seattle Early Scholars Outreach (SESO) program–Gaining Early Awareness and Readiness for Undergraduate Programs (GEAR UP)—which promoted the development of college awareness and readiness for middle and high school students. It was an effort to break the cycle of poverty in areas where the college-going rate was disproportionately low. Seven Seattle middle schools were served where at least 50% of the students qualified for the free and reduced lunch program. Services included tutoring, test preparation, campus visits, career exploration, mathematics review and enrichment workshops, leadership training, and parent meetings.

The decline in enrollment of EOP students notwithstanding, this was the decade when the OMA ship was righted. Vice President Herman Lujan had proposed a bridge program in 1978, but it was never implemented due to lack of funds. When Myron Apilado took the helm at OMA, he, too, felt it was imperative to improve the retention and persistence rate of a subset of EOP students who were most at-risk, but could not secure funding, at least initially.

In 1995, the Office of Undergraduate Education (OUE) became interested in establishing a bridge program for athletes; however, during that time it was believed that such a program might violate NCAA rules. OMA was invited to partner with OUE, and a three-week residential Bridge Program was launched. Students attended classes and sessions on building academic skills and participated in highly disciplined team-building exercises. Participants signed a contract pledging to follow a regimen designed to enable them to successfully navigate the University. A number of these students have gone on to increase diversity in the workforce and make a difference in society. In addition, compared to pre-Bridge students who entered with comparable academic credentials, the retention rates of the Bridge students were substantially higher. In fact, it was during this period when the first-year retention rate gap between EOP students and the rest of UW undergraduate students narrowed from high double digits to low single digits.

Encouraged by these outcomes and a belief that it was time for OMA to begin receiving national attention for its efforts, Myron Apilado and Deirdre Raynor submitted a proposal to give a presentation at the 1997 Minority Student Day Conference in San Antonio, Texas. It was the first time anyone at OMA had done so in its 29 years. Co-presenters were Vice President Apilado and Deirdre Raynor, an IC instructor. The presentation was titled "The Anatomy

Apilado's and Raynor's PowerPoint presentation at the 1997 Minority Student Day Conference in San Antonio, Texas.

of a Comprehensive Academic Support Program." It highlighted a program that was established to recruit, provide advising services, academic support, social support, graduate school preparation, a bridge program, and study abroad opportunities to underrepresented and economically and educationally disadvantaged students. The presentation was well received by attendees who came from all parts of the country. Examples of other presentations were given at LSU, Learning Centers conferences, Northwest Association of Special Programs Conference, and NCORE (National Conference on Race and Ethnicity).

Continuing along the path of being the first, the Early Identification Program staff came up with the idea that would further prepare not only its participants but also participants at other schools for life as graduate students. Under the leadership of the director, Dr. Carlene Brown, soon to be succeeded by Dr. James Antony, the first undergraduate research conference in the history of the UW was held.

Another first at UW was realized in 1998 when a proposal was made and approved to establish a Middle College Program at the UW. Later named Ida B. Wells High School, it would provide students an opportunity to take high school courses in a college environment. Done in collaboration between OMA, Seattle Public Schools, and the College of Education, this arrangement provided an alternative for students who otherwise may not have graduated from high school. Not only did these students graduate, but some also transitioned almost seamlessly into EOP. A number of graduates were admitted to the UW. One alum who ultimately earned a Doctor of Pharmacy (PharmD) degree worked for Costco for a while and now is a business owner.

Although not a first at UW, another opportunity fortuitously fell into the lap of OMA. Professor James Claus approached Bill Baker about forging a partnership with the Classics Department that would provide an opportunity for EOP students to have a study abroad experience designed specifically for them. In 1995, 14 EOP students enrolled in a Classics course titled "Introduction to the Ancient City of Rome." They went abroad to study in one of the most important centers of Western Civilization: Rome, Italy. Soon after other students were afforded the opportunity to study in Japan. "I felt that students going abroad would get to see some other cultures and get some different kinds of feelings about themselves," Myron Apilado recalled in his 2016 interview. He further stated, "Getting people away from the way we live here in the United States is a powerful and wonderful experience." Although these accomplishments were something to be proud of, OMA leadership realized there was no time for complacency. It was necessary to prepare for

Ida B. Wells High School Class of 2010

EOP students studying abroad in Rome through the Classics course in 2016.

impending changes such as court decisions that may affect the accomplishment of long-term enrollment goals. The harbinger of such a change came about with the decision handed down in a case from Texas, known as the Hopwood case. The Fifth Circuit Court of Appeals barred racial preference in the admissions process, essentially rendering a two-tier admissions system illegal. Although the ruling only applied to Louisiana, Texas, and Mississippi, the UW Admissions Office moved proactively to abandon its two-tier admission system (i.e., regular admission and EOP admission), which had survived for 28 years. The UW administration believed that an anticipatory response in a timely manner would improve the chances of a favorable outcome.

Therefore, all undergraduate applications were required to be submitted to the UW Office of Admissions; however, race could still be considered as one of the factors used in admissions. The EOP Admissions program was discontinued, and admissions at UW became a one-tier system. The decision to take this preemptive step was a joint decision between Registrar and Director of Admissions Tim Washburn and Director of EOP Admissions and Recruitment Enrique Morales. Following this change, OMA's focus changed to Recruitment and Outreach. Enrique Morales continued as director for the next five years.

Outcomes

Except for EOP enrollment, great strides were made during this decade. Research by the OMA&D Assessment and Research Unit, using data from the Enterprise Data Warehouse (EDW) and the AnalyticInteg Database (AIDB), showed that while EOP enrollment declined by 13%, URM enrollment increased by more than 38%, due mainly to an almost doubling of Latino student enrollees. EOP retention rates increased by 12 percentage points to within one percentage point of that of the UW student body. Six-year graduation rates increased by 20 percentage points, but a gap of 10% between the EOP graduation rate and that of the general UW student body remained. Degree attainment for EOP students increased by almost 57%, and academic performance in gateway courses improved substantially. Over this decade, two out of every three URM enrollees were EOP students and 60% of URM degree earners were EOP students. These data serve as a strong indicator of the role played by OMA in increasing the face of diversity both in the student body and the graduating classes.

The state budget increased by 20% and the EOP endowment portfolio increased from one endowed fund to 12 funds. What was started in earnest during Kelly's tenure, and continued through the previous decade, also continued during the next decade. EOP students were blessed with monetary gifts of $1,867,441 during the decade, almost triple the amount in gifts received from private sources over the previous decade (President's Reports, 1988/1989-1996/1997). Such success was a clear indication that many individual donors and/or businesses wanted to see EOP students and the OMA family of programs succeed. Based on these accomplishments and apparent unparalleled and broad support, one could conclude that OMA was well on its way to achieving national program status.

STUDENT CASES

LORNE MURRAY. One student in this era stands out, not only because of personal achievement, but because of what he did (and does) for others. Lorne Murray, a student from a single parent household out of Silverdale, Washington, came to the Instructional Center seeking academic support for his math and science courses. The staff almost immediately recognized Murray's quick grasp of complex concepts and his ability to clearly explain these concepts to his peers and share with them effective learning strategies and problem-solving techniques. He soon was recruited to be a tutor in math, chemistry, and biology and became popular with many of his peers over the next three years. He became one the Center's models of success for many of his peers, especially those who aspired to become physicians. His performance in his classes rose to new heights culminating in his writing a perfect final example in one of his organic chemistry courses taught by a professor known to be one of the Chemistry Department's most difficult.

Although busy carrying a full course load and helping others, Lorne Murray also conducted undergraduate research that led to a publication with a well-known hand surgeon. For these accomplishments, he was the first undergraduate UW student to receive the UNCF Merck Scholarship. Besides a $25,000 cash award directly to him, his department (Microbiology) was awarded $10,000. In addition, he received two EOP Recognition Achievement awards, one of which was the President's Achievement Award, that went to the EOP student with the highest graduating GPA.

Murray was accepted by several medical schools but chose Harvard. He later became a Fellow at Cedar Sinai Hospital in Los Angeles specializing in cardiology. It should be noted that this is the hospital of choice for many movie stars, so we who knew him in the Instructional Center nicknamed him "Dr. Hollywood." Remembering the days during his undergraduate years when he struggled financially, and the support he received from key OMA&D staff, prompted Dr. Murray, now a lead cardiologist at an Arizona clinic, not only to donate to other EOP scholarship funds but also to establish an annual $5,000 scholarship awarded to "students who show the most determination, perseverance, and who have overcome the highest obstacles to achieve substantial academic success." It carries the name the Murray, Pitre, Baker, Rosebaugh Scholarship (Herrington, 2018).

TANIA BARRON. Another student who went on to make a difference was Tania Barron. Tania entered the University through the inaugural Bridge Program.

Tania attended Roosevelt High School where she graduated with a GPA that was 0.7 grade points below the UW average of regularly admissible students. Heeding the advice of her EOP counselors and using the academic services on a regular basis, she earned impressive grades over the next two years. She was recruited to serve as a psychology tutor at the IC, participated in undergraduate research in psychology, and went to Rome in the Study Abroad Program. In her junior and senior years, Tania received an EOP Recognition Award for academic excellence and the EOP Vice President's Achievement Award, given to a student whose college GPA is markedly higher than their high school GPA. She received a Fulbright Scholarship, enabling her to share experiences with and learn from the people of Ecuador. Tania graduated from the UW with degrees in social psychology and public health with a cumulative GPA that was a full grade point higher than what she earned in high school. She was elected to Phi Beta Kappa and went on to earn a master's degree in public policy from Harvard's Kennedy School of Government.

After working in environmental services for ten years, Tania decided to venture out on her own. She co-founded The Terron Group, LLC, a consulting firm providing environmental, social and health risk-management solutions, and currently serves as Managing Partner. Two of Tania's siblings are also EOP alumni. One went on to earn a PhD who now works as executive director at Pension Real Estate Association, and a younger brother currently works at Microsoft. Although not an EOP alum, her mother—who graduated the same year as Tania—was an IC alum.

JABARI WALKER. Jabari Walker was another student who would not have been allowed to enroll at UW were it not for EOP and the Bridge Program. Like Tania, he entered the UW with a high school GPA almost one full grade point below the average GPA of the entering cohort of full-time UW students. Undaunted by this status, Jabari aspired to seek admissions into either electrical engineering or computer engineering, both highly competitive majors. These programs routinely denied students who entered UW with high academic credentials. Taking full advantage of the academic support and advising provided by OMA programs, he worked diligently and purposefully toward his goal. Against what seemed like insurmountable odds, Jabari was admitted into both majors. He chose computer engineering and graduated with a cumulative GPA 0.6 grade points higher than his entering GPA. He went on to earn a master's degree in computer science from the University of Illinois Urbana-Champaign. Jabari later shared that he wanted to do well so that the IC staff would speak highly of him in a manner spoken about Lorne Murray, a peer tutor in chemistry who was excelling academically. Jabari did not forget from whence he came. He routinely contributes to the EOP scholarship fund.

CHRISTINA ROBERTS. Another case in point is exemplified in the Christina Roberts story. From elementary school to the ninth grade, Christina lived in an unstable family environment. She dropped out of junior high and thus failed all of her first semester courses. Afterwards, Christina went to live with her grandmother who was a University of Washington librarian. Following up on the recommendations of Christina's former junior high teachers and mentors, her grandmother went to the Upward Bound office on campus and advocated for her granddaughter to be admitted to the program. According to Christina, she was considered a risky candidate for various reasons. She went on to say, "High school was exceptionally hard because of family instability. . . I lived in many places during my high school years. UB [Upward Bound] was a lifesaver. The staff at UB, especially Leny and Donna, went above and beyond to support me and encourage me to persist despite all of the issues going on in my life." Despite these efforts, Christina was denied admission to UW due to a high school GPA that was more than a full grade point lower than the average for freshman enrollees. The impact of this news was compounded by learning heartbreaking news about her mother. Nonetheless, Christina did not give up and through the appeal process was admitted to UW through EOP.

According to Christina, once enrolled, she took full advantage of the support provided by the OMA&D family of programs. The Upward Bound program employed her for three years as a work-study student. She frequently visited the Instructional Center for tutoring in math and participated in the GRE prep course offered to the first McNair Program cohort. "The McNair program was exceptional," said Christina, "From learning how to network to attending conferences, McNair offered me practical and tangible advice, and I received amazing support as I worked toward applying to graduate school. McNair connected me with a faculty mentor in English, and I was also supported in completing extensive undergraduate research. In many ways, because of McNair, I was more prepared than many of my graduate school peers, which was a wonderful head start given the demands and challenges of grad school."

Christina noted that she also used the Ethnic Cultural Center extensively, participating in First Nations, an American Indian student organization. "I am urban raised, and while I was not an enrolled tribal member growing up, I am now an enrolled member," said she. "I have a lot of family in Montana. . . I now consider myself to be a part of the Urban Native community in the Seattle area. I've lived here most of my life and given the fact that 70% of Native people live in urban spaces now, I feel as if I'm a part of a huge community of peoples from many Indigenous nations."

Christina graduated from the University earning degrees in English and Comparative History of Ideas (CHID) with a GPA that was almost a full grade point higher than her high school GPA. She was on the dean's list for two consecutive years and received an EOP Recognition Award for academic excellence. She went on to earn a PhD from the University of Arizona and is now an associate professor and director of an indigenous institute at Seattle University.

More than two decades later, Christina is thankful for the impact that the OMA&D family programs and staff has had on her educational career. She states, "There's no way I can convey through email how grateful I am and how much I benefitted from the environment created at the UW by you [Emile Pitre] and so many others." She went on to say, "I loved my UW OMA&D community!"

CONAN VIERNES. On the other end of the EOP spectrum, some students began to excel academically from the outset. A representative case is the story of a student who attended high school on the Yakama Indian Reservation. Conan Viernes, a student from Wapato High School, was a frequent user of the OMA Instructional Center, where he participated in weekly review workshops that were designed to supplement and complement what was being taught in regular courses. He excelled in these courses. Not only did Conan benefit from participating in these workshops, but he also served as a model of success for other EOP students who were workshop participants. His achievement was recognized when he received the UW President's Medal, awarded to the UW student who earned the highest cumulative GPA as a freshman.

RACHAEL SEYMOUR. Rachael Seymour's story moves from the frozen tundra to Hollywood. Rachael and an older brother grew up in an unincorporated area of the tundra in Alaska 15 miles outside Fairbanks. They lived most of their childhood in a dry cabin—no plumbing, toilet, or shower. Their mother, the daughter of a Tuskegee airman, was Black (with Cherokee/Choctaw ancestry). Their father was American Indian (Athabaskan), but he left home when Rachael and her sibling were young. Not only did they have no running water, but they had to collect snow in a garbage bag, melt it (over a wood stove), and pass the liquid through a strainer before it was ready for drinking, bathing, or other uses. Where they lived was so remote that they had to walk two miles, rain, shine, or snow (mostly), many times in sub-zero conditions, often in the dark and avoiding moose, to catch the bus to school. Although she was very interested in playing the cello, these conditions forced Rachael to abandon the idea because practicing at home was out of the question. The instrument would freeze during the walk to and from home.

Rachael struggled with school, earning a 1.9 GPA at end of her freshman year. As a result, she was relegated to taking remedial subjects for the next two years. Living conditions improved dramatically once her family moved into a house during her junior year. Although there were sports teams for women, Rachael chose football, playing tight end, and lettered on a special team.

After spending her senior year studying in Japan, Rachael set her sights on attending college in the contiguous 48 states. She chose the University of Washington because, according to her, she wanted to study in a place that was much larger than Fairbanks. She was denied admissions due to core deficiencies and lack of strength of her high school curriculum. She was told to enroll at a community college and apply through the Educational Opportunity Program (EOP) after one year, which proved successful.

During her freshman year, she received academic support from the IC, which she remembered was "a real help during the uncertainty of navigating my first college classes." Initially, through the urging of a classmate, she sought out departmental advising. The advice given was to drop one of the courses she was taking. Rachael ignored this advice and sought help from the IC. After receiving excellent grades in each course, she returned to the adviser and asked, "Which course should I have dropped?" When she shared the report of this stellar academic performance with the director of the OMA Early Identification Program (EIP), according to Rachael, Dr. Carlene Brown replied, "Great, keep it up." Said Rachael, "High expectations motivated me to do well, that was what I liked about the support OMA provided. After that, I became addicted to getting good grades."

From then on, Rachael excelled in classes, making the annual dean's list for four consecutive years. Such an excellent academic record resulted in her being named a Truman Scholar. It was around this time that Dr. Brown urged her to consider graduate school. Said Rachael, "I didn't even know what graduate school was when I arrived at UW!"

Her compelling story and her excellent academic record led to her being chosen to receive the EOP Vice President Achievement Award at Celebration 1993. The following year she graduated magna cum laude, was elected to Phi Beta Kappa, and went on to earn a master's degree in public policy from the Kennedy School of Government at Harvard. After graduate school, Rachael served as an analyst for the CIA, but her penchant for writing and acting lured her to Hollywood. Not only has she appeared in roles, usually as a police officer on television shows such as *Scandal*, *Veep*, *Criminal Minds*, and *The Mentalist*, but she has produced shows as well. Rachael has also served on the Screen Actors Guild Board of Directors and is one of the founders of the Beverly Hills Human Relations Commission. In 2019, she served as a screen writer for ABC's hit series, *The Rookie*.

Not forgetting from whence she came, Rachael established the Rachael A. Seymour Most Improved Scholarship which are awarded to selected Fairbanks, Alaska, high school seniors who meet the criteria.

Notable EOP Alumni of the Decade

The number of Notable EOP Alumni designated as such almost doubled compared to the previous decade. As can be seen in the educational and career summaries below, many earned multiple post-baccalaureate degrees. Their educational achievements and professional career accomplishments should leave no doubt as to why these individuals were chosen to be recognized. In terms of educational achievements two out of three earned master's, doctoral, law, and medical degrees. What is most impressive was that two alumni earned an MD/PhD, a rare accomplishment—less than 5% nationally have been so bestowed. In terms of professional accomplishments, many of these alums hold leadership positions as CEOs, presidents, vice presidents, directors/managers in technology, engineering, healthcare, and the legal profession.

Frank Ashby, '88, '98, MPA (UW), '08 EdD (UW)

Gabriel Florentino, '88 (UW)

Michelle Bonam, '89, MBA/MSE (Penn)

Eric Lizarraga Burdge, '89, '96, MD/PhD (Cornell/UW)

Gabriel Gallardo, '89, '93, '00, PhD (UW)

Gayle Johnson, '89 (UW)

Mimi Lam, '89, MD (University of Nevada)

Cornelius Nicholson, '89 DDS (UW)

Wei-Chih Wang, '89, '92, '96, PhD (UW)

David Gandara, '90 (UW)

Lee Garrett, '90, MBA (Penn)

Tri Phan, '90 (UW)

Dean Calloway, '91, MS (Carnegie Mellon), JD (University of Chicago)

Michaelanne Ehrenberg, '91, JD (Boston University)

Debra Morales-Nunez, '91, JD (UW)

Gregory Tyler, '91, MBA (University of Rhode Island), MS (University of Dayton)

Helen Powell, '91, '92, MS (UW)

Cos Roberts, '91 (UW)

Annie Young-Scrivner, '91, MBA (University of Minnesota)

Ahndrea Blue, '92, '95, JD (UW)

Brent Jones, '92, PhD (University of Texas, Austin)

Allan Wu, '92, MD (University of Rochester School of Medicine)

Amy Benson, '93, Phi Beta Kappa (UW)

Ana Bowman, '93 (UW)

Bill Fishburn, '93, MS (UC Berkeley)

Faimous Harrison, '93, MS (Seattle Pacific University), PhD (Oregon State)

David Herrera, '93, JD/MBA (University of Illinois)

Angelique A. Johnson Andrews, '93, MD (UW)

Joelle Segawa Kane, '91, JD (University of Hawaii)

Dale Learn, '93, JD (University of Maryland)

Carlo Melbihess, '93 (UW)

Javier Valdez, '93, MPA (Baruch College, CUNY)

Juan Varela, '93, MS (Georgia Tech)

Barron Willis III, '93, MBA (UW), MSME (UC Berkeley)

Collette Courtion, '94, MBA (Pepperdine)

Roy Diaz, '94, '96, '02, MS, PhD, JD (UW)

Wuaca Luna, '94, '97, MD (UW)

Judy Nicastro, '94,'97, JD (UW)

Rachael Seymour, '94, '93, MPP (Harvard)

Wesley K. Thomas (Navajo), '94,'96,'99, PhD (UW)

Elva Arredondo, '95, PhD (Duke)

Kassa Mekonnen, '95, MSMI (University of Phoenix)

Bruce Joseph, '95, MBA (UW, Bothell)

Angela King, '95 (UW)

Scott March, '95, '96, MSW (UW)

Rion Ramirez (Turtle Mountain Chippewa Band of Indians), '95, '98, JD (UW)

Michelle Billingsley Akpojowo, '96 (UW)

Heather Barry, '96 MPA (Evergreen State College)

Allan Carandang, '96 (UW)

Antoinette Davis, '96, JD (Seattle U)

Debra Dove, '96 (UW)

Tiffany Dufu, '96, '99, MA (UW)

Miki Moore Hardisty, '96, MS (UC San Diego)

Terrence Hui, '96, MS (George Mason University), PhD (George Washington University)

Leo Gonzalez, '96, MBA (Arizona)

Dawncelie Johnson-White, '96 (UW)

Lorne Murray, '96, MD (Harvard)

Zandra Palmer, '96 (UW)

David D. Tran, '96, MD/PhD (Mayo Medical School, Rochester, MN)

Marshall Chalverus, '97 (UW)

Eddie Clopton, '97, JD (University of Illinois)

Heather Dash, '97, MA (Emory)

Danielle Whitener, '97 (UW)

Gina Clemente Willink, '97, MS (UC Santa Clara)

Their adviser, June Hairston, is on the far left. This group was instrumental in getting then-President Richard McCormick to approve funding for needed renovations and for purchasing computers for the computer lab.

CHAPTER 5

1998–2007: The Era of Cross-fertilization and Expansion

[The IC is] "a jewel in the crown of the University of Washington, a model for all higher education to follow. . . [Its distinguishing characteristics include] "comprehensiveness, scope of program offerings, staffing level of credentialed and specialized instructors, caliber of the tutor corps, and program assessment data that informed evaluative decision making"

—visiting University of Michigan senior vice provost, Monts, 2001

". . . she [Rusty] added the title Vice Provost for Diversity. That gave us not only a focus on retention and student success but also diversity or enhancement of diversity across our campus. It began to connect our work with the work of faculty, the work of academic departments. I think that was a significant shift in our work."

—Gabriel Gallardo, 2015

Myron Apilado's tenure as vice president extended into the fourth decade of the Office of Minority Affairs with a positive trajectory. Gifts to EOP/OMA totaled $355,957 for the 1998 fiscal year, an all-time high. The evolutionary journey continued with the establishment of The Early Scholars Outreach Program (ESOP). The aim was to create wide awareness of the need for higher education and for the university and public schools to work together to improve student performance. Funds were provided by the state legislature to partner with nine schools, six in the Seattle/Renton area, three in Yakima, and one on the Quinault Indian Reservation. The program served students from Black, Asian, Latino, Pacific Islander, and American Indian groups.

Word got around that something special was happening in the great northwest. As the IC director, I was invited to be one of the honoraria (paid) presenters at a conference entitled "Mentoring for the 21st Century" at Louisiana State University, Baton Rouge, Louisiana. I also presented at the American Chemical Society Regional Conference in October 1998. Participants were impressed and opined that the Instructional Center demonstrated best practices worthy of national model status. Buoyed by this informal recognition, Apilado convinced the UW provost's office to provide funds to hire a computer analyst skilled in data mining. This acquisition led to the first longitudinal study of the IC conducted by an IC director. In collaboration with an IC statistics instructor and a graduate student in the Economics Department, I sought to determine whether a correlation existed between frequency of IC use in selected 100 and 200 level chemistry courses and grades earned. Based on the data, the conclusion was that frequent use of the IC in nine different chemistry courses could increase students' GPA in these courses as high as 0.8 grade points.

It is significant that the IC was the first program at UW to use an electronic tracking system to record usage of program services by individual students and by specific course. The information acquired made it possible to create a database that could be linked with data in the UW database. This coupling enabled staff to conduct statistical analysis to make informed programming and policy decisions regarding educational outcomes.

It also allowed the IC to engage in extensive assessment work at a time when many institutions were resisting such efforts. Findings were used to determine the overall effectiveness of intervention strategies employed to serve program participants. For the first time in more than two decades, a case could be made for the value of OMA using hard data instead of relying almost exclusively on anecdotes. Disaggregation of the data made it possible to track educational outcomes using descriptors such as ethnicity/race, gender, and freshman/transfer, EOP, low-income, first-generation, and all-UW status over extended periods of time to determine whether intervention strategies were working. If so, researchers could ask to what degree, and if not, the program could implement strategies for improvement and collect evaluative data. A definitive association between improvement in educational outcomes and intervention strategies was used to define best practices. This approach has proven to be truly transformative and made it possible to share these practices at regional and national conferences.

The role of the Student Advisory Board (SAB) evolved as well. The SAB went from primarily serving in an advisory capacity to one of activism. For the first time in OMA's 22-year history, the vice president had a very good working relationship not only with his Student Advisory Board but also with EOP students in general. The SAB worked well with Vice President Apilado, which allowed the group to have a positive influence on then-UW President Richard McCormick. They were able to convince McCormick that the ECC needed to be remodeled and that it was important for users of the facility to have a computer lab available to them. This group also lobbied for an upgrade of the computer lab housed in the IC.

Such accomplishments can largely be attributed to the strong leadership of key members of the group. Out of this group came a student regent, John Amaya, a Latino and Business Administration major who served as president of the SAB. Michael Tuncap, a Bridge student, became an ASUW vice president. Tuncap, along with the support of his community, led an effort to have Hawaiian and other Pacific Islander students officially designated as underrepresented (URM).

Notable EOP Alumni Daya Mortel (left) an Jaebadiah Gardner at the ECC Computer Lab, 2004.

For 30 years, race was allowed to be considered as one of the factors in evaluating applicants for admission. Initiative 200 (I-200), a statewide voter initiative in 1998, forbade giving preference in hiring, college admissions, or other state functions, based on race, ethnicity, or gender.

While these gains were being made, an anti-affirmative action wave was blanketing the entire state of Washington, which, if actualized, would change the makeup of students entering the University. For 30 years, race was allowed to be considered as one of the factors in evaluating applicants for admission. Initiative 200 (I-200), a statewide voter initiative in 1998, forbade giving preference in hiring, college admissions, or other state functions, based on race, ethnicity, or gender. Despite efforts to block it, I-200 was approved by voters. Its passage meant applications would have to be viewed with colorblind lenses. Instead of an average of about 600 new students coded EOP, only about 200 entered the University in the fall of

1999. Specifically, the number of incoming Black, Latino, American Indian/ Alaska Native, and Pacific Islander students decreased by 36%, 21%, 37%, and 71%, respectively. The decline for Filipino students was 44%. However, the overall decline in enrollment of URM students was just over 6% mainly because returning students' enrollment was not affected. The downward trend continued through 2002. Over that same period, Asian, International, and "Not Indicated" student enrollments increased.

Rather than yielding to the notion that nothing could be done if race could no longer be considered, the Minority Think Tank became more intentionally involved. It was a multiethnic group composed of both undergraduate and graduate students that played an integral role in keeping the University true to the cause of diversity despite the passage of I-200. This group, led by Tyrone Porter, Tyson Marsh, Michael Tuncap, Chris Knaus, and Rose James, staged a protest that shut down Highway 520 for roughly four hours on December 3, 1998, to highlight their dissatisfaction with voters on the eastside of Lake Washington who favored the measure (Adam, 1998). Following this move, students met with administrators including the UW president, vice presidents for student affairs and minority affairs, and some faculty members, particularly from the School of Law, to make certain that every effort would be made to mitigate the situation going forward. They wanted assurance that the University would still work to increase minority enrollment and maintain scholarships earmarked for specific minority groups, and that minority programs would continue. After studying the wording of the initiative, UW leaders concluded that there was no stipulation that *recruitment* could not be race specific.

To counteract the precipitous decline in enrollment of underrepresented minority students, an intense effort funded by the President's Office was undertaken to reverse the downward trend in enrollment. Outreach and recruitment staffing grew substantially. The Student Ambassador Outreach Program was established to enhance the recruitment efforts directed toward underrepresented minority students throughout the state of Washington. Student recruiters increased five-fold. Recruitment and outreach efforts intensified statewide using strategies that were race specific (not a violation of I-200). A campaign was launched to increase the number of URM students who took the SAT, translating into increased numbers of high school graduates eligible to apply to the university. This effort proved to be highly successful. These strategies implemented by the leadership

NEWS

SAB PRESIDENTIAL FORUM

On January 28th, the Student Advisory board participated in its annual Presidential Forum at the ECC. This forum was an opportunity for SAB to share student concerns directly with President McCormick. Among the main topics was the possible effect of Initiative 200. Students asked several questions specifically pertaining to this issue including what the possible effects on the university would be if I-200 passed, and what could be done to insure diversity on campus. President McCormick expressed his dedication to diversity, not only for social justice but also in connection with academic excellence, and his willingness to act within the boundaries of the law to preserve this notion.

Renovations on the ECC building were also a topic, and a committee evaluating such needs was a suggestion in resolving this. Questions were asked concerning issues that were not directly within the president's influence, for example the possibility of an ethnic cultural class requirement, but the fact the they were brought to his attention was an important step.

Also invited to the forum were the directors of the Asian, Black, Native American, and Latino ASUW Student Commissions who were also given the opportunity to ask questions. This annual event is one of the most valued activities of the Student Advisory Board because of the direct contact with the President of the University and the ability to bring student concerns to light.

Student Advisory Board members discuss I-200 with President McCormick
at the 1998 Presidential Forum.

would not only increase the number of prospective students but also increase the probability that enrollees would persist and graduate.

Regarding the role played by others during this period, here is what Gabriel Gallardo, interim OMA/D vice president at the time, shared:

> *You know that there were many people that were involved who were not necessarily part of OMA&D that played a role—in the faculty, in administrative ranks. . . . Obviously, the people in the organization carried the load for many years, but it doesn't happen in isolation, and I think that's the message that we want to convey, from presidents to leaders on campus, and community leaders that may not get the recognition, but [who] are also very active in pushing the administration or pushing the organization.*

About Vice President for Student Affairs Ernest Morris specifically, Gallardo said:

> *I think about Ernest Morris [vice president for student affairs 1985– 2005]. He wasn't a leader in OMA&D but, you know, he was one of the few African American leaders on our campus for many years. I think that without his work there are a number of things that we wouldn't have worked out: he was involved in the response to I-200; he leveraged the work of financial aid and admissions to make sure that we were inclusive after I-200. So, there are a lot of people that played a role that were not necessarily part of the organization.*

The OMA leadership was convinced that many of the underrepresented minority (URM) students, as well as economically and educationally disadvantaged students, were at a disadvantage because of relatively lower SAT scores and high school GPAs. Thus, Enrique Morales, executive director of admissions/assistant to the vice president for OMA Outreach and Recruitment, proposed to the registrar and assistant vice president for enrollment management, Tim Washburn, that these students should become affiliated and allowed to take advantage of the tried-and-true services of the family of OMA programs. Washburn agreed and the EOP Affiliation Program was institutionalized. As recipients of these services, the chances of the affiliated EOP students being admitted to graduate and professional schools where they were disproportionally underrepresented improved substantially. These strategies, coupled with serving a larger proportion of the currently enrolled population not in danger of failing to graduate and most likely to graduate with credentials in a major of their choice, would improve the chances of a larger proportion being admitted to either graduate or professional school. Considering there was an outcry calling for a more diverse workforce, these strategies would also improve other chances of students securing employment in a highly competitive job market.

While these events were happening, OMA worked diligently and resolutely toward securing federal funding to serve subsets of the target population. A McNair Program was funded to prepare low-income undergraduate, first-generation URM students, and EOP students with academic merit, for doctoral programs through scholarly activities. Students would have access to faculty mentoring, research opportunities, internships, the Graduate Record Exam (GRE), and graduate application preparation assistance. "We will be able to contribute to the development of a pool of students that will become the future professors and researchers of our nation's higher education institutions" said founding director, Gabriel Gallardo. Funding was also secured which enabled the UW's GEAR UP initiative to launch in the Yakima Valley to break the cycle of poverty and low educational achievement that was (and still is) pervasive throughout Central Washington.

Myron Apilado's tenure came to an end in the spring of 2001. He served in the vice president's role for 11 years, the longest tenure to date. He acted as a consultant to the incoming vice president for an additional year. Although he left with mixed emotions, he was very proud of the accomplishments realized while he was at the helm of OMA. He was most proud of the recognition received by the IC, which he called the flagship much to the chagrin of some staff, just a month before his departure. The IC received not one, but two University Recognition awards in the same year, the first program to do so in the 31-year history of the UW's Recognition Ceremony. One of the awards was for instructional excellence awarded by the Teaching Academy, even though the IC was not connected to an academic department. The other award was for advancing diversity.

Over this period, the double award-winning program hosted visitors from higher education institutions who came to learn how the IC worked.

Visitors came from universities including the University of Alabama, University of Michigan-Ann Arbor, Washington State, San Francisco State, Portland State, Tulane, Louisiana State University, University of Minnesota, Oregon State University, University of Nevada-Reno, Temple University, University of Port Elizabeth South Africa, North Carolina State, and Eastern Washington University.

It is worth noting that, impressed with what he saw and learned on a visit to campus, a senior vice provost from the University of Michigan described the IC as "a jewel in the crown of the University of Washington, a model for all higher education to follow." Distinguishing characteristics that he highlighted included "comprehensiveness, scope of program offerings, staffing level of credentialed and specialized instructors, caliber of the tutor corps, and program assessment data that informed evaluative decision making" (Monts, 2001).

In a 2015 interview Apilado shared this:

I never believed that OMA got the national attention I felt it deserved. It's not the award that's good. What's good is the presentations that you made might enable student affairs professionals at other institutions to replicate programs at their institutions. It has been the right kind of information, about our success, that should have been presented at conferences long ago. The awards that we received were only because our staff was doing serious and effective work with students.

Barceló's Emphasis on Collaboration

Transitioning into the next century (the seventh leg of the evolutionary journey) ushered in new leadership: Dr. Nancy "Rusty" Barceló, the sixth vice president. From the outset, Barceló emphasized collaboration between OMA and campus-wide university entities and achieving excellence through diversity. She often spoke about "embracing community building and promoting collaboration and integration among faculty, staff and students." Further, Barceló emphasized strategic planning that would facilitate the development of a more diverse university. Included in this plan were accountability measures to assess outreach efforts, recruitment, and graduation outcomes.

Soon after her arrival, she conducted an assessment of the status of OMA that included input from staff. The outcome led her to reorganize OMA into a Pre-college and an Academic Advancement unit, broadening her locus of control to include additional assistants to the vice president and directors. It was her impression that "people were working, but they were working in silos and not always as a team." Her intent was to implement practices and procedures that would enable each entering cohort of EOP students to maximize their learning potential such that they would not only persist and graduate at rates comparable to other Research I institutions, but also a higher proportion would gain admission to graduate and professional schools. The

Anthony Rose, EOP alumni, with Dr. Rusty Barceló, OMA&D 6th vice president, at the May 16, 2018, Celebration.

overarching goal was to achieve national model status within a few years. Reaching this lofty goal would first require additional staffing in strategic roles to shore up the infrastructure. Between 2001 and 2003 the staff grew by almost 30%, and the overall staff composition was almost three-fourths minority and two-thirds women. Within this group, 12 people were promoted to key positions.

Achieving model program status would require the development, prioritization, and implementation of a strategic plan. Each OMA program established work plans that would be used as accountability measures to determine program success, as well as intervention strategies that would improve educational outcomes. A determining factor for success was the extent to which intradepartmental and interdepartmental collaboration occurred both on and off campus.

Barceló felt that although nearly two-thirds of the funding streams for OMA came from federal funding sources, it was imperative that a New Initiative and External Funding Unit be established to coordinate grant submissions to national, state, and local funding agencies, as well as serve as a grant writing, management, and administration resource. Another function of

Reflections on Myron Apilado

Myron Apilado left an enduring legacy of respect among people who worked with him. Here are some of their comments, when asked to rate the effectiveness of the vice presidents they worked with:

Long-time staff member Gabriel Gallardo said:

Dr. Myron Apilado

> For me, Myron stands at the top of my list because he gave me an opportunity to work in OMA&D. He opened the doors to this career trajectory, and at that point not really knowing that this would end up being the work that I did the rest of my life. Myron has been a very strong supporter over the years. He's remained connected to OMA&D.

June Hairston (EdD), longtime OMA&D adviser, and current director of the National Science Foundation funded Louis Stokes Alliance for Minority Participation (LSAMP) noted:

> What I liked about Dr. Apilado was that he was not afraid to be intrusive. We started with the Bridge Program, where we took students and intrusively got into the mix. We held them accountable and put them on contracts. We made them come in, and if they weren't compliant then we put them on probation or even dropped them. We created leaders out of that group because we held them accountable, and we held the bar high.
>
> I had the opportunity during that time to be Dr. Apilado's adviser to the Student Advisory Board. I was told before I came that there was a lot of turbulence going on. When I came on board, it was working with this board of 20 students, four from each of the ethnic groups. We changed an adversarial relationship with the vice president to a very supportive and enhanced relationship with the vice president. We revived the Ethnic Cultural Center under that group, remodeled it. The board met with President McCormick [president of the University of Washington 1995-2002] on a regular basis. But that board was very strategic under Dr. Apilado. That board became leaders in ASUW. We had our first student regent from that group—John Amaya [the student Regent 2000-2001]. It was a powerful group that eventually produced doctors and lawyers. It was just a great time. Nine years I did that with

them. It was one of the great times of my term here. That was with Dr. Apilado. He held us accountable.

Dr. Apilado fought against the co-location [moving the OMA counseling staff from Schmitz Hall to Mary Gates Hall, a more central campus location]. He eventually resigned because he couldn't agree with McCormick. That's how passionate he was. He didn't want us to lose our identity. That fear filtered to us as advisers. We thought coming over here would make us lose who we were and that we would have to blend. That's still an underlying current: Is the future about losing who we are and who we serve? And how we serve them? It comes up every now and then. That was Dr. Apilado.

Raul Anaya, a long-time adviser to OMA and OMA&D students, had this to say about Dr. Apilado:

Myron. I like Myron [Apilado]. He was good. I think the challenge that Myron had was when we were morphing into a "them and us" scenario where we were on this side of 15th [in Schmitz Hall] and central campus maybe didn't think of us at first thought when we were talking about diversity of students and recruitment and all that. So maybe his challenge was: how do we become more centralized on campus?

Apilado felt strongly that re-location of OMA counseling services to Mary Gates Hall, which at the time was under the auspices of the dean of the Office of Undergraduate Education (OUE), was the first step toward decentralization of OMA, followed by total absorption. It was a chess match that OMA would lose, he believed.

Mike Tulee, sharing memories of his time as an undergraduate student when he was one of the few Native Americans at the UW, also spoke fondly of Apilado:

For some reason his name seems to stand out more than the others [vice presidents], the reason being that he was always jovial. I'd walk by his office, and he was always joking around with the staff. Somehow, he was seemingly more personable than the others. The others were probably quite personable, but for some reason I was able to chat with him on a number of occasions. The other ones were friendly, but I believe they were more focused on their jobs. But Myron, I felt like he really let his hair down quite often and I would sit in his office and just say "hi." He actually knew my first name, so for an undergrad student I thought that was pretty interesting.

the unit was to promote collaboration with faculty and departments on grant projects designed to positively impact a diverse student population.

In a similar vein, Barceló also realized that it was extremely important to increase funding for financial support for students through scholarships. Barceló brokered a partnership with the UW Office of Development whereby a dedicated development officer would be assigned to OMA. Within two years, funds raised at the annual Celebration banquet increased from $16,000 to nearly $70,000 and reached about $90,000 by the time Barceló returned to the University of Minnesota in 2006.

The self-assessment findings revealed that although the number of applications of URM students continued to increase, the number choosing to attend did not increase commensurably. To address this issue, programs were implemented to increase the enrollment of high-achieving students who had been offered admission (Shaping Your Future) and increase the participation of EOP students in the University's orientation program (Welcome Daze). Welcome Daze, which preceded Dawg Daze (the University's general orientation programming), has endured 19 years. In partnership with the Office of Undergraduate Education, and funded by President Richard McCormick, a residential Summer Bridge Program for Term B was established in 2002.

Although a Bridge program had been in existence since 1995, Barceló felt that it should be larger, should not necessarily require the participation of athletes, and should have buy-in from multiple units across campus. Thus, she convened a group composed of representatives from the Office of Admissions, Dean of Undergraduate Education, Office of the Provost, College of Arts and Sciences, and selected UW faculty to plan the program. This effort also had the blessings of the Faculty Council on Academic Standards. The outcome was that Admissions provided a list of about 1.5% of the total entering freshmen who were eligible for provisional admission (EOP III). A group of OMA staff was assembled to choose the student cohort it felt had the greatest potential to be successful at UW.

Students were offered admission with the caveat that they would need to sign a contract requiring they successfully complete Term B of Summer Quarter, participate in academic sessions, and visit their EOP adviser and the IC for academic support for a prescribed number of times each quarter during their first year of enrollment. A committee was also established to determine whether

Filipino Dance Group at Welcome Daze, September 9, 2017.

Left: Iisaaksiichaa Ross Braine and Kaya Warrior at Welcome Daze, September 21, 2018.
Right: Dr. June Hairston at Welcome Daze September 22, 2017.

the terms of the contract were met. Failure to do so could lead to disenrollment.

In the mornings, students attended classes taught by UW professors. In the afternoon, they participated in sessions at the IC designed to improve competencies in math and writing. An assessment protocol was also put in place to determine the academic progress of the Bridge students. Findings revealed that participants earned cumulative GPAs significantly higher than a comparison group and significantly higher than predicted based on their high school GPA and SAT scores. For the first three cohorts, first-year retention rates were comparable to those of non-Bridge EOP students and were higher than the national average.

Barceló was successful in securing funding for the program from President Richard McCormick's office over the next four years. Once Barceló left the University, it became extremely difficult to secure funding. So, what happened to the Bridge program that was established in 1995? It was designated as Autumn Bridge, since it was operated between Summer and Autumn quarters, and was continued through 2004 when the Athletic department decided to establish a separate program.

Strategic planning and making programmatic decisions informed by assessment of outcomes marked part of the new organizational thrust. Even with this new thrust, Barceló felt the future of the program was not sustainable if the goal was only to maintain the status quo of focusing merely on access and retention. In an interview conducted in 2016, Barceló reflected:

> *Another void I saw, or need, was that there was very little data, over and beyond outreach and retention. There wasn't any data that said: how do we know that diversity and equity is being successful, in terms of not just the climate, but in terms of our policies, etcetera? I thought that was important. The other fundamental thing that we talked about often was that not only should we be a resource to the students that we served, but how could the office and the staff and the people be a resource to the broader university community, in terms of the work that they were trying to do?"*

Barceló saw an opportunity to broaden the focus toward issues of institutional transformation. She felt that the work of equity and diversity should not fall mainly on the shoulders of OMA, but that it should be a shared responsibility of the campus as a whole and that "everybody should provide the leadership," a statement she made frequently to staff, faculty, and administration. Furthermore, Barceló felt that it was important that the leader of OMA work directly with faculty and be more engaged with the academic mission of the institution. She made the case for a joint appointment as vice provost for diversity, thus becoming a hybrid of student affairs and academic affairs. With the advent of this hybrid configuration, diversity research and advocacy for recruitment and retention of a more diverse faculty and staff university-wide became the paramount focus. The leadership advocated for and promoted transforming the curriculum by making diversity an integral aspect of content and pedagogy that not only met the needs of minority students but also the broader student body. This duality of responsibilities resulted in a new title for Barceló: Vice President for Minority Affairs and Vice Provost for Diversity.

The formation of the student affairs/academic division did not go off without a hitch. The incumbent staff, many of whom had worked diligently and purposefully to create a highly successful program for more than three decades, began to feel unappreciated by the leadership. In addition, certain segments of the community wondered whether this dual-purposed approach was a benefit or a hindrance for the population that student activists fought so selflessly for. To remain a benefit for that population would require striking a balance by the leadership, coupled with commitment and support from the president and provost of the institution. What follows is how Barceló said she dealt with the concerns:

> *I just talked about it very directly with people when the issue did come up, whether it be with students, faculty, or staff, because the fact of the matter is that most of us have multiple identities. I'll use myself: I have a disability, I'm a lesbian, I'm a Chicana, and I'm a woman. All of my identities interact. How do we make sure that we're an inclusive office? Not at the expense of the Minority Affairs mission, which was critical. I was very clear about that. All of that was my way to be more inclusive. . . there needs to be a connection to the academic institution. And one might argue that Student Affairs does, but I think it has a very different take when it's a stand-alone, [as opposed to] having a seat in both the academic and the Student Affairs division.*

The end results were that this new hybrid model enhanced the division's relationship with the colleges.

In addition to operationalizing this hybrid entity, Barceló sought to change the name of the student affairs component. The primary issue was that the word "minority" stigmatized the program. She charged a small group of OMA staff to come up with an alternate name. After a series of meetings, the group proposed the name be changed to the Educational Opportunity Office. The President's Minority Community Advisory Committee (MCAC), chaired by Larry Gossett, strongly objected. MCAC had been established by President McCormick in 1997 to provide advice on issues that were of concern to the minority communities such as outreach, recruitment, admissions, enrollment, graduation rates of minority students, minority faculty and staff representation, and the long-standing financial aid challenge. The rationale of the group for rejecting the name change was that a name would signify to the minority communities that the University no longer supported efforts to recruit, retain and graduate URM and educationally/economically disadvantaged students. President McCormick concurred, and the idea was abandoned.

This decision did not go over well with some folks, especially white parents who objected to their students' participation in the Bridge Program, which was run by the Office of Minority Affairs. For 35 years, economically disadvantaged white students and their families did not seem to have a problem. Things had changed. What did not change was that these students were provisionally admitted to UW and Minority Affairs was the only conduit to matriculation.

Unfazed by this veto, Barceló turned her attention toward the state of diversity at the University. "Considering the fact that a campus-wide appraisal had not been done for some time, I felt that one should be done to engage the entire campus community, faculty, staff, and students," said Barceló. At that time, she lamented, "All we had were numbers, in terms of [what the] dropout rate was, and that was all fine, but it was far more complex than that." Thus, she convened a committee to conduct a diversity appraisal.

In the 2006 Diversity Appraisal report, the role of the OMA Vice President and Vice Provost was clearly defined and left no doubt to the importance of that role. It states specifically that: "The Office of the Vice President for Minority Affairs and Vice Provost for Diversity, which is housed in the Office of Minority Affairs, provides university-wide leadership on the development, implementation, and evaluation of diversity programming and policies." In this role, Barceló was to play a key role in the establishment of a diversity research institute. She was instrumental in convincing then-President Lee Huntsman that a diversity appraisal should be conducted that not only encompassed race, ethnicity, gender, and class, but also disability, sexual identity/orientation, religion, age, culture, region/geography, and indigenous status. In terms of class, the appraisal was not at the time defined to include income level and parental educational attainment level.

From the report, it was clear there was no universal systematic approach to determine efficacy across various units, and no benchmarks. It was also clear that while the University was committed to access, there still was a need to increase participation and improve college readiness. Furthermore, it was abundantly clear that OMA under Barceló's leadership carried out the University's commitment to pre-college outreach and recruitment in several ways. OMA provided financial support, student development, and retention assistance by delivering excellent academic and social services to diverse program participants, enhancing mentoring activities, encouraging students to study diversity, fostering the development of diversity curricula, creating interdepartmental collaboration and partnerships, and developing assessment strategies to analyze retention and graduation rates not only in diverse populations but campus wide (tapping into the University database). Furthermore, OMA continually engaged with diverse communities external to the UW.

Barceló felt that it was imperative that there should be central leadership for research and diversity initiatives and that infrastructure should be provided to support the work of faculty and students (Diversity appraisal report, 2004). As a part of this emphasis on research and scholarship in diversity,

Dr. Rusty Barceló at the Inaugural Samuel E. Kelly Distinguished Faculty Lecture 2005.

Quintard Taylor at the April 21, 2005, Inaugural Samuel E. Kelly Distinguished Faculty Lecture.

Barceló established the Samuel E. Kelly Distinguished Faculty Lecture to honor the OMA's founding vice president in 2005. The primary purpose was to acknowledge the work of distinguished faculty whose research focused on diversity and social justice. Quintard Taylor, holder of the Scott and Dorothy Bullitt Chair in American History at the UW, gave the inaugural lecture: *From Civil Rights to Black Power in the West: The Movement in Seattle 1960-1970*.

The results gleaned from the appraisal were used to make improvements in diversity efforts in localized units, such as academic departments, as well as in the institution as a whole. Barceló was appointed chair of the newly established University Diversity Council, which included staff, faculty, students, and community members. The council's purpose was to develop long-term strategies for institutionalization of diversity. One of the community members represented the Breakfast Group (BG) composed of African American businessmen and professionals. The group invited various public officials to their monthly breakfasts, including Barceló, to make presentations and engage in meaningful conversations about efforts to improve the state of

Lorne Murray at Merck Pharmaceutical Lab in 1995, the first UW undergraduate to receive the UNCF Merck Scholarship.

African Americans. The BG was particularly interested in education, including enrollment, retention, and graduation of Black students at the UW and how they could work with Minority Affairs to effect improvement. The relationship blossomed during Barceló's entire tenure and led to several of its members (Ernie Dunston, Charles Mitchell, and Herman McKinney) becoming recipients of the Charles E. Odegaard Award from the FEOP Board.

Inspired by community recognition, OMA&D continued to expand, adding Curriculum Transformation to the fold. The primary goal of the Curriculum Transformation Project was teaching about race, gender, ethnicity, nationality difference, nation, class, disability, sexuality, religion, and their intersections through curriculum development. Seminars, institutes, and projects were the vehicles through which these goals were achieved. "Curriculum Transformation asked faculty members to take a critical stance on power and difference in the classroom, interweave multiple perspectives, and integrate student voices and knowledge into the learning process."

In addition, the Health Sciences Center Minority Student Program, which was established to increase diversity in medicine, dentistry, and pharmacy, and the biomedical and behavioral sciences, was also annexed. Management of the University's most prestigious scholarship program (Diversity Scholars Program) for underrepresented minority (URM) students was brought under the OMA&D banner. Funding for three new programs was secured. Funding efforts were enhanced by the addition of a professional staff position that had as one of its priorities to increase the fundraising capacity of OMA&D. Examples of increased activities included stewardship geared toward increasing the endowment portfolio, connecting donors with scholarship recipients, and securing funds for special projects such as the opportunity to create a documentary about early diversity efforts at the University (another first).

With Director George Zeno joining the team, fundraising was elevated to a whole new level. It was the catalyst that sparked meteoric growth. Funds raised at the scholarship level immediately increased five-fold. Said Barceló, "I think also we became a national model for how to do the work. I was interviewed extensively by other institutions."

In addition to the diversity appraisal, OMA&D participated in a university-wide advising self-study that included all the advisers on campus. June Hairston, a longtime lead OMA&D adviser and self-study member described it this way:

> *They interviewed all the advisers on campus, including our advisers. What they saw was that students were complaining more about the advising model in undergraduate advising. Students were not feeling that satisfaction, that progress to a degree, and there were a lot of complaints. When they saw our model and they interviewed students and staff, they saw a model that was working. It was the holistic model. The holistic model addressed academic advising, personal counseling, career counseling, limited financial aid advising, and we were with the student from the beginning to at least until they got into their major.*

In terms of course sequencing, OMA&D academic advisers used knowledge gained over five decades of experience of both advisers and IC instructors to design a systematic sequence of prerequisites unique to the academic makeup of EOP students.

Hairston further stated:

They saw our model as something to be respected and appreciated on this campus. I don't know that people fully understood our model because the image of our office was not always favorable across campus. I think it was because people were filling in the blanks to the questions that they had, filling in their own blanks, and coming up with their own conclusions. I can say that we didn't do an excellent job of marketing the services that we provided to students. We didn't have anybody to give us a brand or promote the language throughout the campus, so we were always having to defend who we were.

The study was conducted by the UW Office of Educational Assessment. The study found that OMA&D advisers rated their access to administrators and the importance of participating in decision making by their advising unit as moderate, which was the lowest compared to other advising units. Only a few knew of a formal mechanism to provide input at the departmental/college level, and even fewer knew of such at the University level. All advisers suggested that communication needed to be improved across advising units.

In addition, OMA&D advisers thought of themselves and the students they served as family. Their overarching approach was holistic in nature in an effort to serve the whole student. In addition to focusing on academics, they advised students on personal problems, financial aid, and housing. Advisers also attended such events as award presentations, affinity group graduation ceremonies, and weddings. Advisers wrote letters of recommendation for students' applications to majors, for scholarships, and acted as references for internships. In essence, the OMA&D advisers showed EOP students that they cared about all aspects of students' lives. Above all else, students were their number one priority. Another unique feature of OMA&D advising was the amount of time spent during visits; advising visits in OMA&D ran 40 to 60 minutes, which was the highest of all advising units.

Findings also revealed that communication issues, inconsistency of information, and increased workload were challenges that needed to be addressed. The issue of EOP students feeling marginalized and isolated was a concern as well. However, opinions were split on whether OMA&D should remain off campus (Schmitz Hall) or move to a more central location (Mary

Gates Hall). A small group of student respondents suggested the latter. When it came to a student's perception that advisers' comfort level working with students whose ethnicity was different than their own, EOP students rated OMA&D advisers significantly higher than non-EOP students.

Following a review of the findings of the study, and interviewing selected members of each advising unit, external evaluators from the Universities of Arizona and Michigan determined that the approach employed by OMA&D advisers should be adopted as the model and that the UW's undergraduate advising should be centrally located as soon as space was made available.

However, implementation was easier said than done. According to Hairston, the transition could not be realized until differences were bridged, consciousness about diversity was raised, and everyone became allies of social justice. Once division and skepticism were eliminated, the co-location of OMA&D and Undergraduate Affairs advisers would be ready for implementation. That co-location happened in 2010.

While there was an uptick in retention and graduation rates for URM students during this decade, the enrollment among these groups was essentially flat, which meant that the representation gap was not narrowing. Although the general state population was composed of nearly 13% URM citizens, less than 9% of the undergraduate population were URM enrollees. In an attempt to change this dynamic, the University developed a comprehensive admission

OMA&D recruiters at the Winter Pow Wow, January 26, 2013.

review system. "It allowed us to design a system that gave a series of points to students who had come from disadvantaged, low-income, and first-generation backgrounds, but not only that for those who had come from schools where they were underserviced—such things like course availability, AP exams, etc.," said Enrique Morales, who was associate vice president for Pre-college Programs. Morales further stated, "We also included students who had unique hardship, showed leadership traits in their community, etc."

Other strategies implemented included expanding recruitment in rural areas. Recruiters became more visible in the communities of color by attending community festivals and by increasing the number of visits to campus by prospective students of color.

During Vice President/Vice Provost Barceló's tenure, OMA&D collaborated with the UW Office of Educational Assessment (OEA) on a self-assessment to identify areas of strength, concern, and obstacles preventing OMA&D from working effectively, to gauge how well organizational and program goals were being met, and to evaluate an expansion of responsibility with the vice provost components. The findings revealed that faculty in general had positive perceptions of OMA&D but had differing suggestions for how OMA&D could improve their services and integrate faculty into its efforts. The following quotations from the assessment report illustrate how a few of the interviewees felt about OMA&D and its programs:

One respondent wrote:

In general, I would like to commend OMA&D. I have been [closely involved with their work] for a while, and I know that after all the handcuffs that have been put on them, the type of labor that they are doing is almost heroic. They are swimming against the current. They are doing a good job.

Another respondent shared the following:

OMA&D's retention programs have contributed to enhancing the undergraduate experience of low-income, first-generation, and underrepresented students through strong instructional support and advising strategies, experiential learning opportunities, and social and cultural activities. One challenge that the organization faces is "limited" interface between vice president and vice provost programmatic components, which creates appearances that these entities are independent of each other.

The Self-Assessment Committee also provided recommendations which included engaging the entire OMA&D staff and campus constituents toward an understanding of the important symbiotic relationship between the vice president and vice provost responsibilities in addressing student, staff, and faculty concerns.

There was one major perennial concern that Barceló inherited. That concern was how to address the challenge of retaining and graduating URM students once enrolled. In response to this concern, my colleague Catharine Beyer from the Office of Educational Assessment and I, as director for the Office of Minority Affairs & Diversity Instructional Center, collaborated to design a UW attrition and retention study. The purpose of the study was to examine reasons why URM students were leaving the UW without earning a degree at rates much higher than those of white and Asian students. Barceló insisted that a deeper understanding of this issue was imperative to implement effective intervention strategies. Working with other colleagues, we conducted a multi-method research study in 2006 and reported our findings to the provost. The study included cohorts that entered UW between 1999 and 2003.

The major factors that the study found affected retention of underrepresented minority students included campus climate; financial issues; differences between academic needs and family/community/cultural expectations or needs; pre-college and first-year academic experience; waiting/being embarrassed to ask for help; work-related issues; and not getting into one's major of choice.

According to the study, campus climate—that feeling of being in an unwelcoming environment—appeared to have the greatest influence in underrepresented students' decisions to leave. The study suggested that:

- *Black students may feel more isolated*
- *Latino/a may feel a greater cultural need to support family*
- *Native American groups may experience the University as a more "alien place" with values more different from their own and those of their families than other groups might experience*
- *Students from the Pacific Islands may have trouble being far away from family and a culture that centered on family and relationships*
- *Multiracial students are engaged in powerful identity questions while at the UW and they are often pressured to "pick a side"—identifying as mono-racial rather than embracing all parts of their ethnicities* (p.8)

Not only were reasons identified as to why URM students left school, but the study also identified reasons why students persisted and graduated:

- *A sense of commitment to their families and communities helps them stay in college*
- *Having a faculty or staff member on campus who believes in them and shows concern helps them persist in the face of challenge*
- *Students' own motivation, desire, and will pulled them through school*
- *Involvement in community-based activities . . . gave them a sense of belonging and purpose, which in turn helped them continue their educational paths* (pp. 53-54)

Students also expressed a few ideas of what might enhance persistence. For example:

- *Improving the critical mass of underrepresented minority students, faculty, and staff on campus*
- *providing more activities and smaller classes for students so that they might have more contact with faculty and peers*
- *Increasing the size and staff of the Instructional Center (IC)*
- *Formally recognizing students' cultural heritages, such as Stanford University did when it built a longhouse on campus for Native American students"* (pp. 59-60)

The study also gathered and reported faculty and staff suggestions for what might improve the retention and graduation rates of underrepresented minority students. Their suggestions included: "considering ways in which the University can support underrepresented minority students in their use of financial aid services; continuing to focus on advising services . . . and forging better and deeper connections between UW administration/ departments and underrepresented minority students' families and communities" (pp. 60-61).

Based on the quantitative and qualitative data they had gathered, the researchers who conducted the study offered recommendations concerning campus climate (structural, behavioral, and psychological), financial need, differences between academic expectations and family/cultural need, pre-college and first-year academic experiences, asking for help, work-related issues, and not getting into the major of choice. Recommendations included the following:

1. *Develop and implement a plan to increase the numbers of underrepresented minority faculty, staff, and students so that the ethnic diversity of the UW accurately represents the ethnic diversity in Washington State. Researchers argued that "a critical mass of people of color on campus is an important component in improving campus climate for all students."*

2. *Increase faculty/student interaction, for example, by providing opportunities for students to work on faculty research.*

3. *Guarantee that the organizations and support services created for students of color have adequate funding, staffing, and other resources to serve students.*

4. *Begin conversations with OMA about the advantages and disadvantages of locating their facilities more centrally on campus in order to address the geographical marginalization of services for underrepresented minority students.*

5. *Determine ways to help ensure that financial aid packages are more grant-based than loan heavy.*

6. *Use proactive methods to intervene early when students experience academic problems, for example, using the gap between underrepresented minority students' high school and second quarter UW GPAs as a marker for intervention.*

7. *Create a viable pathway for re-entry into the UW for underrepresented minority students who left or were dropped because of academic performance, and re-recruit underrepresented minority students who left the University in good standing.*

8. *Increase the capacity of OMA&D's Instructional Center* (Pitre et al, 2006, pp. 62-64).

The leadership, both OMA&D and Undergraduate Academic Affairs (UAA), acknowledged that the results were revealing and pledged to address the recommendations in the coming years.

Over the years, the institution has made some progress. Diversity Blueprint plans were implemented to address #1. The experiential learning addressed #2 and included a study abroad component. Efforts have been ongoing to address #3, but progress has been only incremental. Re-location of OMA&D services to Mary Gates Hall (#4) was implemented in 2008 (OMA&D administration) and 2010 (advising and experiential learning). Efforts to address #5 have been evolving. Husky Promise, which guarantees tuition for state need-grant and Pell eligible students, was implemented in 2007. The OMA&D Endowment fund (established in 1991) continues to provide scholarships for selected EOP students. However, financial aid packages remain loan heavy. The EOP Counseling Center implemented an early warning system (#6) in 2009. The early warning system mandated that EOP freshman students who earned less than a 2.5 GPA in any given quarter, must see their counselors before registering for the next quarter. A re-entry program (#7) was implemented in 2006. It was named ROAR (Reach Out and Reconnect) and Keoke Silvano was appointed counselor. The aim was to identify EOP students who had stopped out and to contact those students who left in good standing to determine whether there was a viable pathway by which they could resume their undergraduate studies, prioritizing students who had enough credits to graduate within the six-year window. Efforts have gotten underway to address #8. However, to date, capacity has not change due to slower than anticipated fundraising gains.

Essentially, Barceló turned Lujan's dream of OMA being respected by the UW academic community into reality. Gabriel Gallardo, who spent his career in a variety of roles in OMA, and OMA&D, said:

Then, after Myron, Rusty Barceló came to the University of Washington. She brought a lot of ideas about expanding our work around diversity. She made us think more inclusively, so our definition of diversity expanded significantly. It meant not only race and ethnicity but gender, sexuality, geography, religion, all those dimensions. That was an added benefit for the organization because it allowed us to bring the provost's arena into the fold. So, when Rusty was here, she added the title Vice Provost for Diversity. That gave us not only a focus on retention and student success but also diversity or enhancement of diversity across our campus. It began to connect our work with the work of faculty, the work of academic departments. I think that was a significant shift in our work. One of the things that we used to do in the early days is that we strived to work from the periphery to the core. That was, I think—for

Reflections on Dr. Rusty Barceló

Rusty Barceló spent five years leading the efforts of OMA, three of which also specifically included expanding the reach of diversity. What follow are reflections staff made about her.

June Hairston, one of the lead advisers in OMA&D, spoke extensively about Vice President/Vice Provost Barceló:

Dr. Rusty Barceló

I loved Rusty in a very special way because Rusty came with an inclusive mentality at the grass roots. What do I mean by that? Rusty carried the same tradition. She would come and speak to us, maybe not every day, but enough for us to feel like Rusty was in the house.

Rusty would respect the advisers' input. Any time she had to give a presentation to a large audience, Rusty would come down to our office, catch us in the hall, and say, I just need about five or 10 minutes, I need you to hear this sentence. What do you think? Let me know, be honest. We advisers loved that. We loved that she wanted to hear what we had to say. And we were clear about suggesting changes: "No, you don't want to say this, say it this way."

She had our ear, and we were thankful for the connection. The other thing I liked about Rusty was for any policy that would impact change, Rusty would have an all-staff meeting maybe a couple of times a year. We would all get together, and she would have us brainstorm on issues that were important for this organization. And it wasn't like an hour. It was an afternoon or a full day. Rusty would periodically come to our adviser meetings. She would not let the directors be in that meeting, our director, so she could hear our heartbeat: "They're not here, say what's on your mind. Let's talk." Her agenda was: "How can we make the whole organization successful?" I really appreciated that style of leadership.

The other thing is, she was challenging. Rusty is the reason that I have my doctorate. When she first came on board, she said: "I want to get as many of you who want to go to graduate school—I want to encourage that." She put me on committees that my director should have been on. I would go to these committee meetings and all of these directors were listed. They even put me down one time as director of either the Instructional Center or the Counseling Center. And I was just an adviser; not "just"—I was an adviser. Every year I was on a significant committee, not realizing that being on those committees is what informed my candidacy for the doctoral program because I had the opportunity to show how, what, the College of Education was doing in terms of theory, ideas, and concepts—we were doing in terms of application, and how we could marry the two together. Rusty encouraged quite a few to stretch, and I was one of those who accepted that challenge and stretched.

Raul Anaya stated:

Rusty, she again brought up the conversation about where do we best serve students from? And that was cause for us to contemplate that, and talk about it, and agree that, yes, Mary Gates [Hall] was the best place to put ourselves on central campus and be part of campus as opposed to apart from campus. The diversity audit was another accomplishment I would say that she brought about.

Adrienne Chan said:

Rusty. She had the vision of adding research components, making the OMA and EOP more academic. I don't know if that's happened or not, but I thought that was a very insightful way of adding some academic dimension, some quote-unquote "scholarship," to our program.

the staff it was validating. It was something that they took great pride in. I think it began to build great partnerships with colleagues and units across the University.

A Decade of Building Respect and Campus-wide Diversity

Following Barceló's resignation to return to the University of Minnesota, UW Provost Phyllis Wise appointed Sheila Edwards Lange interim vice president for minority affairs and vice provost for diversity in 2006. A group of students publicly opposed this appointment. They felt that a staff member of more than 25 years (and at the time serving as an associate vice president) should

have been the choice. Led by EOP student Lull Mengesha, a small group of students assembled in front of Schmitz Hall in protest on the day the appointment was made public. There was speculation that the staff member, who was very popular with the students, had "put them up to it." This staff member was urged by Barceló to speak with the protesters to defuse the situation. The staff

Dr. Sheila Edwards Lange, 7th OMA&D vice president at the May 7, 2015, Celebration.

member complied, but to no avail. Mengesha's response was that in his position, the staff member was expected to ask them (the students) to cease and desist on behalf of the administration.

Lange chose to come to the protest to directly engage the students and assure them that in her new role, she would be student-centered. "Instead of making it a fight, she accepted their concerns," said June Hairston. Not satisfied, students chose to protest both on social media and at events including a town hall meeting convened by the provost. "It was a big, big turbulent time . . . [but] we still had significant people in the organization that we looked up to that gave us a sense of security in the midst of transition." Long story short, the associate vice president assured Provost Wise that he had no desire to serve in a role that had been offered to someone else, and that he had no problem with her selection for the interim position. Soon afterwards, students abandoned their resistance to the appointment.

During this interim period, the OMA&D self-assessment was finalized. When asked from her vantage point a decade later about what was learned in terms of strengths and improvement, Lange shared the following:

We learned that student services [were] a real strength; that we had the ability to bring in external dollars, and we had a very diversified funding stream, a long history of those programs. Where we needed to improve was on the other part of diversity, so looking at the faculty and the staff and the institutional change and culture piece was something that needed work.

We discovered we were really the national model in terms of access and support for low-income and students of color. We were always asking about who's doing it better. I remember Jose Moreno, the external guy, came in, and there were a number of books that were coming out at the time about best practices for providing access for low-income and underrepresented students and then supporting them. We found that a lot of the things that we were already doing in that arena were best practices and a national model.

The other thing that we discovered was that we weren't fully integrated into the broader mission of the institution in a way that people felt connected to it. So, really trying to figure out how the work of the office contributes to the overall mission of the University. This was at a time that the Michigan case had just been decided. The Bollinger case. [Reference is to the Supreme Court's 2003 decision in the case Grutter v. Bollinger, which allowed the use of affirmative action in law school admissions at the University of Michigan as long as it did not qualify as a quota system.] *So just as I was coming in, we were starting to ask questions about . . . how is this work connected to the institutional mission? Is it really clear? And would it meet the Supreme Court case test? I think that we as a team could articulate how it was. But it wasn't broadly known outside of OMA&D how it was really connected to the institutional mission.*

Despite the protests, Lange stayed the course, applied for the permanent position, and was appointed the seventh vice president for OMA&D and the second vice provost for diversity. Thus, the eighth leg of the evolutionary journey began. She worked purposefully to assure the students that she had their best interests in mind and went on to enjoy a rapport with students comparable to that enjoyed by Myron Apilado during his 11-year tenure. When asked how she was able to achieve such rapport, here is what she said:

It was not easy. But, you know, I think it's mutual respect, and willingness to listen to what their concerns are, and a genuine attempt to try to figure out how we could address what we were hearing. Then, when some of the things that they were asking for were unreasonable or impossible, just being straightforward about that. That's one thing, but the other thing is—I do this work for students. I love working on a college campus because I love the students. I love the engagement that they bring, the intellectual curiosity that they bring, the passion that they bring both inside and outside the classroom. I like working with that sort of more traditional age as people are really starting to question what they believe in, either confirming what they believe in, questioning what they believe in, trying to come to terms with themselves as leaders and individuals. It's just an interesting time to work with young people. I think students pick up on that, I just generally love being with them. It invigorates me. I learn a lot from students.

I think that students always know that I've always had their best interests in heart because I want them to be successful. I want each and every one of them to be successful, and I see this office and this university as owing them everything that we have so that they can be successful. Anything that I can do—either institutionally to provide pathways, or programs, or services, or counseling, or advising—that's going to help each and every one of our students be successful, then I'm going to be successful, our community is going to be successful.

I still believe that this work is political work. Education is political work, and I've believed that since I was a young girl because if we can educate people, we can give them the tools to go out and change the world and change the community. If a student is educated and can be able to have a living wage job and take care of themselves, have a career, they'll be more likely to vote, they'll be more likely to volunteer to serve on community groups, they'll be more likely to question the status quo out in our community, and less likely to use social services.

The New Regime

An organizational restructuring ensued soon after Lange's appointment became permanent in 2007. Roles and responsibilities of the administrative leadership were redefined leading to promotion of selected staff. While the pre-college unit remained intact, fiscal, human resources, and technology were subsumed under new leadership (assistant vice president). The academic advancement unit was also reorganized under new leadership and renamed the Student Success Unit. Assessment became a stand-alone unit, and a new Community and Public Relations unit was established. Furthermore, to increase and retain more faculty of color

The documentary "In Pursuit of Social Justice," an oral history of the early years of diversity efforts at the University of Washington, won a Silver Telly and an honorable mention for videography at the 28th Annual Telly Awards, 2007.

at the UW, an associate vice provost reporting dually to the OMA&D vice president/vice provost and the provost's office was established. Professor Luis Fraga, formerly of Stanford, was appointed to this position as well as being named the Russell F. Stark Professor in the Political Science department. Faculty and staff affinity groups (Black, Latino, Asian, for example) were added and supported.

Lange very strategically moved to allay any lingering apprehensions the OMA (student affairs) side of the house were holding onto about the new hybrid structure that Barceló had instituted. Lange chose to change the name of this hybrid unit to the Office of Minority Affairs & Diversity (OMA&D), which clearly distinguished functional differences without sacrificing one for the other.

Outcomes

A wide range of OMA&D assessment studies, reports, and internal documents tell the outcomes story. Fueled by intense recruitment efforts, and the implementation of the affiliates program, EOP enrollment increased by

Instructional Center (IC) Brotman Awards for Instructional Excellence and Diversity, 2001.

67% over the decade; however, URM enrollment increased by a modest 8%. Nonetheless, EOP made up two-thirds of the URM enrollment. EOP degree earners increased by 25% compared with those of the previous decade and represented 57% of URM degree earners. Over the decade, EOP retention increased by four percentage points and resulted in achieving parity with the UW student body. The six-year graduation rate for EOP students entering from high school increased by ten percentage points, bringing the rate to within five percentage points of the UW student body. The six-year graduation rate for EOP transfers increased as well, and the gap was even better, narrowing to three percentage points.

The budget and staffing grew by 30% and 40%, respectively. There was a five-fold increase in funds raised at the EOP scholarship dinner Celebration. Five new endowments were added to the OMA endowment portfolio. In addition, three federally funded programs were added to the OMA&D family of programs.

STUDENT CASES

ALFREDO CEJA, MARIA SOLEDAD CEJA, AND MIRIAM CEJA. Over the years, several families have supported multiple EOP alumni members. Siblings Alfredo Ceja, Maria Soledad Ceja, and Miriam Ceja all focused on STEM disciplines. They graduated from Wapato High School in Wapato, Washington. Their parents only completed eighth grade in Mexico and worked as farm workers in the agricultural fields. In addition to working in the fields, their mother also worked in the Del Monte plant sorting vegetables. "Going to college for us was the goal, and getting good grades throughout college was a must to help obtain scholarships. We did get approved for federal and Pell grants and utilized them to help support our first few years of college," wrote Miriam. According to Miriam, the siblings' interest in math was inspired by their high school math teacher. He had earlier inspired three Wapato High School alums (and notable EOP alums as well), Conan Viernes and brothers Gerald and Roman Flores, to pursue NASA internships through ALVA (Alliance for Learning and Vision for Underrepresented Americans). All three went on to earn degrees in engineering, one in electrical and two in mechanical. That pursuit piqued their interest in engineering disciplines.

Even before the three siblings enrolled at UW, they were aware of the support services available to them having visited the UW campus while still in high school. "I was introduced to the IC and the other services in previous college visits," Miriam stated. Both of her siblings, Alfredo and Maria, used these services and spoke very highly of them. "When I first began to visit to the IC, I felt like I already had a leg up on the other freshman students since my siblings would tell me who to go to for my specific homework concerns," said Miriam. She went on to say, "Later, in my college career, this place became a new home to me. I worked there, tutored incoming students, and also used this place to do my homework and study for exams. The commitment of the staff and tutors that worked there was instrumental to my college years, and I honestly believe I would not have been able to graduate in engineering if it weren't for the IC and the support I received from everyone there." IC usage data show that all three siblings used the center extensively, especially Miriam.

The Ceja siblings graduated in successive years with degrees in Mechanical, Materials Science, and Chemical Engineering, respectively. After graduating in 2002, Alfredo moved to Richland, Washington, to start his job with Bechtel and is still employed there after 20 years, currently serving as a supervisor at Bechtel National, Inc. Maria Soledad, who graduated in 2003, chose to continue her education, earning a master's degree in Materials Science and Engineering from UCLA. Shortly after graduating from UCLA, she was hired by Intel in New

Mexico. After two years, she transferred to the Oregon campus and is currently serving as a senior process engineer. Miriam graduated from UW in 2004 with a Chemical Engineering degree. She began working for the Intel Corporation in Oregon as process engineer shortly thereafter and is employed as a tech transfer manager. We salute the Ceja siblings who make the OMA&D family and their parents proud.

JORGE ROBERTS. A second student case story includes romance. EOP students often referred to UW support programs as homes away from home. The close relationships they forged with each other were mainly in the form of friendships. In some cases, relationships blossomed into romance. One such relationship came about between a Spanish tutor and an IC user not enrolled in a Spanish class, but who had graduated from a high school in Mexico.

After attending college in Mexico for a year, Jorge Roberts immigrated to the US to live with his father, an American who at the time was fighting liver cancer while living on Social Security and food stamps. Despite not having attended college, his father urged Jorge to pursue a college degree as a means to a better life. Jorge took his father's advice, using need-based grants, subsidized student loans, merit-based scholarships, and earnings from various part time jobs to fund his education. His father passed away during winter quarter of his junior year leaving Jorge totally on his own but for the support of his extended family at the IC and the EIP (Early Identification Program). He immersed himself in his studies and campus activities, serving as vice chair of the Student Advisory Board (SAB) for the University's Vice President for Minority Affairs. In this role he began working with the Board to develop outreach programs to counteract the decline in minority applications after Washington State voters passed I-200.

Jorge's leadership opportunities did not end with his participation in SAB. In 2000, he became the first Latino in the 100-year history to be appointed Finance & Budget Director by the Associated Students of the University of Washington (ASUW). During his tenure, he was responsible for solving the organization's looming financial crisis, establishing guidelines that would sustain solvency in future years. He also founded the Washington State Model UN Conference—a two-day simulation of the United Nations. The program has endured for 19 years and is the largest program of its kind in the Pacific Northwest, benefiting more than 5,000 high school students and over 1,000 college students.

For his academic and leadership successes, Jorge received the EOP President's Achievement Award as the highest achieving graduating UW EOP senior. He graduated from UW with two degrees, a BS with distinction in Economics and a BA in Business Administration with a lot of coursework in math.

For the last 16 years, Jorge has been married to Maryah Nijm, whom he met at the IC during the summer of 1999. At that time, Maryah was a Spanish tutor at the IC. She received the Mary Gates Leadership Award for starting a co-existence group between Jewish and Arab students. She graduated from the UW with a BA in Spanish Literature and a minor in Near Eastern Studies. She subsequently received her certificate in Arabic language from the Middle East Institute in Washington, DC, She has worked in many jobs, including the World Bank, non-profit development, as a fitness instructor and most recently in landscape architecture. Jorge shared proudly that, "Today, Maryah and I have four children: a 13-year-old girl, 10-year-old twin boys, and a seven-year-old boy." At the time of this writing, the family resided in Northern Virginia.

After three years of conducting statistical analysis with big data and research in economics for the Federal Trade Commission's Bureau of Economics Anti-trust Division, Jorge decided to enroll in the MBA program at the Harvard Business School. "Upon graduation from Harvard Business School, I worked in mergers and acquisitions for Merrill Lynch's Investment Banking team in London," said Jorge.

Since 2007, Jorge has worked with major institutional investors such as the Canadian pension OMERS, The Carlyle Group, and Goldman Sachs Infrastructure. For more than three years, Jorge has served as CEO of AvPorts, a US-based and -owned airport management company with more than 650 employees. He also volunteers with Management Leadership for Tomorrow, an organization with a mission to increase minority and women representation in corporate America. Besides serving as a board member for Airports Council International-Latin America and Caribbean, he serves on the board of the Friends of the Educational Opportunity Program (FEOP).

In correspondence with me, Jorge stated, "I am eternally grateful to the UW, Office of Minority of Affairs & Diversity, and OMA&D's Instructional Center (IC) for providing me the tools and confidence to succeed."

HOANG NHAN. Hoang Nhan, the oldest of four children, grew up in Vietnam. According to Hoang, during the first 17 years of her life she was confused about her identity. Even though she was born and grew up in Vietnam, she was rejected by the Vietnamese society because of her Chinese heritage. After the Vietnam War, the Chinese were oppressed and persecuted, especially if they owned a business as her father did. His business went bankrupt in the early 1990s, and, after experiencing severe hardship and on the brink of giving up altogether, the family decided to emigrate in 1996 in search of the American dream.

However, the dream turned into a nightmare. The family's financial instability and her parents working through a divorce, left her mother with the responsibility of raising four children. Nhan, being the eldest, had to work two part-time jobs to help support her family while still in high school. The circumstances were further exacerbated by the fact that Nhan encountered difficulties communicating because Cantonese and Vietnamese were her primary languages. According to her Merage Institute Fellowship essay, "English was... nothing but a strange sound to me." Despite encountering such adversity, Hoang was determined to not settle for a high school education or an associate degree. She wanted to finish a college degree. She worked on improving her competency in English as well as saving money to fund her education. She gained admission into UW for the fall of 1999 as a first-generation and low-income student.

That summer, an EOP adviser, Pat Butler invited Hoang to join the OMA family. Hoang recalled: "I did not know that joining EOP would give me the passport to numerous wonderful services." She credited George Bauer with providing the support to improve her writing skills and Leah Spence for encouraging her to discover her own love for literature. "All the A's I earned in my science and math introductory courses, I owe them to the Chemistry, Physics, Biology and math tutors [instructors] at the IC." Through the Stipends for Aspiring Researchers/Bridges4 program, Hoang was bitten by the research bug and was proud to have her name appear on two publications and several abstracts in neuroscience. It did not stop there. She was introduced by June Hairston to the McNair Program giving her access to more research resources and opportunities to attend conferences. Before becoming a Merage Fellow, Hoang was the recipient of other scholarships, including the Prestigious Goldwater Scholarship, Presidential Scholarship, EOP Merit Scholarship, and Mary Gates Training Grants.

Hoang graduated Cum Laude from the UW with bachelor's degrees in neuroscience and English (no longer just sounds!). She was accepted into graduate school at UC San Diego. Said Hoang, "And regarding recent acceptance to UCSD's Neurosciences PhD program, I owe it to Dr. Gabriel Gallardo and all the wonderful McNair staff." Since earning her PhD, Hoang has worked as a Product Scientist II at 23andMe and as of this writing as a Biomarker Operations Project Manager at an American biotechnology corporation, providing operational expertise across oncology clinical trials across the globe.

At the end of a stellar undergraduate career, Hoang said: "My obstacles have trained me to be a hard worker; my accomplishments have taught me to be grateful; and my failures have taught me to be humble."

JANELLE SAGMILLER PALACIOS (Salish Kootenai Nation). Janelle Sagmiller Palacios grew up in Montana on the Flathead Reservation where she picked cherries in orchards around Flathead Lake, working on farms with migrant workers in Washington's Skagit Valley in later years. As early as middle school, she had her sights set on a medical career, participating for three summers in INMED (Indians in Medicine) at the University of South Dakota. For two quarters she struggled until connecting with the services of the OMA family of programs. There she found her niche in OMA's Partnership for a Seamless Education projects at an elementary school where she, along with a fellow UW student and the teachers, developed a project to facilitate the reconnection of American Indian students and their families to the culture and history of northwest tribes.

In her junior year, Janelle was admitted to the highly competitive UW Nursing program. There, she was mentored by Dr. June Strickland, an American Indian who had served on the faculty since 1983. According to the *Contact* newsletter article about her, Janelle was "sponsored by Nursing faculty and with other UW Nursing students, [she] initiated the UW Teen Parent Mentorship for students at Seattle's Chief Sealth High School, giving teenage parents not only pre-and post-natal advice, but working with them to gain admissions and financial aid for college." During that same year, she was accepted into the Minorities in Medicine Educational Program at Yale, Columbia, and UW, but chose UW. Soon afterwards, Janelle was recruited to become a participant in the McNair Scholars Program at OMA&D, a program designed to prepare first-generation and low-income undergraduate students for doctoral studies. Janelle said that her experience in this program changed her career trajectory. She was bitten by the research bug.

Janelle graduated from UW with a BSN (Bachelor of Science in Nursing) in 2003. Instead of applying to medical school, she decided to pursue a graduate degree in nursing at the University of California, San Francisco, where she earned a PhD in 2008. The focus of her dissertation was the childbearing experiences of young adult American Indian women (Heads/tails, 2019). Janelle went on to complete an MSN and became a CNM (Certified Nurse-Midwife) in 2011. Along the way, she was awarded two post-doctoral fellowships to conduct research in women's health and health disparities in vulnerable populations. For eleven years and counting, Janelle has served as a nurse midwife at Kaiser Permanente in the Bay area. Dr. Palacios is to be commended for her lifelong interest in enhancing the wellness among American Indian families.

Notable EOP Alumni for the Decade

The academic credentials of the EOP alumni who made this list were by far the most impressive of the 40-year history of OMA&D in terms of holders of medical degrees, juris doctor degrees, degrees in dentistry, and doctoral degrees. Besides careers in healthcare, the legal profession (partners, shareholder, assistant attorneys general (two), education (six professors), and engineering/technology, there were vice presidents, book authors (one multiple prize winner), a managing partner, an attaché, and a national political analyst.

Dan Espinoza, '98, JD (Stanford)

Ryan Kezele (Chickasaw Nation), '98, DDS (UW)

Ada Limon, '98, MFA (NYU)

Mercy Laurino, '98, '16, MS (University of Denver), PhD (UW)

Thi D. Nguyen,'98, DDS (UW)

Christopher Peinado, '98, MD (UC San Diego)

Heather Wilson Ramirez,'98, JD (Seattle U)

Carmen Sammy-Sacquitne McDermott, '98. '04, MD (UW)

Derek Neequi Takai, '98, '02, DDS (UW)

Gerado (Jerry) Flores, '99 (UW)

Amalia Martino, '99 (UW)

Julien L. Pham, '99, MD (UW), MPH (Harvard)

Rahwa Ghermay, '99, MD (University of Michigan)

R. Omar Riojas, '99, JD (Stanford)

Janelle Amador, '00, MS (UW)

Tania Barron, '00, Phi Beta Kappa, MPP (Harvard)

Samarah Fortson Blackmon, '00, PhD (UCLA)

Patrick Keola Ching, '00, MS (San Jose State)

Maryjane Fielding Banks, '00, MBA (UW)

Somnit Lee, '00, '07 MD (UW)

Yael Varnado, '00, MD (Cornell)

Nora Vasquez, '00, '06, MD (UW)

John Amaya, '01, '05, JD (UW), LLM (Georgetown Law Center)

James Curtis, '01, '05, JD (UW)

Jennifer Devine, '01, PhD (UC, Berkeley)

Roman Flores, '01 (UCLA)

Tony Korolis, '01, MS (Santa Clara)

Allison Leighton, '00, MA (Columbia)

Tyson Marsh, '01, MA (UCLA), PhD (UCLA)

Ruchi (Nayyar) Mehta, '01, MD (Ross University School of Medicine)

Arthur Plata, '01 (UW)

Christina Roberts, '01, PhD (Arizona, 2007)

Eddie Rhone, '01, MS (UW)

My Le Shaw, '01 '08, MD (UW)

Leo Valladares, '01 (UW)

Kenneth Washington, '01, MBA (UW)

Emilyn Alejandro, '02, PhD (University of British Columbia)

Ona Anicello, '02, MS (UW)

Marie Apsay, '02, JD (Gonzaga)
Felix Cabrera, '02, MD (UW)
Amanda Isbell, '02, MD (American
University of the Caribbean)
Seila Kheang, '02, MS (Carnegie
Mellon)
Mariana Loya Linck,' 02, PhD (UC
San Diego)
Karen Luu, '02 (UW)
Sidney Nelson III, '02, MD (Howard)
Nisha Patel, '02, PharmD, (UW)
Jorge Roberts, '02, MBA (Harvard)
Angela Rye, '02, JD (Seattle U)
Jessie Ryker-Crawford
(Chippewa), '02, PhD (UW)
Michael Tuncap, '02, MS (UC
Berkeley), PhD (UC Berkeley)
Mario Villa, '02, MBA (Seattle U)
Danica You, '02, JD (Cornell)
Miriam Castro, '03, MD (UW)
Ivan Cazares, '03 (UW)
Rita Gobran, '03 (UW)
Aaron Horn, '03 (UW)
Paulette Jordan, '03 (UW)
Zahid Khan, '03, MS (UW)
Dakotah Lane, '03, MD (Cornell)
David Lara, '03, MPA (University of
Texas, Austin)
Janelle Sagmiller Palacios, '03, PhD
(UC San Francisco); MSN (UC
San Francisco); Postdoctoral
Fellow (UCLA); Postdoctoral
Fellow (UC San Francisco)
Monika Parashar, '03 (UW)
Ebony Peay Ramirez, '03 (UW)
Jabari Walker, '03, BS, MS
(University of Illinois, Urbana-
Champaign)

Aliseya Wright, '03, MS (UC
Berkeley)
Gabriela Condrea, '04, MEd
(Chestnut Hill College)
Parker Haley, '04, DDS (UW)
Jarman Hauser, '04, MS (UW)
Leilani Sharpe, '04, MD/PhD (Johns
Hopkins)
Luis Tulloch, '04, MD (UW)
Venus Kennedy, '04, MBA (Harvard)
Aysa Miller, '04, MA (Johns
Hopkins)
Hoang Nhan, '04, PhD (UC San
Diego)
Ruth Nistrian English, '04, DDS
(Creighton)
Martha Sandoval, '04, JD (UW)
Jamal Whitehead, '04, JD (Seattle U)
Sonca Viet Thi Nguyen, '04, PhD
(Michigan)
Vuthy Leng, '05, MD (Ross
University)
Anthony Rivisto, '05, (UW)
Chalia Stallings-Ala'ilima, '05, '08,
JD (UW)
Sumona Das Gupta, '06, '09, EOP
Honors, JD (UW)
Vikash Patel, '06, PharmD
(Massachusetts College of
Pharmacy and Health Sciences)
Martin Acevedo, '07, MBA (Seattle U)
Natalie Hoover, '07, MD (Saint Louis
University)
Vincent Humphrey, '07, JD
(University of Idaho)
Juan C. Pinzon, '07, '08, MS (UW),
MS (Wisconsin)

Emile Pitre, Carl Miller, Billy Jackson, Larry Gossett, Eddie Walker (left to right),
40th Anniversary Celebration, 2008.

CHAPTER 6

2008–2017: Toward National Model Status

*We discovered we were really the national model in terms
of access and support for low-income and students of color.
We were always asking about who's doing it better.*

—Lange, 2015

OMA&D's fifth decade of the evolution marked the second year of Sheila Lange's tenure and the 40th anniversary of the founding of OMA&D. The Friends of the Educational Opportunity Program (FEOP) board had a precedent of choosing a group, rather than an individual, with the 35th Charles E. Odegaard Award. Inspired by the reception for a documentary titled *In Pursuit of Social Justice: The Early Years of Diversity Efforts at the University of Washington* (Hinckley, 2007) which previewed in early 2007, Lange recommended to the FEOB that the 1968 BSU be considered for the award.

Years before, at Celebration 1993, the 25th anniversary of the sit-in of 1968, OMA&D had publicly acknowledged the 1968 BSU members for their historical efforts with a small number of founders in attendance. That celebration paled in comparison to what Lange proposed to commemorate the fortieth anniversary. Lange charged the Community and Public Relations unit, led by Assistant Vice President Stephanie Miller, to convene a committee to plan a celebration for May 20, 2008. The date marked the occupation of the University president's office by the BSU and its supporters. Six months in the making, the commemoration was titled "Celebrating 40 Years of Diversity: 1968-2008: The Journey Continues . . ." An entire afternoon of events was scheduled on Red Square, including music and performances by individuals and groups. EOP students who were on the Dean's list for the two previous quarters of the school year proudly marched through Red Square as the crowd enthusiastically cheered. A DJ played music popular during the late 1960s and beyond.

The formal program was moderated by EOP alumnus Cameron Wong, of Fox News, and included Lange and UW President Mark Emmert. Emmert gave remarks and introduced Larry Gossett, Martin Luther King County Councilmember, who was joined on stage by BSU founders Carl Miller, Billy Jackson, Eddie Walker, and myself. While Gossett spoke to a cheering crowd, Walker and I stood proudly with fists raised, symbolic of the Black Power movement of the late 1960s and early 1970s. Two panel discussions took

Select EOP students on the Spring 2008 Deans List.

place in the Walker-Ames Room of Kane Hall. One was composed of EOP student leaders—Third Andresen, Precious Aure, Iisaaksiichaa Ross Braine, Roy Diaz, Sabrina Fields, and David Moore-Reeploeg—and moderated by Professor Rick Bonus. They reflected on the state of diversity during their time at UW. The other panel was composed of four former OMA vice presidents—Samuel E. Kelly, Herman Lujan, Myron Apilado, and Rusty Barceló—along with Sheila Edwards Lange, current OMA&D vice president/vice provost. Moderated by KTCS 9 anchor Enrique Cerna, they discussed 40 years of visionary leadership.

Also included at the event were student photo exhibits, a resource fair, and food booths featuring ethnic cuisine provided by local restaurants. The celebration ended with a VIP reception in the Walker-Ames Room. Leading up to the events, Vice President/Vice Provost Lange and Associate Vice President Pitre were interviewed by Eddie Rye, Urban Forum Northwest-1150 AM KKNW host and a longtime community activist.

During Lange's tenure, assessment outcomes were used extensively in the decision-making process. The data OMA&D collected became an invaluable asset in making the case for improvement in services for program participants, in supporting the rationale for re-envisioning program goals and objectives, and in making the argument for national model status. Educational

Herman Lujan, Myron Apilado, Sheila Lange, Samuel Kelly, and Rusty Barceló
(left to right) at Celebration 2008.

1968 BSU Founders and Roberto Maestas at Celebration 2008.

Panel of past and present students for the 40th anniversary Celebration.

Polynesian dance group performing for the "40 Years" Celebration in 2008.

outcomes of program participants were not only compared to those of the general student body but also disaggregated to detect disparities across ethnicities, as well as gender, low-income, and first-generation dimensions of diversity. This approach allowed for group-specific intervention strategies to address disparities. Educational outcomes of program participants were compared to those of student bodies at peer institutions; ethnic group to ethnic group comparisons were also made to gauge how well institutions were doing in retaining and graduating their minority student populations.

Kathleen Halley, Garry Owens, and Eddie Walker at the 2008 Celebration.

The 2008 Odegaard Award honoring the 1968 Black Student Union.

The leadership also took steps to mitigate the feelings of marginalization and isolation by students and staff. Select OMA diversity programs moved to central campus, thus achieving the UW provost's goal of "one-stop-shopping" where relevant services could be provided to all pre-majors in one location. While this centralization approach was welcomed by students and staff, there was also general concern by veteran staff and communities of color that it was an assimilation and absorption strategy by the administration. This apprehension first surfaced eight years earlier, which led to Myron Apilado leaving his position as VP.

According to Lange, she too had reservations: "I was afraid that although I had Phyllis Wise, who was the provost at the time. . . I had her solid commitment that it was not an attempt to merge the office with undergraduate academic affairs, that fear was very real for the staff and even for me." Lange thought that the commitment may not last if Provost Wise left the institution. Of utmost importance to Lange was that the distinct identity of OMA&D not be compromised. Impelled by the legal mandate from the Michigan case that diversity must be a central component of the institutional mission and concerned about the staff's perception that being housed on the margins of the institution impeded efforts to effectively support EOP students, Lange decided to take a leap of faith. Once the decision was made, more needed to be done to move forward. Lange recalled:

> We had facilitators come in and work with the EOP advisers and the UAA (undergraduate academic advising) teams—actually, the first year programs, and experiential learning, all of them—but primarily the two advising teams, to try to facilitate conversations about how is the work different, why the work [is] different, and to have both sides better understand the work that each was doing, and how this co-location could actually strengthen what they were doing, that it would be better in this co-location.

Many accomplishments were realized during the Sheila Edwards Lange era. One that stood out most for her concerned OMA facilities. "There just wasn't enough space for the number of people as we were adding grants. There was nowhere to really put them, and nowhere to expand and grow for new opportunities," said Lange. This was partly achieved by moving OMA&D administration, advising, and experiential learning components to Mary Gates Hall, essentially from substandard space to a state-of-the-art facility. Furthermore, as the size of population served by OMA&D grew, so did the number of student organizations competing for space at the Ethnic Cultural Center. Finally, after what Lange described as fits and starts of proposals to merge it with another classroom or move it from its location, and other battles, funding was secured via student fees to rebuild the ECC at its original location.

One of the battles that arose was whether, or how, to save the more than 20 murals laden with asbestos. Latino students and community members, later joined by Black students and supported by King County councilmember Larry Gossett, insisted that every effort should be made, cost notwithstanding, to preserve these historic works of art created by minority students. The alternative was to have a likeness of each of the four ethnic room murals etched on glass windows of the new building. After much discussion with various segments of the ethnic communities, funding was secured to abate the asbestos and render the pieces safe for mounting in the new building.

Once the building was complete, questions developed as to how the larger rooms would be assigned. Students from groups whose predecessors had fought for the creation of OMA&D, including the ECC, felt the larger rooms should be similarly assigned to the "legacy" groups that played a critical role in establishing the original Special Education Program (SEP). The Black Student Union, MEChA, First Nations, Filipino American Student Association, Polynesian Student Association, and Micronesian Island Club were designated as Legacy Groups and had previously shared the larger designated rooms.

Students from the Pacific Islander group insisted their group should have its own room in the new building, rather than share a meeting space with Asian student groups. Using tactics employed by activists reminiscent of the late 1960s and 1970s, the group staged a rally to show that they would not take no for an answer. In Lange's view, there was no need for such tactics; a meeting to propose a Pacific Islander room would have been sufficient.

According to Lange, "There are now 102 registered student organizations affiliated with it. When we were doing the planning, we thought it would be 60 or 70. So already we just can't accommodate everybody who wants to be in the building."

In 2013, a new building with triple the space was completed, dedicated, and named the Samuel E. Kelly Ethnic Cultural Center, honoring OMA's founding vice president, who served from 1970 to 1976.

There was also a facilities-related issue that had not been addressed successfully for four decades—the need for a longhouse-style building to serve the American Indian students on campus. After seven years of planning (a working group, designated by then-President Mark Emmert, met every other week) beginning with Interim President Phyllis Wise, a herculean effort by the OMA&D advancement unit (specifically David Iyall), and approval of the Board of Regents, the gathering hall was built and given the name wəɬəbʔaltxʷ from the Lushootseed language. The name in English, which is more commonly used on campus, is Intellectual House. The grand opening took place on March 12, 2015. Since its opening, that facility has become one of the most popular meeting spaces for minority student groups as well as many campus events, including two State of the University addresses by President Ana Mari Cauce.

Samuel E. Kelly Ethnic Cultural Center

Left: Interior of the Samuel E. Kelly Ethnic Cultural Center, April 20, 2019. Right: OMA&D Student Advisory Board and ASUW presidents cutting the ribbon to open the new Cultural Center, January 2013.

Opening Ceremony festivities.

Ribbon Cutting for longhouse-style gathering hall for American Indian students, March 12, 2015.

Exterior of the Intellectual House.

It should be noted that one facilities issue did not get resolved, much to Lange's regret. "The IC [Instructional Center], I still didn't solve that. If I had to say my greatest failure, it would be that I did not solve the IC problem before I left. The IC building is falling apart, and all of the major systems are failing," said Lange. Despite these dire conditions, including losing a third of its tutor budget, this double-award winning center, continues to attract more than 2,100 unique student visitors annually.

Another important aspect of the Lange legacy, as she stated, was "moving diversity to the center of the institution, and then positioning diversity as a shared responsibility."

Lange emphasized at every opportunity that it was not just OMA&D's responsibility to promote diversity, equity, and inclusion, but it was the responsibility of every vice president, dean, department chair—and especially new hires and appointees—to "know something about diversity, speak to diversity as a value" and support the efforts of OMA&D. In essence, everybody should be doing the work.

Lange further stated:

> When we did that [diversity] blueprint, we really tried to make it clear that although we have a central office. . . and we did some focus groups around what people wanted to see for a diversity office looking ahead, trying to project ahead 20 years. And folks said, yes, we're going to need a diversity office. But we have to figure out how to empower the Foster School [of Business], the College of Built Environments, the chemistry department. All of those places need to be better equipped to teach diverse learners and to diversify their faculty, and a central office could not do that work for them. They actually had to build their capacity to be more welcoming and inclusive in all of our departments and administrative units, not just academic units.

The Diversity Blueprint is a document prepared by the University Diversity Council (led by the OMA&D vice president and vice provost) describing the goals, priorities and action steps designed to embed diversity at all levels of the University of Washington on all three campuses (Bothell, Seattle, Tacoma) and specifies the various institutional entities responsible. The University Diversity Council was composed of administrator, faculty, staff, students, and community representatives.

THE DIVERSITY BLUEPRINT

An excerpt from the 2015 University of Washington Diversity Blueprint:

Goal: Attract, Retain, and Graduate a Diverse and Excellent Student Body

Recommended Priorities and Action Steps-1

- *Ensure continued progress toward achieving diversity in the undergraduate student body.*
- *Establish collaborative relationships between central recruitment and outreach services and departments to better coordinate K-12 pipeline programs and initiatives and to connect potential students to academic departments for follow-up.*
- *Explore multiple mechanisms and funding opportunities to expand recruitment and retention of underrepresented and low-income students; explore sliding scales for services and differentiated tuition for students based on ability to pay.*
- *Expand outreach to state, community, two-year, and tribal colleges, and to educational organizations working with high-performing students to expand the pipeline of underrepresented students.*
- *Expand collaboration and coordination among departments and central diversity units in order to improve scholarship packages offered to underrepresented minority students upon entry to UW.*
- *Monitor demographic trends in high school student population to prepare for shifting priorities in outreach and recruitment.*

Recommended Priorities and Action Steps-2

- *Improve retention and graduation rates for underrepresented undergraduate students to reach rates comparable to all UW undergraduate students.*
- *Provide comprehensive financial aid packages that will enable students to earn degrees and implement proactive advising of students to ensure financial literacy and management of resources.*
- *Enhance advising strategies, such as early warning and intervention systems, for underrepresented students and create opportunities for sharing best practices among advisers serving different constituencies.*
- *Develop strong partnerships among diversity units and academic departments to secure outside funding for projects to increase the success of underrepresented students.*

In addition, Lange accomplished much more in her tenure. She enjoyed great working relations with the OMA&D Student Advisory Board, which at this time encompassed a broad spectrum of diversity, as well as with the Native American Advisory Board. She established quarterly meetings bringing together OMA&D administrators and Legacy groups to address issues important to their constituents and assuring students the organization was committed to providing effective services and advocating on their behalf.

Lange also worked in earnest to grow the OMA&D endowment portfolio, increasing it from 18 to 35 endowments. Not only did the number of endowments increase, but the principal of selected existing endowments increased. This in turn increased the funds available to award scholarships to deserving EOP students. One of the endowments was the Friends of the Educational Opportunity Program (FEOP) Legacy Endowment, which took advantage of matching funds made available through the University fundraising campaign initiative. The size of monetary gifts reached an all-time high.

In addition, the reach of OMA&D was extended through its newsletters and website and the budget grew substantially through additional federal grant attainment. Also added to the OMA&D family of programs at that time were programs serving students from migrant families (College Assistance Migrant Program) and students who were foster care youth and alumni (Champions program).

Lange said:

> *Diversity is a core value of the institution, and if we truly believe that is the case, then we should be doing it and we should be doing it together.*
>
> *–Lange, 2015*

STEM diversity was something that we were doing, some of it. But bringing in the Mathematics, Engineering, Science, Achievement and Louis Stokes Alliance for Minority Participation grants, the Student Support Services STEM, and the Upward Bound STEM... So, we were really bringing that STEM focus to what we were doing.

The reason why we were able to do those things was because of the sort of shared responsibility. I could say to a dean, "Diversity is a core value of the institution, and if we truly believe that is the case, then we should be doing it and we should be doing it together."

Another aspect of Lange's legacy was the advantage of using the premise of the entire institution valuing diversity when articulating about challenging issues. A case in point was a proposal to build a new structure to house the UW police department. It had to move from the location it had occupied for years on West Campus onto a site across the street from the new Kelly Ethnic Cultural Center. Lange's argument was, "We say we value diversity, but we built this ECC and we're going to bring students and their families who right now don't have the best of relationships with police. . ." The proposal to locate a new UW police building across from the ECC was abandoned in favor of a different location. Lange articulated the case in a manner that was compelling for those responsible for making the final decision. By doing so, a confrontation between concerned students and the administration was avoided.

When asked in 2015 how the story should be told regarding the merger of minority affairs with diversity, Lange said:

I think it is still evolving. Part of the reason why I really felt it was important to add "diversity" was because diversity is broader than race and ethnicity, first of all. "Minority" implied that it was just race. We had never in the history of OMA just been about race, so it really was broader than race and ethnicity. But it also was about more than the student piece. So, [it was also about] the faculty, the curriculum, and transforming policies and practices that were happening. As I was talking about what we needed to do in terms of building capacity out in the units, that's the "and diversity" piece because the OMA is sort of our traditional student services, the piece that we were doing always. "Diversity" is bringing in all of those other units, all of those other folks who have responsibility to be partners with us.

As I think about it in the next five years, it would be collaborations between OMA&D with the Foster School and the medical school or something. We've done some of that. For example, the EOP program in the Foster School is a great collaboration. Seeing more of that in other units, it would be having Student Life in their divisional work take on better understanding of implicit bias, and how that impacts their hiring of both student workers but also the folks who are leading student services on the campus. We're seeing some of that already in the partnership with Institutional Research. They're trying to figure out how they can build databases that will allow us to tell a better story about what's happening to low-income, first-generation students of color, even how we define those things, how we disaggregate data.

So, what is it about this program that has impacted the lives of so many students? Lange gave the most notable response:

One of the things that I was struck with when I was here was that, for many of the staff in OMA&D, this is more than a job. The staff in the IC who are there until midnight, sometimes one o'clock in the morning, they're not compensated for that. The staff who advise students and go to meetings after hours, they're not compensated for that. People actually generally just believe in the mission of educational opportunity and broadening access for more folks. I think over the history, as you've talked to people, you'll find that people who've sat in my chair—but also the people who have been EOP advisers or who have been tutors [in the IC] or assistants in the ECC—everybody cares about the mission, and it's more than a job. I don't know that that's the case in other units across campus. It's more than a job. It's personal. It's about our community, and this team behaves that way every day. I want people to know that over time it has always been that way. I think that's why we've been able to make a difference.

People actually generally just believe in the mission of educational opportunity and broadening access for more folks.

—Lange, 2015

Asian Community Luncheon, October 2013.

The Southeast Asian Dilemma

With success also comes challenges. One such challenge was the question of whether apparent successes of the broadly defined Asian student group was uniform throughout. In 2012, a small group of UW students and select members of the community surmised that was not the case, especially when it came to Southeast Asian students. The first step in addressing this issue was to identify the sub-groups, followed by defining which of these sub-groups should be identified for further analysis. Cambodian, Hmong, Laotian, Burmese, Cham, Mien, Bhutanese, and Vietnamese students were initially identified based on their shared experience as refugees or children of refugees for whom there exist opportunity gaps, especially degree attainment.

In 2013, a Southeast Asian Recruitment and Outreach Counselor was hired with temporary funds to focus on these sub-groups. By the end of the recruitment cycle, valuable information was gained regarding how the OMA&D Recruitment and Outreach team could partner with Community Based Organizations (CBOs) and increase the number of Southeast Asian student ambassadors to boost enrollment numbers for Southeast Asian sub-groups even though the census data showed none of the sub-groups were underrepresented when compared to their distribution in the general state population.

Lange also recommended the establishment of a Southeast Asian advisory group and the addition of a community member to the Minority Community Advisory Committee. The student and community groups were pleased regarding the proposed recommendation but insisted that a recruitment and outreach counselor be hired. After several meetings, one including the OMA&D vice president, the UW provost, and the UW president, the decision was made to finalize the appointment of a recruiter/adviser, and select Southeast Asian sub-groups were designated as underrepresented. Once again student and community activism prevailed. Lange's two recommendations were implemented as well.

Lange's storied career at OMA&D and UW did not go unnoticed by other institutions, especially on the West Coast. When the presidency at Seattle Central College became vacant, she was highly recommended to fill the position on an interim basis. It was an opportunity to become her own boss. Confident that she could successfully compete for the permanent position, Sheila Edwards Lange resigned from the UW to become the interim president of Seattle Central College. Gabriel Gallardo was appointed to take her place for the interim. Gallardo had been employed in Minority Affairs since 1996 and had moved up through the ranks to become the associate vice president for Student Success.

Having served as second in command for eight years, Gallardo had quite a bit to say about Lange:

> *Under Sheila's leadership we began to really elevate the work to a new height in terms of our connection with the community, in terms of our work with campus partners. In about 2007, 2008, we started to have this conversation about the co-location of advising and our experiential learning frameworks under one space. We worked on that for several years, and in 2010 our advising group co-located with undergraduate academic advising downstairs in Mary Gates Hall, and then our EIP McNair Program co-located with the undergraduate research program. So, this brought together all these units under one space to work collaboratively to support all students. This was done in concert with Student Life, Career Services, obviously first year programs, and so we envisioned it as a suite of*

programs that supported the entire student experience from the freshman year all the way to graduation.

That was also a significant shift in how we viewed our work because it made us integral to supporting student success. We were not a peripheral entity, just operating over there in Schmitz Hall, but we were at the center of campus in the building that carries the Gates last name and, you know, has significance for the entire campus community. We also in that process felt validated for our work that was carried out in obscurity for many years. But now it came to the forefront in the 2010–2011 period. Sheila did a lot of work with community partners and stakeholders.

When asked to reflect on challenges and accomplishments over the last 20 years, Gallardo shared the following regarding challenges:

I think the worst of times, it's always around resources. The declining state support in [2008–10] was a big, big negative for our organization. We had to reduce our budgets by about 15-20% for a period of three or four years. We lost some FTEs [full-time equivalent staff]; we lost one major program that we had, our summer bridge program. That was a $300,000 per year effort, but we had to reduce that to less than $10,000 per year, from a residential program that took place over four weeks to maybe a week non-residential program with limited resources. [Two federal grants—from the Department of Education and the National Institutes of Health—were discontinued during this period as well.] So that was a big blow to the organization. We've had to make adjustments to continue the operation.

Ensuring that we work effectively with our partners across the campus and increasing the size of a cadre that are sympathetic and sensitive to the issues of undocumented students. We're investing a lot of energy and trying to develop a framework that will allow other folks to have that same sympathy for the students and understanding of the issues they are facing.

Another challenge was improving access and retention for Native students. [To address these issues] we have to make sure that we bring students from those [Native] communities, to talk to them [as prospective enrollees] about what they're experiencing, and make sure that we have a supportive climate that students can thrive, that they can be successful being away from home. Our Intellectual House, I think, offers us a great opportunity to showcase a space that's designed for supporting Native learning and research and community building.

As for accomplishments, Gallardo said that he was particularly proud of student successes:

I think establishing a culture of evaluation and assessment for the organization and for tracking student success. . . . Emile was involved in that work early on, and then that kind of filtered through the entire organization. I think it's important now in terms of making the case for additional support and funding, and for actually measuring the impact of the resources that we commit to this work. The other thing is the ability to leverage the great work that we've done on our campus and seek out federal funding for a lot of our efforts.

The National Science Foundation, National Institutes of Health, and Department of Education funding were given as examples. Gallardo went on to say, "All of these things have kind of helped to broaden participation of underrepresented students." Gallardo also spoke about OMA&D's ability to bring in highly talented and caring staff who are committed to student success as a major factor. Echoing some of the same sentiments that Lange had noted, Gallardo said:

That is one of the things that I'm most proud of—that there's an ethos of support and care among the staff, and that is not replicated in any other organization in the entire university because people are committed, they understand the challenges that students bring, they're committed to their success.

He continued:

Our retention rates are among the top in the country for URM students and for mainstream students, between 90 to 94%. That's phenomenal. Our graduation rates have increased significantly since the early days of the program, where we were graduating maybe 25% of the students, now to between 75 and 80%, depending on the differences between populations. So that is a significant pride point for us as an organization and for the work that we do in retention. We have a great reach across the state, and we continue to do a lot of work with our GEAR UP programs and our outreach programs to ensure that students from diverse backgrounds feel like the University is a place for them, there's an environment of support, that they can thrive here, that they can have a successful Husky experience.

On the issue of survival as a self-contained model, Gallardo stated:

I guess the other thing is that there's always been the threat of absorption or elimination or eradication of OMA&D, in the worst case. You know, we were always vigilant about that, and trying to make sure that we remain relevant, and that the work that we do has value for the institution. I think with the race and equity initiative that President Ana Mari Cauce has launched, that really underscores the value of diversity and the work that we still need to do in terms of bridging some of those gaps between different groups, and our understanding of race and equity.

Enrollment Growth

We often look to math to provide the vocabulary to tell the story of the wonderful, the unexpected, or the inexplicable. At times, it provides the phrasing to tell the story of equity and change. *Figure 1* shows the enrollment trend of minority, EOP, and underrepresented minority (URM) students over the 50-year period that OMA&D has been in existence. From 1968 to 1980 EOP enrollment and minority enrollment increased at about the same rate. But from 1980 to 1998 EOP enrollment steadily declined while minority enrollment continued to trend upwards. This decline in EOP enrollment occurred despite intensified recruitment efforts.

The primary reason for this decline is attributed to three changes in the admission policy over that period. The first occurred in 1982, when regularly admissible minority students were not allowed to enter the University through EOP. In 1988, the state Higher Education Coordinating Board instituted an admission index algorithm that used test scores, a weighted GPA, as well as a strict high school core requirement, making it more difficult for URM and economically and educationally disadvantaged students to gain admission to UW. The downward trend was further compounded when race could no longer be used as a factor in the admission process after the passage of Initiative 200 in 1998.

FIGURE 1

UW SEATTLE CAMPUS
1969-2017 AUTUMN QUARTER ENROLLMENT BY STUDENTS GROUPS (2-YR INTERVAL)

YEAR (Aut)	MINORITY*	URM**	EOP***
1969	1,578	714	506
1971	2,441	1,311	1,349
1973	3,160	1,712	2,175
1975	3,407	1,739	2,607
1977	3,679	1,542	2,621
1979	4,198	1,574	3,033
1981	4,460	1,541	3,123
1983	4,977	1,507	3,092
1985	4,892	1,459	2,808
1987	5,235	1,686	2,903
1989	5,701	1,758	3,013
1991	6,510	2,009	3,036
1993	7,028	2,224	3,070
1995	7,445	2,345	2,738
1997	7,953	2,456	2,626
1999	7,841	2,194	3,059
2001	8,175	2,101	4,396
2003	8,676	2,119	4,575
2005	9,189	2,397	4,490
2007	9,963	2,799	4,563
2009	10,671	3,119	4,647
2011	10,933	3,351	4,883
2013	11,461	3,610	5,163
2015	12,317	3,923	5,258
2017	13,218	4,426	5,850

Enrollment Growth: Autumn Quarter OMA&D, 1969–2017.

In summary, as admission policies changed, so did the percentage of minority students who enrolled in EOP. The proportion went from more than two out of three during the 1974–1975 school year, to one out of two during 1988–1989, to one out of three during the 1999–2000 school year. The precipitous decline in EOP enrollment was thus influenced by the decline in the enrollment of URM students following the passage of I-200 and the change in EOP designation criteria, which reduced the participation of Asian students by one-half.

To counteract the effects of the latter change, President Richard McCormick provided funding that enabled staffing to grow substantially. Student recruiters increased five-fold and recruitment and outreach efforts intensified throughout the state of Washington using strategies that were race- and ethnic-specific. At the same time, a campaign was launched to increase the number of URM students who took the SAT. As a result, the number of high school graduates eligible to apply to the University increased significantly.

This effort proved to be highly successful. Between 1999 and 2016, four times more URM students took the SAT in 2016 than those who took the test in 1999, ranging between two times more for American Indian/Native

Alaskan and six times more for Latinos. In addition, OMA secured federal funding that allowed for the implementation of pre-college programs that increased the number of college-ready students. OMA arranged more campus visits for middle and high school students. Diversity scholarships were made available through generous funding from private sources, such as Costco, Chateau Ste. Michelle Winery, and Safeco.

Also, the UW implemented a holistic admission review process considering personal qualities (e.g., community service, cultural awareness, work experience, perseverance despite personal adversity, disability, economic and educational disadvantages) in addition to grades and test scores. These efforts resulted in a three-fold increase in incoming URM freshmen and transfer students between 1999 and 2016. Black and Latino enrollment increases accounted for a substantial portion, increasing by 165% and 228% respectively.

Over this same period, the overall enrollment of UW incoming freshmen and transfers was just one-fifth the rate of increase for URM students. The same was the case for the total student body enrollment figures (All-UW versus URM). Thus, it can be argued with confidence that the increases in URM enrollment in both instances were not just a matter of keeping pace with the increase in overall UW enrollment, because URM enrollment outpaced UW enrollment by a substantial margin.

Along with the increased URM enrollment on the Seattle campus, URM enrollment in EOP increased substantially as well. For example, four out of five URM students chose to become EOP participants to take advantage of the services provided by the OMA&D family of programs. At the same time 15% of Asian students and 6% of white students sought to become EOP students. These students were low-income and would be the first in their families to earn a bachelor's degree, therefore, qualifying as economically and educationally disadvantaged (EED) students. The increases in URM and EED students' participation, coupled with a marked increase in federally funded programs and Husky Promise scholarships funded with private gifts, made it possible for OMA&D to serve a substantially higher number of students, thereby improving their chances of persisting and graduating.

The spike in enrollment of EOP students between 1999 and 2002 was due mainly to 120% and 88% increases in participation by white and Asian students, respectively.

These changes translated into more than 50,000 students being the beneficiaries of a program that was established as a response to a small group of students who insisted that the face of diversity on the UW campus needed to change.

Since the passage of I-200, URM and female students comprised about 70% and 60% of EOP enrollees, respectively. Most (90%) students in entering cohorts came from within the state. They graduated from top feeder public high schools such as (rank ordered) Franklin (Seattle), Garfield (Seattle), Roosevelt (Seattle), Cleveland (Seattle), Mariner (Everett), Ingraham (Seattle), Kent-Meridian (Kent), A.C. Davis (Yakima), Henry Foss (Tacoma), Foster (Seattle), Federal Way (Federal Way), Renton (Renton), West Seattle (Seattle), and Kentridge (Kent), to name a few of the more than 1100 high schools.

Other students transferred from two- and four-year in-state schools such as (rank ordered) Seattle Central, Bellevue, Shoreline, Highline (Des Moines), South Seattle, Olympic College (Bremerton), Edmonds (Lynnwood), Green River (Auburn), and Tacoma, to name a few of nearly 190 institutions.

Almost half of the EOP enrollees came from low-income backgrounds and half would be the first in their families to graduate from college. It is important to note that of all low-income and first-generation students enrolled at the UW, four out of five were non-minority.

All in all, the number of incoming underrepresented minority (URM) students increased almost five-fold even though it was much more difficult to get into the University now than it had been 50 years earlier. For example, roughly three out of four URM applicants were admitted in the early years compared to just one out of two in recent years.

In summary, over this 50-year period, the number of students (EOP) served annually by OMA&D went from 257 to more than 5,700, a 22-fold increase. The overall representation of minority students at UW Seattle grew from 5% to nearly 37% over the 50-year period, a more than seven-fold increase. These changes translated into more than 50,000 students being the beneficiaries of a program that was established as a response to a small group of students who insisted that the face of diversity on the UW campus needed to change.

Rounding Out the Final Two Years of the Half Century

In May 2016, UW president Ana Mari Cauce announced Rickey L. Hall, who at the time was vice chancellor for Diversity and Inclusion at the University of Tennessee, as her choice to become the eighth vice president of OMA&D and the first University Diversity Officer for all three campuses. The University and OMA&D were not strangers to Hall; he had visited the campus in earlier years during his tenure as assistant vice president for Equity and Diversity at the University of Minnesota. In fact, he was so impressed with the work being done at the OMA&D Instructional Center that he adopted that name for the study center at Minnesota.

During an interview, Vice President Hall spoke about his vision for OMA&D:

> *My vision, as I talked about a bit as I was interviewing, but since I've been here certainly, is for the Office of Minority Affairs & Diversity to be a leader, a national leader in terms of access and opportunity for underrepresented minorities, first-generation, low-income students. When I say opportunity, I also mean the support piece, too. I always say that access isn't enough, and it's not real opportunity unless there's proper support there, meaning academic support—certainly, we do that through our Student Success efforts—but also financial support. So, those are the areas: access, academic, and financial support. I want us to be leaders in how we do that for underrepresented minorities and first-generation [students]. Hopefully, that leads to us being leaders in outcomes for those populations as well.*
>
> *One of the things I say now is that in order for us to achieve that vision, it certainly has to be about the individual units within OMA&D. If we're going to be a national leader that means the ECC needs to be a national leader, and that really means the Instructional Center needs to be a national*

Rickey Hall at Celebration 2017.

leader. Now, what I've also said is that some of our units are already that. Our Instructional Center, I would argue with anybody, I'd put up against any tutorial program around the country. It IS a national leader, and I think that there are others that are also there, or close to being there, that we could put there.

OMA&D's data collection system, for a program of its kind, not only leads the nation, but also is a leader within the institution. However, the one thing we haven't done a good job of is telling our story. I want the leadership to do this by getting out and going to national conferences and presenting, sharing what we're doing, because we should be caring about this nationally. . . . Let's share those stories so that others can maybe learn some things that they can maybe replicate or tweak to work in their particular context. When you look at us and how we're structured, I can't think of another that is resourced in the way that we are.

When Hall initially joined OMA&D, he was told Filipino students were neither recognized by the University nor the federal government as one of the groups designated as underrepresented. Thus, to receive services, applicants had to apply as either first-generation college or low-income students. The Filipino community was not pleased with this requirement. In the early period of OMA when the program was organized by ethnic student divisions, these students were recruited and routinely served. In fact, this group was

Filipino American Student Association 100th Anniversary Officers.

classified by the EOP Admission Policy Committee to be underrepresented for recruitment purposes. But over the years that policy was abandoned as the group's numbers grew. It was argued that, based on the grandfather clause, these groups should be automatically EOP eligible. Vice President Hall concurred, and now Filipino students are again automatically eligible for services and opportunities provided by the OMA&D family of programs.

Hall was well aware of the rich history of OMA&D. In less than a month on the job, he convened a committee and charged its members with planning a 50th anniversary celebration. Jeanette James was appointed chair.

In the ensuing eighteen months, OMA&D 50th Anniversary buttons were made and distributed widely, and a six-page spread was featured in the March edition of *Columns* magazine, a publication distributed to more than 270,000 UW alumni. A commemorative OMA&D 50th Anniversary photo gallery was created on the third floor of Mary Gates Hall, where the administrative staff is housed along with the Information School Dean's office and computer classrooms. In addition, an online timeline was featured on the OMA&D 50th Anniversary website and an OMA&D 50th Anniversary Exhibition was displayed in the North wing of the Allen Library for six weeks.

OMA&D 50th Anniversary Historical Display in the North Lobby of the Allen Library.

The 2018 BSU Executive Board for the 50th Anniversary exhibition.

Three days before the exact day of the founding of OMA&D, a reception was held on campus in wəɬəbʔaltxʷ (the Intellectual House) and attended by more than 150 individuals. Following the reception, a UWTV Video of a conversation with me about the 50-year history of OMA&D was produced before a live audience of approximately 300 that included the president of the University as well as five founding members of the Black Student Union. The talk was also highlighted on the OMA&D web site. In addition, the 50-year celebration was featured in the student newspaper, *The Daily*, and in *The Seattle Times*. To date no other institution in the country had ever celebrated the founding of similar programs with such depth and breadth. It set the gold standard!

The celebratory activities did not detract from the work of the family of OMA&D programs. During the first two years of Hall's tenure, the four most diverse classes ever enrolled arrived at UW Seattle; the Celebration banquet set fundraising records for two consecutive years; 10 additional endowments were added to the OMA&D portfolio; the EOP retention rate gap narrowed to less than two percentage points; and more than 5,700 URM and EED students were supported by the OMA&D family of programs. Federal funding for three additional programs was secured resulting in the largest budget in the 50-year history of the program.

In addition, the Board of Regents and the UW Foundation Board created a Diversity, Equity, and Inclusion Committee, and a Diversity and Inclusion Committee, respectively. Hall attributes such impressive accomplishments to timing, readiness, and a president, Ana Mari Cauce, whose priorities differed from a couple of presidents who preceded her. He also credits deans and other leaders committed to advancing the efforts that led to these outcomes. In terms of the fundraising piece, here is what Hall said:

> *I think on the fundraising side, I just saw a lot of opportunities there, because I had been talking so much about that in my previous positions that I thought that really people were ready and poised to give to diversity. In terms of things, I'd like to see during my tenure . . . I really would like for us to reach the priorities that we've established. I really would like for us to meet the $25 million goal for programming support for the Instructional Center. I'd like for us to get the funding to build the second phase of the Intellectual House (wəɬəbʔaltxʷ). Also, one of the things I'd*

love to see is for us to get a transformational gift just for diversity. When I say transformational, I mean, from one or two individuals, $20 million plus that goes into an endowment for broad diversity, because we have these other challenges.

Hall is also credited with coining the phrase "50 Next" in pledging to "keep evolving to meet the changing needs of current and future students." In that vein, he alludes to emerging populations, such as undocumented, multiracial (the fastest growing segment of the state population and projected to continue to grow), and underrepresented groups such as LGBTQ students, as well as students who are veterans and those coming from the foster care system. General shifting demographics, which translate into a significant increase in the population that OMA&D has historically served, will substantially impact the capacity to adequately deliver such services.

Outcomes

Throughout the more than nine-year tenure of Sheila Edwards Lange, OMA&D remained organizationally intact. Minority Affairs, Student Life, and Undergraduate Academic Affairs became a triumvirate working in concert for the benefit of all university students. Experiential learning (research and study abroad) for program participants soared to heights never witnessed before. EOP students were afforded the opportunity to participate in OMA&D-partnered study abroad programs in Australia, Barbados, Brazil, Ghana, Iceland, and Tahiti. Programs with a STEM (Science, Technology, Engineering, Math) focus and geared toward increasing participation of URM and economically and educationally disadvantaged (EED) students multiplied with the help of funding secured from the Department of Education and the National Science Foundation. Programs to support the matriculation through the University of children of migrant farm workers and children who were a product of the foster care system were added to the family of OMA&D programs. A community and public relations unit was established to highlight the "good work" that OMA&D and its family of programs were doing.

According to OMA&D budget reports and research conducted by the OMA&D Assessment and Research unit on enrollment, retention, and graduation, the budget increased by about eight million. EOP and URM enrollment increased by 16% and 54%, respectively. The retention rate gap closed to within two percentage points and the graduation rate closed to within six percentage points for EOP students. The retention and graduation rate gaps for URM students closed to within three and ten percentage points, respectively. The number of EOP and URM degree earners increased by 15% and 83%, respectively.

During Hall's tenure, the budget increased by approximately $13 million. Sixteen endowments were added to the OMA&D portfolio and of those, three have reached one million dollars or more. URM and EOP enrollment increased by 20% and 75%, respectively. The retention rate of EOP student exceeded that of that of the UW student body. The graduation rate gap for URM students closed to 7% percentage points. And for IC users, it closed to 2% percentage points. The number of EOP and URM degree earners increased by 4% and 16%, respectively.

STUDENT CASES

ELIJAH AND RUBEN BURBANK. Imagine two-year-old twins living in a household where one of the parents just died from a drug overdose, and the mother is left with no stable source of income, living in the inner city of Tacoma in an area known for rival Crips and Bloods gang members. What is the likelihood that these two young children would not only survive, but excel in high school, be awarded Costco Diversity scholarships, major in biology and neurobiology and neurosciences? Such was the case with Elijah and Ruben Burbank. During their studies at UW, these young men, who had attended Wilson High School, paid it forward by tutoring EOP students at the IC. They helped other students in courses, such as introductory biology, that posed the greatest challenges for students aspiring to be medical doctors, dentists, biochemists, and bioengineers. Elijah graduated with one of the highest cumulative GPAs of EOP graduating seniors and, as a result of service to others and overcoming significant obstacles, was chosen to receive the EOP President's Achievement Award. Ruben also earned a high GPA and received an EOP Recognition Award during his junior year.

After graduating, both were accepted to the UW School of Medicine with full financial support. At the time of this writing, Elijah was a physician/naval medical officer and an anesthesiology resident at UW, now married to a fellow EOP alumna **Josephine Quitugua** (also an EOP Recognition Award recipient). They are the proud parents of two children (boy and girl). Ruben did his residence in surgery at Morehouse School of Medicine and was awarded the "Beyond the Call of Duty" Award 2014. He went on to practice as a general surgery specialist in Portland, Oregon.

ANISA IBRAHIM. With the civil war raging in Somalia, Anisa Ibrahim's family of five had no other choice but to leave to save their lives. Where they would go was dictated by which countries were accepting refugees and by proximity to Somalia. They fled to Kenya where the United Nations High Commissioner for Refugees (UNHCR) had set up a camp. After a year, Anisa's family immigrated to the US, settling in Seattle where she attended elementary, middle, and high school in the Rainier Valley area. In her correspondence with me, Anisa said: "While I had a good experience... education inequities were abundant." She also said, "I participated in the UW [OMA&D] Upward Bound program during high school, which was a godsend. I found counselors who believed in me, my potential, and encouraged me to pursue higher education fiercely. They also gave me the tools and guidance through the process (taking SATS, personal statements, etc.)."

Anisa was admitted to the University of Washington, the first in her family to attend college. With excellent grades and high financial need, Anisa was awarded a Costco Diversity Scholarship. Said she, "I do not know how I would have been able to afford college had it not been for this scholarship."

About her experience at UW, Anisa said: "College can be an isolating experience. I had no mentors who had done it before me, no one to look up to that clarified my path, and no one to show me the ropes. I encountered people who doubted me [when went to general counselor instead of an EOP counselor] and people whose biases led them to tell me 'weed out' courses would get the best of me." Fortunately, she learned about the OMA&D family of programs through EOP and other students she met at the IC.

While taking nine different chemistry courses, Anisa worked with Scott Fung and E.J. Burks who saw her as a highly motivated individual, one who demonstrated the thoroughness and perseverance to succeed as a STEM major. Scott said, "I am extremely proud of Anisa, as she is a role model for so many of our program students at the IC, especially students of color and from immigrant backgrounds." She also worked with Brian McLain in mathematics and Carolyn DuPen in biology, and George Bauer in the IC who worked with her in writing and her personal statement for medical school. She credits all of them with contributing to her success. Proud and grateful, Anisa said, "My IC tutors [instructors] supported me when the difficulties of being a first-generation college student became overwhelming and celebrated with me when I reached my accomplishments. I CANNOT say enough about how special this place was and how much it contributed to levelling the playing field."

While at UW, Anisa received other scholarships including OMA&D's Lee and Virginia Huntsman Scholarship. She graduated with a BS in biology and physiology in 2009 and went on to earn a medical degree from the UW School of Medicine in 2013. She was featured in a CNN article in 2019. About the OMA&D family of programs, she stated: "I cannot say enough how having a 'home' and community at the UW contributed to my personal well-being and success. Due to this, I was able to dream big and am now in a position that I never imagined would be possible." She is currently the medical director for, Harborview Pediatrics Clinic and a clinical assistant professor in the Department of Pediatrics at UW.

Notable Alumni of the Decade

This group of alumni is the smallest in size since the 1968–1977 decade. They graduated fewer than 10 years ago and it takes time to build an enduring successful career. Their selection is based, in part, on a trajectory toward distinguished careers.

Alula Asfaw, '08, MPhil (University of Cambridge), JD (Yale)

Mohamed Bulale, '08 (UW)

Elijah Burbank, '08, '12, MD (UW)

Ruben Burbank, '08, '12, MD (UW)

Anthony Durazo, '08 (UW)

Melon Feleke, '08, MBA (Harvard)

Rachel Gillum, '08, PhD (Stanford)

Laurel James, '08, MS (UW) PhC (UW)

Desiree Omli, '08, JD (California Western School of Law), MPA (Seattle U)

Alvaro Presenda, '08, MSC (Albert-Ludwigs-Universitat Freiberg im Breisgau), PhD (Universitat Politecnicade Valencia)

Lula Samuel, '08, MBA (University of North Carolina, Chapel Hill)

Asia Quince, '08 (UW)

Heather Rastovac, '08, PhD (UC Berkeley)

Cyrus Ansari, International Studies, '09, JD (NYU)

Patricia Dixon, '09, MBA (Seattle U)

Charmaine Felix, '09, DDS (UW)

Jaimée Marsh, '09, MSW (Michigan)

Iisaaksiichaa Ross Braine, '09, '15, MSIM (UW)

Jared Watson, '09, PhD (University of Maryland)

Turquoise Young, '10, JD (NYU)

Lorne Arnold, '10, PhD (UW)

Julia Bruk, '10 (UW)

Yashina Burns, '10, JD (UC Irvine)

Eddie Calaunan, '10 (UW)

Tavis Dickerson-Young, '10, MD (UW)

Joel Estrada, '10 (UW)

Cody Johnson, '10 (UW)

Katelyn Keyloun, '10, PharmD (UW), MS (UW)

Brendan Lazarus, '10, (UW)

Amber Sims, '10, MS (University of Maryland)

Alexandra Zaballa, '11, MD (UW)

Maxwell Walker, '12 (UW)

Jesse Elijah Johnson, '12, '16, MEd (UW)

Bryan Dosono, '13, PhD (Syracuse University)

Tony Vo, '14, MS (Harvard Graduate School of Education), EdD (Seattle U)

Dulce Gutiérrez, '15 (UW)

Savannah Romero (Eastern Shoshone), '15, MPA (NYU)

Ruben Reyes, '16, DDS (UW)

Starla Sampaco, '17 (UW)

The Samuel E. Kelly Award presented to OMA&D, October 2008. Emile Pitre, Gabriel Gallardo, Linda Jardine, Steve Woodard, Candace Fries, Kris Hohag, Torrance Powell, Sheila Edwards Lange, Mick Richter (left to right).

Filipino American Student Association Graduation, 2017.

CHAPTER 7

The Fruits of a Half-Century of Labor

A long-time academic counselor, in OMA&D observed, "I think our program can stand up to any of the great programs across the nation."

—Hairston, 2016

"Every positive experience I have had here has come through OMA. They are more than a support. They are like your family on campus."

—unidentified focus group student, 2006

After 50 years of operations, how does one know whether efforts were successful? The OMA&D has a long history of assessment and the use of assessment findings to inform program design and improvement. Some of the indicators used to measure success include the following:

1. *Growth in URM enrollment*
2. *Retention outcomes, specifically narrowing retention rate gaps over time, not only for EOP but also for underrepresented minority (URM) students*
3. *Students' academic performance*
4. *The extent to which the program supports EOP students through scholarships and other forms of financial assistance*
5. *Graduation outcomes, including narrowing the graduation rate gaps for EOP and URM students; narrowing the graduation gap within disaggregated race/ethnicity groups; comparison of graduation rates of UW program participants with those of other flagship state universities and Research 1 institutions; the number of degree earners compared with degree seekers; and growth in the number of degree earners in high demand majors*
6. *Post-baccalaureate degree attainment at UW and the number of top universities that have admitted UW EOP and URM students into graduate and professional programs*
7. *EOP alumni accomplishments, including the number of students who have received national scholarships and fellowships, the number of EOP students who have served in top leadership positions at the UW, and examples of notable alumni*
8. *Firsts—programs that have been recognized nationally and are considered national models*
9. *The growth of the program over time*
10. *Student satisfaction*

EOP Alumni Accomplishments

In the early years of OMA and the EOP many participants, their community, and high school counselors believed that being coded as an Educational Opportunity Program student was a stigma. This belief came about because many minority students being told by their high school counselors, high school classmates, UW students, and others that the only reason they were admitted to UW was because they were minorities. Remnants of this belief continue today. To counter this idea, it is important to share information about notable accomplishments former EOP students have realized. Not only did EOP students assume leadership roles in ethnic-specific student organizations, but they also participated in student government and held institutional leadership positions. For example, eight students have served as president of the Associated Students of the University of Washington (ASUW) over the years, including the first Latina, Alexandra Narvaez, and the first Filipina/Pacific Islander, Daniele Mempin Menez. According to ASUW alumni files, five alums have been elected to the position of ASUW vice president, and at least 28 have held other positions in ASUW. Three EOP alums have served as Student Regents.

After graduation, several EOP alums got involved in politics. Three went on to serve in the Washington State House of Representatives, and one to the Idaho legislature. Two served on the Seattle Public School Board; one was the first Asian to hold that post. Eight have served on city councils. Four served on the Seattle City Council; one on the Oakland, CA, City Council; one on the Federal Way, WA, City Council; one on the Tukwila, WA, City Council; and one on the Yakima, WA, City Council. It is also important to point out that two, African Americans in the predominantly white city of Seattle, served as mayors. (See Appendix D for a complete list of OMA&D alumni elected to office.)

The President's Medal is the epitome of academic excellence. One EOP alum (Conan Viernes) was awarded the UW's Freshman Medal for outstanding academic achievement. Another EOP alum, Narmina Sharifova, received the President's Medal for distinguished academic achievement during her senior year and was recognized at Commencement in 2018.

Besides the scholarships that OMA&D has awarded since 1973, EOP students have competed for and were awarded national scholarships and fellowships. One EOP Alum, Alyssa Lamb, was awarded the Rhodes Scholarship

Left: Former Seattle Mayor Norm Rice at the Awards of Excellence Ceremony, June 8, 2017.

Right: Regent Joanne Harrell and (current) Mayor Bruce Harrell as the Odegaard Award recipients at Celebration 2017.

and studied at the University of Oxford. Jennifer Devine was awarded the Marshal Scholarship and studied at the London School of Economics.

According to UW Office of Merit Scholarships records, over the first half-century of OMA&D's existence, at least 25 were awarded scholarships or fellowships such as the Goldwater, Truman, Udall, Fulbright, Bonderman, Beinecke, Rangel, and Merage awards. At least 200 were awarded UW scholarships and grants, which include Mary Gates Honors, Research, and Leadership endowed scholarships; Honors Program scholarships; NASA Space grants; Carlson Civic Fellowships; and Gerberding scholarships. In addition to being recipients of the prestigious awards mentioned above, eight EOP alums were awarded the UNCF-Merck Scholarship, five of whom received it since 2010.

Were it not for the existence of OMA&D programs and the dedicated commitment of staff, many students with high potential and low academic credentials would not have had the opportunity to enroll, persist, graduate, and go on to meaningful careers. Stories abound of EOP Alumni who otherwise would not have been admitted to the University, like that of Jabari Walker (Chapter IV Student Cases), if OMA&D did not exist.

Corey Ray Thomas, on the other hand, was an economically disadvantaged white student who entered UW through the EOP. She sought help at the OMA&D Instructional Center because she was not doing well academically and felt hopeless. She had been enrolled at UW off and on for more than six years before seeking help. In 2015, she wrote a letter to me, her former IC chemistry instructor. It read in part:

Corey Thomas at Emile Pitre's retirement gathering.

I have often wondered if you know what a profound difference you made in my life. Almost 30 years ago now I was a street kid, my parents were on drugs, I had no resources, and very little education. I had attended an alternative high school that required little effort to graduate, and I applied to the UW and was admitted through the EOP. I would not have graduated without the instructional center and your guidance in particular. I don't know if you remember me, but I spent all day every day at the IC . . . After a few years I was hired by the IC where I tutored chemistry for several years. It felt amazing to help other students, and I loved being at the IC. Now, 30 years later, I am still married to the same man (you attended our wedding), have two lovely daughters, and have been a high school chemistry teacher for over 25 years.

Over the course of the years many students have asked me why I went into teaching, and I always say, "I love teaching and I love kids but what really started me on this path was an amazing teacher" . . . that teacher is you. You are the person that helped me recognize my passion in life. When I started at the University, I never thought I would be good at chemistry. You showed me that if I was determined [to] learn, you were determined to teach. I now love chemistry and how it is fundamental and connected to so many other sciences. I have taught over 2,000 chemistry students and even though I can't remember all their names, I know I cared about each one. Last year, all of my AP Chemistry students earned 4s or 5s on the AP Test, and many said it was the hardest class they had in high school, and the one that taught them the most about themselves. . . . It's an amazing feeling to touch so many lives.

She went on to say:

So, here is what I want you to know: Your dedication to students, your genuine affinity for teaching and learning, your authenticity when working with a student is so profound that I know you have changed the lives of many, many students, not just mine. . . . Your expectation of excellence and achievement inspires students to work harder than they thought possible. . . . Think about all the lives you have touched through your teaching and then all of the lives that they have touched. . . . Your efforts have had a profound effect on my life and the lives of my students. I am forever grateful.

Nelson and Suzanne Del Rio at a Vice President's gathering, 2013.

Corey, Jabari Walker, Nelson Del Rio, and Tania Barron are prime examples of the legacy of students who entered UW with low academic credentials and high academic potential and have gone on to make a difference in society.

Data-driven Decision Making

Over the last 10 years the continuous use of data and research to make informed decisions regarding what is working well and, if something is not working well, strategies to make a course correction, has been at the forefront of OMA&D planning and institutional leadership. The data-driven and also highly personal approach was taken to intentionally send the message that there is a solid infrastructure to support URM and EED students from the time they enter the institution until they graduate. But it does not end there. We have, and we must endeavor to grow, a cadre of URM and EED students for transition into graduate and professional school. This can be achieved by further strengthening OMA&D's partnership with the Graduate

Opportunities and Minority Achievement Program of the UW Graduate School and by involving currently enrolled graduate students to serve as mentors for those undergraduate EOP/EED students who aspire to attend graduate school and who can serve as role models who might inspire others to consider graduate education for the first time.

Retention Outcomes

With the enrollment and funding growth, how have the educational outcomes improved? Let's first examine retention rate trends of EOP students in comparison to the UW student body. As shown in *Figure 2*, the gap between the percentage of entering EOP freshman students and entering UW freshman students returning for their sophomore year was 13 percentage points for the 1981 cohorts. The widest gap recorded was 17 percentage points for the 1984 cohort. For the most part, the gap remained in double digits for the next eight cohort years. Then it narrowed to an average of five percentage points over the next five cohort years. For the following 21 cohort years (between 1995 and 2015), the gap closed to an average of one percentage point.

While there is no statistical analysis pointing to why this retention gap closed, it is likely the intervention strategies employed by the OMA&D family of programs played a significant role in student retention. These intervention

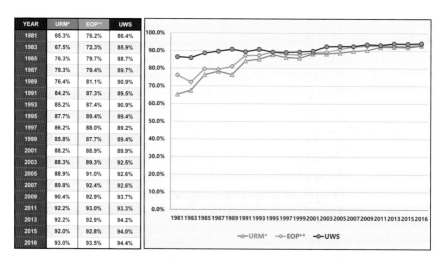

Figure 2. First-year Retention, Autumn Quarter, 1981–2016.

strategies included informed use of assessment data, recruitment of a more college-ready group of students, more intentional mentoring and social support programming, implementation of two different bridge programs (one in 1995 and another in 2001), the launching of the Diversity Scholarship program in 2001, the growth of EOP endowed scholarships, and the accrual of enough interest to support academic excellence as well as emergency funding for students in need of immediate financial support. In addition, holistic advising practices reached a wider swath of students.

Robust academic support in math, science, social science, and writing courses continued to evolve, as well. In fact, for those students who sought such support on a regular basis, the probability of freshmen returning for their sophomore and junior years was as high as three times greater than those who did not seek support. Furthermore, when the average freshman retention rates for EOP students are compared with the average freshman rates for the 54 flagship state universities, the 2006–2009 EOP freshmen cohort rate (92%) ranked seventeenth. Put into perspective, the 2006–2009 UW freshmen cohort rate (94%) ranked eleventh (*US News & World Report*, 2017 ed.).

Graduation Outcomes

One of the goals of institutions of higher learning is to graduate a high percentage of its entering freshman enrollees in a reasonable length of time—usually in six years, which is 150% of the expected time to degree, i.e., four years. The same is expected for EOP students, regardless of extenuating circumstances. One measure of success used by OMA&D administration, especially since 2003, is the size of the six-year graduation gap between EOP cohorts and UW student body cohorts. Data has been accessible to make such a comparison since 1981. Rather than look at a small sample of cohorts, the OMA/OMA&D approach has been to make the comparison over an extended period. By doing so, statistical aberrations are avoided. The cohort year (1983), when the rate was lowest, was chosen to determine the progress that has been made over the years. For this cohort year, the gap was almost 34 percentage points (See *Figure 3*). Less than one-quarter of EOP enrollees were graduating after six years. In subsequent cohort years, the graduation rate for entering EOP freshmen increased at a rate that was faster than the increase experienced

Pacific Island Student Commission Graduation, 2011.

by the general student population. As a result, the graduation rate gap after 29 cohort years has narrowed substantially.

For the 2011 freshman cohort, the gap was less than five percentage points. It is important to note that although the gap has been smallest for cohorts that enrolled since the passage of I-200, narrowing began much earlier. As can be seen in *Figure 3*, the graduation rates for URM cohorts are essentially the same as EOP cohorts up to 1997. The rate declined until 2002. Afterwards, the rate increased to just below that of the EOP cohort. The rate gaps for transfer cohorts parallel those of the freshman cohorts with three exceptions. The widest gap was 28 percentage points; the gap closed at a more rapid rate, and there is essentially no gap for cohort year 2011 for EOP students (See *Figure 4*).

For the URM cohort on the other hand, there remains a gap. It goes without saying that these outcomes are noteworthy, but it should also be noted that there were extenuating circumstances that dampened the extent to which the gap might be narrowed, especially for the freshman cohorts. For example, a relatively high percentage of the cohorts were first-generation and low-income; were required to work the kind of long hours research shows negatively affect grades (Kreighbaum, 2017); were more likely to stop out for financial and

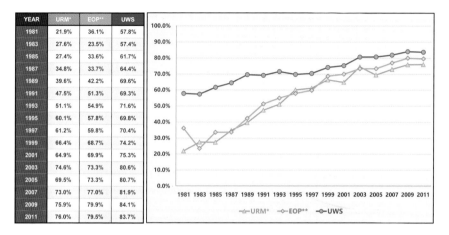

YEAR	URM*	EOP**	UWS
1981	21.9%	36.1%	57.8%
1983	27.6%	23.5%	57.4%
1985	27.4%	33.6%	61.7%
1987	34.8%	33.7%	64.4%
1989	39.6%	42.2%	69.6%
1991	47.5%	51.3%	69.3%
1993	51.1%	54.9%	71.6%
1995	60.1%	57.8%	69.8%
1997	61.2%	59.8%	70.4%
1999	66.4%	68.7%	74.2%
2001	64.9%	69.9%	75.3%
2003	74.6%	73.3%	80.6%
2005	69.5%	73.3%	80.7%
2007	73.0%	77.0%	81.9%
2009	75.9%	79.9%	84.1%
2011	76.0%	79.5%	83.7%

Figure 3. Six-year Graduation, Entering Freshman Cohorts, 1981–2011.

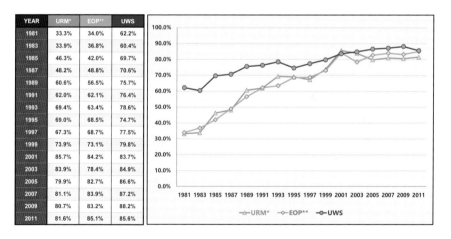

YEAR	URM*	EOP**	UWS
1981	33.3%	34.0%	62.2%
1983	33.9%	36.8%	60.4%
1985	46.3%	42.0%	69.7%
1987	48.2%	48.8%	70.6%
1989	60.6%	56.5%	75.7%
1991	62.0%	62.1%	76.4%
1993	69.4%	63.4%	78.6%
1995	69.0%	68.5%	74.7%
1997	67.3%	68.7%	77.5%
1999	73.9%	73.1%	79.8%
2001	85.7%	84.2%	83.7%
2003	83.9%	78.4%	84.9%
2005	79.9%	82.7%	86.6%
2007	81.1%	83.9%	87.2%
2009	80.7%	83.2%	88.2%
2011	81.6%	85.1%	85.6%

Figure 4. Six-year Graduation, Entering Transfer Cohorts, 1981-2011.

personal reasons; and were graduates from high schools not considered to be high-performing schools. Considering these factors, this graduation outcome is even more impressive.

Similar to the improvement in retention rates, many factors contributed to this notable success in graduation rates. In addition to these factors already discussed, evidence shows that students who use the comprehensive services of the OMA&D Instructional Center are more likely to persist and graduate than those who do not take advantage of the services.

Besides being able to determine the success of OMA&D participants by comparing the EOP cohorts' six-year graduation rates to those of the UW student population, comparisons can also be made to the graduation rates of student bodies at other Research I public institutions. The data shows that when an aggregate cohort (2006-2009) of EOP entering freshmen is compared to the graduation rates of the 54 flagship state universities' entering freshmen cohorts, the rate for EOP students is tied for nineteenth with Michigan State and the University of New Hampshire. EOP graduation rates were ahead of such institutions (rank ordered) as Indiana, Minnesota, Vermont, Massachusetts, South Carolina, Colorado, Iowa, Missouri, Buffalo, and Oregon, to name a few. It is important to note that the UW aggregate cohort ranked thirteenth. Also, as more than 75% to 80% of EOP students were URM students, it was considered instructive to see how the rates of URM students measured up to these same institutions. The outcome was that the rate for URM students tied for twenty-fourth with Massachusetts outpacing six of the institutions shown above (NCAA Graduation Rates).

Another way of determining the graduation success rate of URM students is to compute the graduation success ratio. Using the graduation rates of the 2006–2009 aggregate cohorts of EOP students and the student body yielded a ratio of 0.91, which is highly commendable since a ratio of 1.0 signifies total gap closure.

Although the graduation rates of EOP students measure up well with cohorts at other research institutions, Vice President Lange often stated that the OMA&D administration was not satisfied that over 20% of OMA&D students did not earn a degree within six years. Neither was she satisfied with the fact that other institutions graduated a higher percentage of their freshman cohorts.

So, what were the likely reasons for the higher graduation rate outcomes of those institutions (e.g., Virginia, Berkeley, UCLA, Michigan, North Carolina, Florida, Penn State, Georgia, Illinois, Maryland, Wisconsin, and Ohio State) that outpaced those of UW EOP students? Several come to mind. All of these institutions were highly selective; most accepted less than half of their applicants and some selected less than 30% of applicants, compared with the UW, which had a 53% acceptance rate for all students and a 59% acceptance rate for Washington State residents. Also, a higher proportion of their enrollees graduated in the top 10% of their high school classes than those at the UW. In addition, many of these institutions enrolled substantially fewer first-generation and low-income students. The academic credentials (grades and test scores) of admitted students are relatively high, and those institutions offered more competitive financial aid packages (*US News & World Report*, 2018 ed.).

What is most impressive about student outcomes at the University of Washington is that a wide cross-section of the citizenry is served not only by one of the top universities in the country, but by one of the top in the world, ranking fourth among public universities (Academic ranking of world universities, 2019).

While six-year graduation rates are a key measure of how well an institution does in graduating students over a prescribed period, the stories of students who take longer than six years to graduate essentially go untold. It could be argued that a more comprehensive measure of success would be the total number of degree earners over an extended period of time—the longitudinal success rate. Such information looms large in evaluating the success of a program such as OMA&D.

It is also interesting to see how the numbers of degree earners changed between 1970 and 2017. As can be seen in *Figure 5*, the trend was upward for all three categories. Although not shown in this table, the trend was also upward for the general student body. The rates of increase were 1.6, 5.2, 5.4, and 6.5 times the initial numbers for the UW student body, URM students, EOP students, and minority students, respectively. An even more pronounced increase occurred after 2001. This impressive growth rate translated into more than 29,000 EOP degree earners since OMA&D was established. This number represents more than three out five of the students who went through the program.

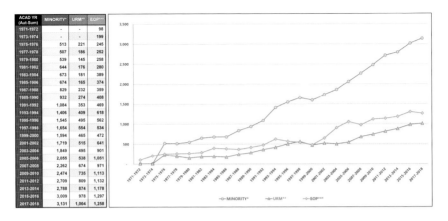

ACAD YR (Aut-Sum)	MINORITY*	URM**	EOP***
1971-1972	-	-	98
1973-1974	-	-	199
1975-1976	513	221	245
1977-1978	507	186	252
1979-1980	539	145	258
1981-1982	644	176	280
1983-1984	673	181	389
1985-1986	674	165	374
1987-1988	829	232	359
1989-1990	932	274	408
1991-1992	1,084	353	469
1993-1994	1,406	409	618
1995-1996	1,545	495	562
1997-1998	1,654	554	534
1999-2000	1,594	465	472
2001-2002	1,719	515	641
2003-2004	1,849	495	901
2005-2006	2,055	538	1,051
2007-2008	2,262	674	971
2009-2010	2,474	735	1,113
2011-2012	2,709	809	1,132
2013-2014	2,788	874	1,178
2015-2016	3,009	978	1,297
2017-2018	3,131	1,004	1,258

Figure 5. Number of students (Seattle campus) Earning Bachelor's Degrees by Group and Year, 1971–2018.

It is important to note that many of those EOP students who left the institution without earning a degree did not leave for academic reasons. Anecdotal evidence shows that students transferred to other institutions where the chance of getting into the major of their choice was greater. Also worthy of note is that some non-EOP students benefited from OMA&D programs designed to serve EOP students. Of those, more than 10,000 earned degrees. The data also show that two out of three of the nearly 20,000 underrepresented minority students (i.e., American Indian/Alaska Native, Black, Latino, and Hawaiian/Pacific Islander) who earned bachelor's degrees from the UW were EOP students.

The breakdown of EOP degree earners by ethnicity shows an interesting picture. The distribution was 2.3% Other, 2.5% Hawaiian/Pacific Islander, 5.7% American Indian/Alaska Native, 8.4% Filipino, 10.1% Caucasian, 17.7% Black, 20.8% Latino, and 32.5% Other Asian. This ethnic/racial distribution, coupled with the fact that most of the degree earners were also economically and educationally disadvantaged (about 70%) and women (58%), is also indicative of inclusivity. Although causality cannot be proven, there appears to be a strong association with these outcomes and the services provided to these students by OMA&D during their undergraduate studies.

The common denominator for the educational attainment of the underrepresented and economically and educationally disadvantaged citizenry of the state of Washington is, indeed, the Office of Minority Affairs &

Diversity. But what did the distribution of majors look like? Were the numbers skewed toward less competitive majors? And, knowing the BSU's original demands called for the establishment of a Black Studies Program, now the American Ethnic Studies (AES) Department, were there a preponderance of EOP degree earners majoring in AES?

The answer to less competitive majors, was yes, but only slightly, and AES ranked ninth among the 50 most popular majors. By category, 17 were in social sciences, 14 were in STEM (science, technology, engineering, math), five were in business, five were in humanities, three were in social services (such as social welfare, social work, and public health), and six were in others.

In terms of numbers, social sciences ranked first with the most popular being sociology; STEM ranked second, with biology being the most popular; and business ranked third, with business administration being the most popular. Social welfare was the most popular major of the "others" category. With funding from the National Science Foundation, the number of degree earners in STEM has doubled since 2008. In addition, the number of degrees earned by EOP students in nursing, public health, environmental health, and environmental studies have increased substantially.

Black Graduation, 2018.

La Raza Graduation, 2010.

Academic Performance

Considering their impressive array of accomplishments, it comes as no surprise that a substantial number of EOP alums graduated with relatively high GPAs. Since 1984, almost 4,000 (one out of seven) graduated with a GPA of 3.5 or higher and more than 14,000 (three out of five) graduated with a 3.0 GPA or higher. For many of these EOP graduates, there is one commonality. They were users of OMA&D services. In fact, four out of five EOP students who entered the UW from high school, and one out of two EOP transfer students, used the IC during their undergraduate years. It is well documented that receiving supplemental instruction, participating in review workshops, and group study are highly associated with users receiving higher grades in biology, chemistry, math, and physics compared to non-IC users. The results of a longitudinal program assessment conducted with data collected from 2001 to 2015 bear this out. EOP students who spent 100 hours per quarter studying in select gateway courses at the IC could expect their grades to increase from 0.2 to 1.2 grade points.

Grade increases were not limited to gateway courses only; in an earlier study using data collected between 1991 and 1999, the findings showed a positive impact on the graduating GPA for EOP students who majored in engineering, natural sciences, and humanities for example. Compared to the EOP non-user cohort, the difference ranged between 0.2 and 0.4 grade points with the largest difference among engineering majors. In general, a higher percentage of EOP IC users graduated with GPAs of 3.0 or better than their non-user counterparts. Furthermore, the findings also showed a high correlation between the number of quarters students who entered from high school received academic support and their graduating GPAs.

The upshot is that academic support delivered by the IC had both a short- and long-term positive effect on the academic performance of its participants. The fact that URM students often *chose* to join the program attests to the effectiveness of services provided, the welcoming atmosphere of the center, and the users' desire to maximize their academic performance, improve their chances of persisting, graduate in the major of their choice, and gain admission to graduate and professional school.

In addition to fostering improved graduation and retention rates among students of color, and thereby helping spread the message across campus that success comes in many colors, there is another aspect of diversity to which the IC has contributed. The IC has given an increasing number of Caucasian students the opportunity to participate in a learning environment where the concentration of underrepresented students is higher than that of almost any class they will attend. These students are encouraged to become active participants in an atmosphere where a highly diverse group of students work together—in study groups, achievement workshops, and review sessions— toward the common goal of maximizing their academic potentials. While many *speak* of the value of studying among a diverse group of people, at the Instructional Center, more and more Caucasian students are having the opportunity to reap the rewards *of doing so.*

Beyond the Bachelor's Degree

For many EOP alumni, educational attainment did not end with a bachelor's degree. More than 2,000 earned graduate and professional degrees at UW Seattle alone. Since 1984 (the year the data was first available electronically) through 2018, EOP alums earned 1,548 master's degrees, 121 juris doctor (JD) degrees, 114 degrees from the Medical School, 108 degrees from the Dental School, 117 degrees from the School of Pharmacy, and 114 doctoral degrees. The five most popular majors for master's degree earners were social work, education, engineering, business, and accounting. The top

Instructional Center Mathematics Drop-In Center, circa 2012.

The IC Delivers

The IC is a place to believe in, not just by students:

- *Administrators from the University of Minnesota were so impressed with what they learned after a campus visit, they went back and changed the name of their academic support unit to the Instructional Center.*

- *According to the OMA&D self-assessment report in 2006, alumni also thought very highly of this program, at a rate of 97%. The following quote by an IC user speaks to the sentiment of many IC users: "IC is more than academic assistance. It is a wonderful supportive environment for minorities seeking a successful and worthwhile experience here at UW."*

- *Select faculty also think highly of the IC. Here is what one said about the center: "The flagship is the IC. What they do is extraordinary. I've worked with a lot of instruction-type centers with athletics in the Big 10 and the Pac 10, and the IC is on a level beyond the best instructional center I've ever seen. They just do incredible work."*

five disciplines for doctoral degree earners were Rehabilitation Medicine, Education, Nursing, Engineering, and Audiology.

What is striking about the areas in which EOP students sought advanced degrees is that they appeared to be degrees geared toward serving humankind in general and their communities in particular. Not only do EOP alumni now have careers in business, engineering, the arts, technology, law, healthcare, and government agencies, they also are leaders in local, state, and international arenas.

In addition to their UW degrees, many EOP students also earned post-baccalaureate degrees from other highly ranked universities, such as Harvard, MIT, Stanford, Pennsylvania, Columbia, Duke, Washington U., Johns Hopkins, Michigan, UC San Francisco, Cornell, Emory, UC Berkeley, NYU, USC, UCLA, UC San Diego, Illinois, Carnegie Mellon, Wisconsin, Texas, and Tulane.

Financial Support

As early as 1971, the first vice president of OMA realized that in addition to the academic and social adjustment challenges underrepresented students faced, college affordability was a key factor in recruitment and retention of EOP students. To address this issue, funds were solicited from faculty, staff, and businesses. In addition, the Friends of the Educational Opportunity Program (FEOP) was established as the fundraising arm. Funds raised have been used to supplement other financial aid awarded to students and to reward EOP students for academic excellence. Since 1973, the Friends of the Educational Opportunity Program has sponsored the Celebration of Excellence banquet in the spring of each year. Over that 45-year period, about 1,400 hundred students were awarded scholarships at the Celebrations. By May 18, 2022, the number will have increased to more than 1,500. Worthy of note is that these scholarship recipients graduated at a rate that was 14 percentage points higher than the rate for the general UW student body.

It should also be noted that the 1,400 awards were just a fraction (less than 10%) of the students who met the eligibility criteria. The number of recipients chosen depended on the availability of dispensable funds. Funding for these scholarships came from revenue generated from three sources.

One source was revenue from sales of tables (of various sponsorship levels) and individual tickets to the annual scholarship dinner attendees. Funds raised at the FEOP Celebration have totaled more than $3.1 million since 2003,

Celebration May 16, 2017

the year a position for fundraising was created for the first time in OMA&D. More positions have been added since and have developed into a team effort led by UW Advancement in partnership with OMA&D. The addition of this team has elevated fundraising to a whole new level.

A second source of scholarship funding is revenue obtained each year from contributions directed toward what is called current-use scholarships.

A third source is interest accrued from endowments.

Parallel to the meteoric rise in the amount of funds raised at Celebration is the tremendous growth in endowments. To date, OMA&D has in its portfolio 55 endowments, the first of which was established in 1987 by a longtime FEOP Board member, Nancy Weber. Twenty-four were added since 2003. The market value of 30 endowments presently exceeds $100,000. Eight endowments were named for OMA&D staff (former and present); four were named for former EOP students; three were named for UW presidents (two former); and two were named for former FEOP Board members. In addition to their dedication and commitment to serving EOP/OMA&D students, four endowments were named for former EOP students, one of which—the Gary D. Kimura Family Endowed EOP Scholarship—is the sixth largest in the OMA&D portfolio. As of this writing, the total market value of the endowment portfolio was $11M which is comparable to several historically Black Colleges and Universities (HBCUs) such as Southern University and A&M College, South Carolina State University, Grambling

Students Fabiola and Ruta on Red Square, October 11, 2013.

"One thing I like about my counselor is that if she can't find solutions for a problem I have, she is going to start calling people, talking to different advisers, doing whatever it takes to find the answer for me."

—unidentified student, 2006 student focus group report

Men Promoting Change, February 13, 2015.

Phi Beta Sigma, Inc Kappa Lambda at Stroll Competition, November 11, 2017.

State University, Mississippi Valley State University, University of Arkansas Pine Bluff, Langston University, and West Virginia State University (National Association of College and University Business Officers, 2016).

Student Satisfaction

To determine the students' level of satisfaction, a survey was administered as part of a self-assessment in 2006. The results revealed that 75 to 85% of the students were very satisfied or satisfied with the services offered by each program, with the EOP Advising/Counseling Center and the Instructional Center garnering the highest ratings, respectively. Also worthy of note is that the academic counselors were rated high on accessibility, approachability, and adaptability to students' schedules (Lange and Gallardo, 2006, p. 56).

Besides survey responses, student focus groups revealed specifically how they felt about what the different programs meant to them. According to the focus group report, one student said: "One thing I like about my counselor is that if she can't find solutions for a problem I have, she is going to start calling people, talking to different advisers, doing whatever it takes to find the answer for me" (p.6). The report also noted that students appreciated the assistance they received in securing scholarships and other means of financial aid.

The focus group study reported that students praised the IC for helping them to succeed in difficult courses and for giving them the confidence that they could be successful in their academic pursuits. One student said: "The IC was my second home the freshman year. I probably couldn't have survived my math classes without it" (p.3). Another student, speaking of the IC, said: "I started living in the IC my sophomore year, and that's when my grades went up. I started leaning on the tutors then and asked them how they did it. Now it is rewarding to have students doing that to me—asking me things and spending time with them to answer their questions. You need the advice of someone who has actually gone through it" (p. 4). Other students noted that working in the IC gave them confidence in their knowledge and abilities, which they were able to take with them into their classrooms (p.4). One student said that involvement in OMA gave her support, even when she was feeling like she was doing badly. Another student said that "... the University was a huge campus and that being involved with OMA made it feel smaller, which was necessary for success" (Snyder and Beyer, 2006, p.4).

MEChA members celebrating, March 6, 2015.

Students celebrating sisterhood, October 21, 2015.

Regarding the social benefits of participation, students also spoke of the 'networking' benefits of getting together with others like themselves. They noted that social networks, such as those developed by participating in OMA programs and services, helped them feel less isolated on a campus

Raven's Feast event, June 14, 2019.

where they always find themselves underrepresented" (p.3). Students also spoke of the ECC as a safe haven. One said:

One of the things I like about the ECC is that I can leave my bag out there in the lounge and no one will touch it. But if you did that in one of the libraries, it would be gone. I feel safer here on the edge.

The research scientist also noted that:

Students pointed to the value of having a place where they could meet new friends and socialize with others who were facing similar issues. Students pointed particularly to the ECC in this regard (p.3).

According to the researchers, one student said:

I think a big part of retention that people don't talk about is the social part of it. It's helped me to be part of the student groups in the ECC. Everyone is looking out for everyone here. I would like it if the whole University of Washington was more like OMA (p.3).

Overall, students thought that OMA programs enhanced their academic development, especially the Bridge program, the Instructional Center, the Ethnic Cultural Center computer lab, the PIPE (Pacific Islander Partnerships in Education) mentoring program, the IMSD (Initiative for Maximizing Student Diversity) program, and the EOP Counseling Center.

Students rally for the Diversity Requirement, April 25, 2013.

CHAPTER 8

Beyond 50 Years (50 Next)

*"How could we have come so far and
yet still have so far to go?"*

—Henry Louis Gates, 2013

The establishment of an organization that would be flexible rather than rigid was required to meet the needs of an ever-changing population. For instance, as the staff became aware of the level of academic preparedness of the early cohorts, academic support went from a cadre of mostly volunteer tutors managed by a tutoring office to a cadre of paid tutors and an appointment-based tutorial center. This grew to the addition of a reading study skills center to address writing, reading, and math skills. These changes led to the merger of the two centers into the Instructional Center, which offered discipline-specific drop-in centers offering workshops, adjunct courses, and exams taught by professional instructors. In addition, the IC began a monitoring system to determine the effectiveness of its support.

In addition, an ethnic cultural center was built and expanded to address social and cultural needs. It was flexible enough to honor space and address students' spiritual needs.

To address changes in admission policies, outreach and recruitment staff intensified their efforts to make sure prospective students not only met core requirements but were aware of the need to take a college prep curriculum, take the SAT/ACT, and to participate in campus visits throughout high school. Grants were also secured to focus on preparing middle school students for college. A bridge program was established to improve the persistence rate of differentially prepared students.

Recognition of the need to supplement students' financial situations led to the securing of federal grants to address the advising, academic support, and graduate school preparation needs of first-generation and low-income students as well as the establishment of an endowment portfolio managed by an advancement group. In addition, a re-entry program for students leaving in good standing, but without a degree—often for financial reasons—was instituted.

The OMA&D, which may not have been established to last long-term, has evolved into an entity markedly different than it was 50 years ago in structure,

Students walk out in support of the Black Lives Matter movement and to address diversity issues on UW campuses and in the greater community, 2015.

but steadfastly similar in its overarching goal of providing educational opportunity to a subset of the state of Washington citizenry—a real and honest opportunity to reach for graduation and the potential of becoming local, regional, national, and global leaders.

Why OMA&D Must Continue Its Work

So why does a program such as the Office of Minority Affairs & Diversity still exist after 50 years? And why should it continue in the future?

Here is how Rusty Barceló, the sixth vice president for OMA and the first vice provost for diversity answered those questions:

People are questioning, talking about reverse discrimination, if there is a need for these programs. And as long as there is any form of discrimination, especially racisms and all the -isms, there's still a need for this office. I think the whole issue of accountability is going to be even more important in the future, with legislators, etcetera, because communities are going to [hold] them [accountable].

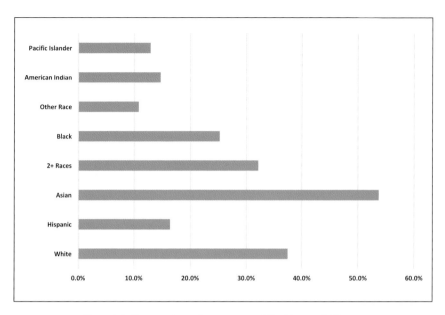

Figure 6: College graduates by race, state of Washington, 2022.

Somehow there's this feeling that diversity is a problem to be solved versus a value to be added. I think the future has to find us positioning these programs, not as a political right, but as an educational objective for the institution. This needs to be seen as [a] national imperative in the next 10 years. This is the reality of this country, of the world. That it is a diverse world. And if ever there was a need for these kinds of programs, it's now, because it's about training all people to do this work. I would argue, and I just said this at a meeting with a group of presidents, that we all need to be multiculturalists if we're going to be successful for the rest of this century.

There are gaps in academic performance in gateway courses, retention and graduation rates, and STEM participation/degree attainment between URM and economically and educationally disadvantaged (EED) students and the general UW population. The gap is even wider when the comparison is made between URM/EED students and white and Asian students. This educational outcome, coupled with an educational attainment gap as high as 41 percentage points (see *Figure 6*) between URM racial groups compared to that of non-

URM groups, is profound. It is indicative of the fact that much work is needed to achieve incremental gains. It goes without saying that if parity was not reached in the last 50 years, it is not unreasonable to believe many more years will be required to achieve the desired outcome.

The Elusive Critical Mass

We must not let up when it comes to recruitment and convincing prospective URM students that this predominantly white institution is committed to achieving a critical mass of each URM group on campus. One definition of "critical mass" is as follows: "A 'critical mass' of students from a distinct racial or ethnic group means a sufficient number to represent a variety of points of view and to avoid such small numbers as might create a sense of isolation" (Student diversity in recruitment, 2004). This sense of isolation is exacerbated when members of these groups are enrolled in classes where their representation is extremely low, especially in gateway courses to STEM and pre-professional majors.

A reasonable target to aim for might be the percentage of URM students comparable to that of the state population of 18- to 24-year-olds. However,

Professor Ralina Joseph moderates a UWAA lecture panel of Emile Pitre, Verlaine Keith-Miller, Larry Gossett, Sharon Maeda, and Rogelio Riojas, May 17, 2017.

Kids MLK Day at the UW, 2003.

as the definition suggests, it may be necessary to aim for percentages higher than those that exist in the state for groups with relatively small populations to begin with. What is the current status of this representation? Presently, the proportion is 26% as can be determined from the 2020 US Census. According to UW demographics, the proportion of URM undergraduates enrolled at UW Seattle is 16%, which translates into an enrollment success rate of 62%, or a gap of ten percentage points. If the institution were being rated, as one agency has done, the conclusion would be that the institution falls 22 percentage points below the top quartile for success in terms of minority student access (The Education Trust, 2010). At some point, the admission process will need to be revisited and reimagined.

In terms of outreach and recruitment, the strategies that have proven successful are robust pre-college initiatives that began as early as middle school and continued throughout high school. Such initiatives endeavor to make students aware of college while at the same time provide them and their families with information and contacts to help them make every effort at being college ready. One aspect of this approach is campus visits, where prospective students meet students who look like them and learn firsthand what college

Chinoso Opara (center) and Teri Ward at the McNair/EIP 22nd Annual Pacific Northwest Spring Research Conference, May 2014.

life is like, participate in campus tours, and observe college classes in session. Learning—about the admission process, about what they can do to improve their chances of being admitted, as well as learning about the wide range of support that is available to them—is crucial. Once admitted, students who are likely to have multiple offers from other universities can be invited to campus to meet select administrators, faculty, staff, and students who will share with them the many benefits of attending this world-class university.

These efforts have so far resulted in incremental progress toward closing the enrollment gap for incoming freshman cohorts over the past 17 years and have led to a corresponding increase in the proportion of URM enrollees in the undergraduate population. These gains are encouraging, but it is important to point out that more than one out of three URM high school students who were *admitted* to the UW chose not to *enroll*. We know that one of the reasons for not enrolling is that other institutions offer more competitive financial aid packages. Not only is the low enrollment yield counter to closing the enrollment gap, but since a large number of potential enrollees are high achieving, choosing not to enroll is also counter to closing the degree attainment gap in STEM majors. Increasing the number of merit scholarships and the implementation

IC Chemistry Drop-In Center

of an innovative marketing plan will require a concerted campus wide effort led by OMA&D.

Another critical mass issue is that of URM faculty in general and particularly in STEM departments campus wide. It can be argued that not only will retention in these departments improve, but so will the retention rates of URM. Student satisfaction will be positively impacted as well. Greater representation of URM faculty and administrators, more mentors, and role models' availability will be needed to enhance their college experience. In essence, the university must be unwavering in its efforts to remove the barriers to diversity in the faculty and administrative ranks.

The STEM Challenge

One can argue that increased degree attainment in STEM majors as well as in other high-demand majors will have a direct effect, not only on increasing diversity in the workforce but will also lead to closing the wealth gap between communities of color and white and Asian communities, thus improving the state's economy (Long, 2017). As can be seen in *Figure 7*, the income GAP is as high as $55,000 for URM families.

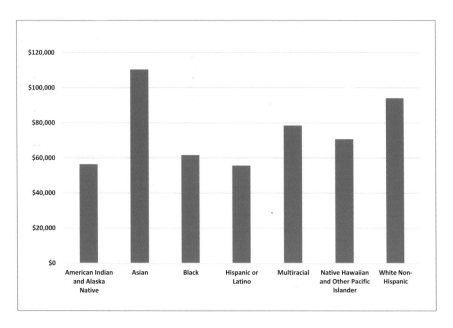

Figure 7: Median income by race, state of Washington, 2022.

At the time of this writing, STEM degree attainment for URM students at UW Seattle increased from 4% to 8% since 2008; a gap of at least six percentage points remains (Knaphus-Soran, et al., 2018).

Closing the STEM participation/degree attainment gap for URM is perhaps the most challenging task, since high academic performance in gateway courses combined with a high cumulative GPA is an essential requirement. Thus, proper course sequencing, course load balance, hours spent studying and preparing for quizzes and exams are critical. For URM students, of whom four out of five are EOP, it is imperative that advising (both professional and peer) and academic support provided by highly committed, dedicated, and credentialed staff, are available, especially for the first two years. Good preparation in the first two years is especially needed to improve students' chances of acceptance into STEM and other high demand majors, such as business and nursing. This entails proper course sequences, frequent use of academic support services, intrusive advising, implementation of early warning system, and mentoring for success. For more than 40 years, the OMA&D family of programs have provided such support.

One strategy that has proven most effective is the implementation of supplemental instruction in introductory biology, chemistry, math, and physics courses. Instructors have begun to use learning science research findings to improve services. Use of technology to reach a wider swath of students should also be considered. To a lesser extent, collaborating with select faculty on teaching and learning strategies has been welcomed and appreciated but more is needed. One example is partnering of select OMA&D instructional staff with faculty in the Department of Biology to determine whether a change in teaching strategy might close the substantial achievement gap between EOP and non-EOP students enrolled in introductory biology.

Academic performance data that led to the idea to conduct the experiment was initially mined and analyzed by OMA&D staff. The results showed that disproportionately lower grades were being earned in many gateway courses. The findings from the experiment were that while all students' grades improved when intense practice and active learning activities replaced lectures EOP/EDD students' grades improved even more, thus narrowing the academic performance gap (Haak, et al., 2011). Use of studies such as this one to examine how low academic performance in specific introductory courses could determine whether students will either continue or discontinue their pursuit of a STEM/high demand major are important, especially when the results are used to modify the way in which these bottleneck courses are taught.

Closing Educational Outcome Gaps

As is indicated by the data, OMA&D has played a critical role in leading the effort that has resulted in marked improvement of educational outcomes for underrepresented students at the UW. Thus, OMA&D's continued leadership and programmatic best practices will be needed to reach parity and ensure sustainability. If projections by the Western Interstate Commission for Higher Education are accurate, the demographics of high school graduates will undergo a dramatic shift over the next 10 to 15 years. The increase in the number of URM graduates from Washington state public high schools is projected to be one-and-a-half times larger than it was in 2016. One out of every three graduates will be an underrepresented minority by 2027–2028 (Bransberger & Michelau, 2016). Furthermore, based on Washington State data covering 10 years, it is estimated that at least one out of two of these

EOP Spring Recognition Ceremony Awardees, May 4, 2017.

graduates will come from low-income families (Washington Office of the Superintendent of Public Instruction). A ripple effect will no doubt carry over to the incoming freshman classes at UW over that 10- to 15-year period. The strategies and interventions that have proven effective in the past will need to be scaled and modified to address the needs of this larger and more internally diverse population.

Based on the in-depth analysis of retention and graduation rates of EOP students, one can conclude that up to this point, OMA&D has done an admirable job in facilitating gap closures. Intervention strategies that provide a blueprint for success include: an orientation program where students are told in no uncertain terms that they are expected to graduate; opportunities for social/cultural/leadership development; mentoring; holistic advising; peer advising; intrusive advising; programming to provide support to unique population subsets; comprehensive academic support; increased funds earmarked for current use scholarships; a re-entry program for stop outs; freshman retention scholarships; a substantial endowment portfolio coupled with a long-standing institutional commitment; and effective partnering with the Office of Admissions. All of these factors effected these positive outcomes. It is important to emphasize that best practices that have emerged out of the efforts of the OMA&D family of programs should be acknowledged and selectively adopted campus wide.

Ever a Concerted Effort

Ideally, OMA&D, working in tandem with Undergraduate Academic Affairs, Student Life, as well as with administrators, select faculty, and staff across all three UW campuses, will positively affect the lives of students and their learning, *while at the same time* completely close disparity gaps. This is especially important for URM males, whose retention and graduation rates are lower than those of URM females. In other words, the strategies and interventions employed would need to have a disproportionately positive effect (logarithmic vs. linear) on the educational outcomes of all EOP/EED students.

To push success forward, all hands must be on deck. This means the entire University, with a cadre of programs and committed and dedicated individuals leading the way, must strive to ensure that the environment for all students is welcoming and supportive. OMA&D has a long history of delivering positive results, despite what seemed to be insurmountable odds. The leadership is in place. The next step is complete involvement of key schools and colleges as well as key administrative offices. The unabashed commitment to diversity and inclusion by the Board of Regents is a must. Staying ever vigilant in pursuit of faculty diversity is a must as well. Community engagement and accountability must also be a part of the equation. Transparency, accountability, and responsibility should be the rallying cry!

Paul Fletcher, Marie Hall-McMurtrie, Carmelita Adkins, Garry Owens, William Daniel Keith, William Jackson (left to right).

Black Graduation, June 8, 2018.

Acknowledgments

This project began in May 2015 when Sheila Edwards Lange, at the time Vice President and Vice Provost for Minority Affairs and Diversity, appointed me to lead an effort to write a book about the rich history of the program that has endured for almost five decades. I am grateful that she opted to do so.

I am also grateful for the preliminary work done on the book project by Quin'Nita Cobbins, who at the time was a graduate student in the History Department at the University of Washington. Her work heavily influenced how the body of the manuscript for this book is organized. Her unpublished paper entitled "History of the Office of Minority Affairs & Diversity, 1968-present" was written in 2013.

I was very fortunate that Antoinette Wills, a historian by training, and one who is well versed in searching the archives to elicit invaluable information, chose to work with me pro bono. As one whose background is in the natural sciences, I had no idea how to go about conducting this type of research. Antoinette not only guided me along the way but collected valuable information through research she conducted throughout the process. Part of this undertaking was to conduct oral history interviews to supplement and complement information gleaned from searching through many boxes of documents at UW Libraries Special Collections. Once the interviews were done, Antoinette laboriously and systematically sifted through each recording and created a spelling guide for the transcribers to facilitate the transcription. She then edited each document and created a cover page with a vignette about the interviewee and a summary of the interview. These transcripts now reside in the UW Libraries Special Collections. I am also indebted to Antoinette for the countless hours she contributed and for graciously volunteering to edit and format the manuscript.

Antoinette also introduced me to John Bolcer and Lisa Oberg, University of Washington librarians and archivists whose expertise and willingness to help is very much appreciated. John Bolcer played a key role in this project by providing the personnel to transcribe 22 interviews. Thank you, Adrienne Antonsen and Joseph Hopkins, for the outstanding job done transcribing the audio recordings.

I am also grateful to the following individuals who participated in the oral history interviews: Rogelio Riojas, Bill Hilliard, Larry Gossett, Sheila Edwards Lange, Rusty Barceló, Myron Apilado, Herman Lujan, Raul Anaya, June Hairston, Enrique Morales, Larry Matsuda, Gabriel Gallardo, Nori Mihara, Tim Washburn, Steve Garcia, Jim Morley, Karen Morell, Adrienne Chan, Lette Hadgu, Rickey Hall, Mike Tulee, and Tekie Mehary. This book would not be a reality without their participation. Brief biographies of the interviewees are included in the Sources section of this book.

A huge thank you goes out to select founding members of the 1968 Black Student Union (BSU), including Carl Miller, Eddie Demmings, Emanuel James "E.J." Brisker, Jr., Verlaine Keith-Miller, Kathleen Halley, Marcie Hall-McMurtrie, Carmelita Laducer Adkins, Eddie Ray Walker, Garry Owens, and Jesus (Jesse) Crowder. They gave me valuable feedback and played a critical role in filling in gaps and perspectives only they could have provided. I am especially grateful to Carl Miller for providing information about the roles various individuals played in the movement and identifying the contents of many photos, some of which appear in the book. A special thank you goes out to Eddie Demmings for his timely quotes and his critical analysis of the contents of various chapters.

I am also deeply indebted to Jimmy Garrett, cofounder of the first BSU in America, for the historical background he provided and for the critical role he played in the development of the entity that changed the face of the UW campus for many years to come.

Thank you to Robby Stern, 1968 president of Students for a Democratic Society (SDS) at the UW, for sharing the white student activists' perspective on the Black student movement on the UW campus and for his and other members' support leading up to and during the 1968 sit-in/occupation described in Chapter I.

I would like to especially thank Arlyn Arquiza for the data that went into creating the graphs and charts in this manuscript. Since 1998, this highly competent colleague has summarized numerous data points facilitating my ability to present strong evidence of the positive impact the Office of Minority Affairs & Diversity family of programs has had on thousands of participants.

I am truly grateful for the unwavering support and encouragement of my wife, Barbara McCants-Pitre who believes there is nothing that I cannot do if I put my mind to it. That faith and confidence in me has been a source of inspiration for four decades.

Without the support of Sheila Edwards Lange and Rickey Hall, who succeeded Sheila as Vice President for Minority Affairs, the opportunity to share this story would not have come to fruition. For that I am eternally grateful.

And last but not least, I wish to thank those who denied my request for assistance, delayed an opportunity to publish sooner, and the detractors who wanted to see us fail. Resistance builds strength and character and fuels the desire to prevail.

—*Emile Pitre*

OMA&D History Timeline

Before 1968: Setting the Stage

1959. President Charles Odegaard issues a memorandum regarding the UW affording equal opportunity to students, faculty, staff, and administrators regardless of race, creed, or color.

1960. Student Nonviolent Coordinating Committee (SNCC) emerges out of an organized Southern Christian Leadership Conference youth conference.

1961. E.J. Brisker joins SNCC, where he becomes an ardent participant and a skilled organizer.

1963. UW President Odegaard and Board of Regents members notice visible lack of Blacks at 1963 Commencement and call for faculty to address this tragedy.

1964. E.J. Brisker meets Jimmy Garrett while working in SNCC.

1965. Dr. Odegaard establishes a Committee on Special Educational Programs, appointing Dr. Eugene Elliot Director of Special Educational Programs.

1966. Educational Opportunity Programs are implemented at University of California Berkeley and University of California Santa Barbara to encourage low-income and minority students with recruitment, admissions, financial aid, tutoring, counseling, and advising programs.

Bill Somerville, first director of EOP at Cal Berkeley, coins phrase "educational opportunity."

UW Department of Education funds an Upward Bound program to prepare low income and first-generation high school students for college.

At the behest of students at Seattle Central Community College, led by Carl Miller, SNCC headquarters sends E.J. Brisker to Seattle to help organize a group called SNCC Freedom Riders.

Afro-American Student Society is founded at the UW to initiate dialogue between Black UW students and African students. According to Larry Gossett, a founding member, there were 63 Black students on campus in 1963 when he entered the UW.

Larry Gossett leaves UW after two years of undergraduate to join VISTA (Volunteers in Service to America) and returns to Seattle 18 months later with a consciousness embracing the Black struggle in the US and of third world people in America and abroad.

The first Black Student Union is founded by Jimmy Garrett, Jerry Varnado, and Tom Williams at San Francisco State College (now University) with a focus of recruiting Black students to college.

1967. A white student group brings SNCC chairman Stokely Carmichael to speak at the UW. E.J. Brisker and Carl Miller help get Carmichael to speak at Garfield High School. It is a defining moment for Black UW students as well as many members of the Black community in Seattle.

Fourteen Black students from the Upward Bound program enroll at UW, bringing the total number of Black students to 150.

A group of Seattle and Tacoma students travel to Los Angeles during Thanksgiving weekend to attend a youth conference organized by a UCLA group and then return inspired to organize BSUs at middle schools, high schools, and college campuses. They are also charged by group leadership to establish an ethnic cultural center and a Black Studies program, as well as recruit Black students, faculty, and staff.

1968: The Black Student Union leads a protest that begins to transform the University.

1968. On January 6, about a month after returning from the youth conference in L.A., a vote is taken by some members of the UW Afro-American Student Society to establish the Black Student Union. Modeled on the BSU at San Francisco State, it is focused on recruiting Black students to the UW campus in Seattle.

On April 26, 1968, the UW chapter of Students for a Democratic Society (SDS), led by Robby Stern, demands admission requirements for Black students be waived until the proportion enrolled at UW equals the proportion of Black casualties in Vietnam, and likewise for Black faculty and staff.

Jimmy Garrett, former SNCC Freedom Rider, co-founder of the BSU at San Francisco State, and national Black Panther Minister of Education, speaks on the Black Struggle at a symposium on the UW campus, April 25–27.

On May 6, the BSU submits a letter to President Odegaard containing a list of five demands.

The BSU leadership votes to stage a sit-in at the Administration Building.

On May 20 at 4:50 p.m., a group of students led by the BSU crashes a Faculty Senate Executive Committee meeting and Dr. Odegaard agrees to the demands after four hours of negotiations.

BSU president E.J. Brisker is invited by Dr. Charles Evans, Chair of the Faculty Senate, to speak at the full Faculty Senate meeting on May 23rd and receives a standing ovation.

On June 3, returning UW student Bill Hilliard is hired to coordinate the recruitment of minority and economically disadvantaged students to attend the University. He hires eight UW student recruiters.

In the fall, the Special Education Program, under the direction of Dr. Charles Evans, is established to recruit and support the 257 minority and disadvantaged students admitted to the University under special admission criteria.

Autumn Quarter enrollment at the UW includes 465 Blacks, 100+ American Indians, and 90+ Mexican Americans, including students in the Special Education Program and students who are not part of SEP.

1969. Students from the Asian Coalition for Equality (ACE), supported by a group of minority students and members of the Asian community, confront Dr. Charles Evans demanding that Filipinos and needy Asians be recruited and be allowed to participate in the Special Education Program (SEP). Dr. Evans agrees to the demands.

A Policy Advisory Board of twelve faculty, eight students, and one non-academic staff member is appointed by President Odegaard to provide policy guidance to administrators of the Special Education Program.

1970s: "Dr. Sam" Kelly Builds the Foundation for the Office of Minority Affairs. During his tenure, staffing grew from 10 to 60 people, the budget grew from $50,000 to just under $2 million, and EOP enrollment grew from 882 to 2,633 (a nearly 300% increase).

1970. June 1, 1970, Samuel E. Kelly assumes the role of vice president for the new Office of Minority Affairs (OMA). The name "Special Education Program" is changed to the "Educational Opportunity Program."

1971. Vice President Kelly forms a relationship with Dean Philip Cartwright of the College of Arts and Sciences to recruit and support minority graduate and professional students.

Herman McKinney is named special assistant to the vice president for minority affairs and assistant dean of the Graduate School.

Vice President Kelly establishes the Friends of the Educational Opportunity Program (FEOP) to serve as community advisors and to raise private funds to make college more affordable for economically disadvantaged students. The first annual EOP Scholarship Fund Drive is launched.

Sam Kelly proposes the mechanics of EOP admissions be assigned to the Office of the Vice President for Minority Affairs.

Vice President Kelly establishes the Student Advisory Board, composed of three student representatives from each ethnic student division, to advise the Vice President for Minority Affairs on issues concerning their constituents and to share the VP's position on these issues.

The Reading Study Skills Center is established to complement existing OMA Tutorial Center offerings to address the academic needs of EOP students entering the University.

Biology professor Dr. Leonie Piternick develops a course to assist EOP students in learning the biological sciences and conducts workshops at the Reading Study Skills Center.

Vice President Kelly is successful in getting UW Athletics to donate revenue from the seasons' 11th football game to the OMA budget. The 11th football game is prominent among the fundraising activities of the FEOP.

1972. The Upward Bound Program moves from the College of Arts and Sciences to the OMA. Funding for the program continues through 1976.

Both the Ethnic Cultural Center and Ethnic Cultural Theater open for business, marking the first such centers in the country to have a multi-ethnic focus.

Funding is garnered and the Resident Release Project is launched to help a select group of men make the transition from prison to education for employment.

1973. Dr. Charles Odegaard is honored at the second annual FEOP meeting in April and the Charles Odegaard Award is established at a dinner.

The 1973 Celebration is the first that honors the achievements of OMA students.

1974. The Asian and Poverty Student divisions are reorganized into the Asian Student Division, directed by Michael Castillano, and the Economically Disadvantaged Student Division, supervised by Judy Carr.

1975. The Board of Regents issues a formal policy statement at its January 13th meeting upholding its commitment of access to higher education by minority and disadvantaged groups.

Larry Gossett receives the first Charles Odegaard Award "Unity" sculpture created by noted artist George Tsutakawa.

OMA undergoes a budget cut for the first time due to legislative cutbacks.

1976. A three-quarter physics sequence is added to help prepare EOP students for physical sciences prerequisites. Professor Lillian McDermott leads this effort.

Dr. Sam Kelly resigns as Vice President for Minority Affairs.

Dr. Ewaugh Fields is named the second vice president for minority affairs, but resigns after seven months due to, among other things, resistance from OMA staff to a plan to reorganize the ethnic student divisions.

1977. Steps are taken to professionalize the instructional staff at the Reading Study Skills Center.

Of the approximately 6,800 EOP students who have attended the University, 1,100 have graduated with either a BA or graduate degree.

Following Dr. Fields' resignation, President Hogness names an ad hoc committee to evaluate the Educational Opportunity Program. Hubert Locke, vice provost for academic affairs, is named committee chair.

The EOP Instructional Center is created from the merger of the Tutorial Center and the Reading Study Skills Center. J. Nathan Ward is named founding director.

1978. Dr. Herman Lujan from the University of Kansas is appointed the third vice president for minority affairs.

To date, the Friends of EOP organization has raised $670,000.

UW MEChA occupies the Chicano Student Division of the OMA and organizes a sickout to protest the proposed reorganization of the EOP.

A four-to-six-week summer bridge program is proposed to give underprepared EOP students an early start on managing the rigors of the university curriculum.

Dr. Millie Russell, a faculty member in the biology department and later a key OMA&D staff member, joins the board of the Friends of EOP.

1979. Following a review of the US Supreme Court's Bakke decision, which affected affirmative action programs based on race, the UW Board of Regents reissues a policy statement emphasizing the importance in any educational program of the exchange of information and life experiences through a culturally diverse student body, with special attention paid to traditionally underrepresented constituencies, including minority groups and women applicants who have been the objects of past societal discrimination.

Prison Education Program, directed by Karen Morell, is established to conduct research and report findings on the Resident Release Project.

Contrary to popular belief that nearly all admittees enrolled, 1974–1978 data showed only one out of two students admitted through EOP actually enrolled: for Asian students, three out of four enrolled.

An EOP Admissions Office is established to process admissions application received by each ethnic student division and to handle financial aid matters, instead of having ethnic student divisions handle this work. Dr. Mira Sinco is named first director.

Selected staff from the ethnic student divisions are organized into an Academic Counseling Center unit with Elaine Miller serving as the first director. This newly formed unit is ethnic specific.

The President's Achievement Award is established by the FEOP in honor of UW President John Hogness.

The Vice President's Achievement Award is established.

The CR Merriwether Scholarship Award for a junior class student of Architecture, Engineering, or Urban Planning is established for Celebration 1979.

1980s: Vice President Herman Lujan Leads OMA through a decade of change and turbulence.

1980. On May 21, 1980, Chicano and Asian students occupy the office of Vice

President Lujan in protest of the implementation of admission requirements for EOP students. More than 70 students are arrested.

On June 4th, Vice President Lujan is burned in effigy on Red Square by student protesters.

Responding to claims that the University was attempting to get rid of OMA, UW President William Gerberding reiterates his commitment to the EOP and to minority admission to the University.

President Gerberding creates a task force to review EOP admissions practices which concludes the University should keep the OMA and its programs.

Universal Placement Testing is implemented to provide informed placement of EOP students in introductory math and writing composition courses, and to address math and English deficiencies.

The Special Services for Disadvantaged Students Program is established to provide counseling and instructional support for first-generation and low-income students. Fall orientation sessions and regular workshops and presentations are offered.

1981. OMA loses the authority to admit some students who qualified academically for regular admission and the EOP becomes a special admit program. Enrollment for Group I students went from 1,475 in 1980 to 662 in 1983, a 55% decrease.

1982. After 12 years, the ethnic student divisions are reorganized into a single, multicultural academic counseling unit.

Biology professor Dr. Millie Russell is appointed special assistant to the vice president for minority affairs to serve as liaison to Health Sciences, the Biology Program, and the Black Professional community.

The Resident Release Project loses its funding from the Department of Corrections and is discontinued.

1983. The Upward Bound Program returns to OMA with a grant from the Department of Education, with Karen Morell serving as director.

2,855 students have earned degrees since the EOP was founded in 1970.

1984. The OMA and selected community colleges establish the Community College Transition Program

The Universal Placement test is implemented for all students to determine proper placement of students in courses.

The inaugural Instructional Center Tutor Recognition Ceremony is held to recognize contributions made by peer tutors.

1985. Educational Talent Search is established to provide specialized support to first-generation and low-income junior high and high school students.

1986. The first EOP Student Recognition Ceremony is held to highlight the outstanding accomplishments EOP freshman and transfer students.

1987. Modeled on a program at the University of California Irvine, the Early Outreach Program is established to support underrepresented and other disadvantaged Middle School students and their parents through increased awareness of college opportunities and early preparation.

1988. The State Higher Education Coordinating Board (HECB) establishes a new admission policy for all state colleges and universities based on an Admission Index. The index is used to predict the probability of students earning a C average at the end of their freshman year, allowing for 15% of the entering class to be admitted by an alternative criterion (special admits).

The EOP Admissions Policy Committee classifies Filipinos, Pacific Islanders, and some Southeast Asian subgroups such as Cambodian and Laotian, as underrepresented and establishes a policy to refer inadmissible Washington State applicants to the Community College Transition Program to improve their academic deficiencies.

Dr. Herman Lujan resigns from OMA to take a position in the UW Provost's office. Over his ten-year tenure, the biennial budget grew from 2 million to $3,038,641.

1989. Dr. Robert Pozos is named the fourth vice president for minority affairs, his tenure lasting just one year.

The EOP Counseling and Advising Services undergoes a transformation from ethnic specific advising to a multiethnic model.

The OMA and the UW Alumni Association launch a mentoring program for EOP entering freshmen.

The FEOP establishes the Athletic Award to recognize the achievement of a scholar athlete.

1990: Under Vice President Myron Apilado, OMA grows and matures. Educational outcomes and student graduation rates improve, and private support increases.

1990. Dr. Myron Apilado is named the fifth Vice President for Minority Affairs.

1991. UW TRIO Training is established to train TRIO program staff across the country in the effective use of technology.

The EOP Scholarship Fund becomes an endowed fund.

1992. The Early Identification Program (EIP) holds the first undergraduate research conference at the UW.

1993. The Samuel E. Kelly Endowed Scholarship is established.

1994. The Multicultural Alumni Partnership (MAP) is founded by Larry Matsuda and Vivian O. Lee to support the EOP and to take a leadership role in addressing issues of equality and equity through mentoring, lectures, and reaching out to the university community.

1995. OMA and the Classics Department establish the Rome program for EOP students to study abroad.

The Office of Undergraduate Education and the OMA launch a three-week Bridge Program designed to provide the most at-risk students a head start on their academic pursuits.

1996. OMA, Seattle Public Schools, and the College of Education collaborate to establish the Ida B. Wells High School, an alternative Middle College program for students who may otherwise not graduate from high school.

1997. A statistical analysis by an IC instructor and a graduate student determines there exists a positive correlation between IC workshop participation in selected math courses and grades earned.

After 29 years of operating a two-tier admission system, all undergraduate applications are now required to be submitted to the UW Office of Admissions. Race can still be considered as one factor for admission.

1998. The IC is invited to be one of the honoraria (paid) presenters at a conference entitled "Mentoring for the 21st Century" at Louisiana State University, Baton Rouge.

A longitudinal study is conducted by the IC to determine if a correlation exists between frequency of IC use in selected 100 level and 200 level chemistry courses and grades earned. Results showed frequent use of the IC in nine different chemistry courses could increase students' GPA in these courses 0.1 to 0.8 grade points.

Over the fiscal year, gifts to EOP/OMA totaled $355,957, an all-time high.

Funded by the US Department of Education, the UW's GEAR UP initiative is launched in the Yakima Valley to break the cycle of poverty and low educational achievement pervasive throughout Central Washington.

The Student Advisory Board plays a key role in convincing the University to remodel the existing Ethnic Cultural Center and securing funding for a computer lab in the facility.

1999. Seattle Early Scholars Outreach GEAR UP (Gaining Early Awareness and Readiness for Undergraduate Programs) is established to enhance middle school student readiness in communities historically not pursuing higher education.

In response to the passage of Initiative 200, the Student Ambassador Outreach Program is established to enhance recruitment efforts of underrepresented minority students in Washington. This and other outreach and recruitment efforts are substantially funded by UW President Richard McCormick.

Minority Think Tank creates EMPOWER (Encouraging Minority People to Overcome with Education and Respect) to prepare underrepresented high school students with leadership potential to express their perception of social justice, reflect on multiculturalism, and prepare for their transition to college.

The McNair Program, funded by the US Department of Education, is created to prepare low-income college students for doctoral programs through research and other scholarly activities.

The EOP Affiliates Initiative is implemented to ensure underrepresented minority students and economically and educationally disadvantaged students would still be eligible for support from OMA&D programs.

2000s: Vice President Rusty Barceló expands OMA's role in the academic life of the UW. University-wide leadership in diversity is added to OMA's mission and name.

2000. Partnerships for a Seamless Education, an outreach program across the state of Washington is established.

The Minority Think Tank student group, the OMA, Board of Regents, and the UW president partner to provide mentoring tools through the EMPOWER program to help students become leaders.

2001. The OMA Instructional Center becomes the first minority program to receive a University Recognition Award, winning the Brotman Award for Instructional Excellence and the Brotman Award for Diversity. Two recognition awards in one year by one program is also a first.

Dr. Nancy "Rusty" Barceló from the University of Minnesota is named the sixth vice president for minority affairs.

The Curriculum Transformation Program, initiated with a Ford Foundation grant in the 1990s, is annexed by the OMA.

A residential Summer Bridge Program for Term B is established in partnership with the Office of Undergraduate Education.

Essence of Success, an outreach effort to recruit Black high school students with high academic potential to the UW, is established.

A senior vice provost visiting from the University of Michigan declares the IC a jewel in the crown of the UW and a model for all higher education to follow.

2002. Vice President Barceló reorganizes administrative units emphasizing assessment, strategic planning, program efficiency, and new initiatives.

The Student Outreach Ambassador Program receives the Brotman Award for Diversity.

2003. Vice Provost for Diversity is added to VP Barceló's responsibilities, with emphasis on the academic side of the University as it relates to diversity. The OMA becomes the Office of Minority Affairs & Diversity (OMA&D).

A director of development position for OMA&D is created. The Development Office's George Zeno adds OMA&D to his fundraising portfolio.

Shaping Your Future is implemented to increase the number of admitted underrepresented minority students to select the UW for enrollment.

The Health Sciences Center Minority Student Program becomes part of OMA&D.

2004. OMA&D creates Welcome Daze to increase EOP student and parent participation in the Autumn Quarter Dawg Daze activities, especially Freshman Convocation, to introduced them to continuing students, OMA&D staff, faculty, and administrators, as well as student and campus groups.

OMA&D participates in a campus-wide advising self-study resulting in recommendations that the OMA&D advising model be adopted by undergraduate advising and that EOP advising relocate to Mary Gates Hall where other undergraduate academic advisers are located.

2005. The Samuel E. Kelly Distinguished Faculty Lecture is established. Professor Quintard Taylor, holder of the Scott and Dorothy Bullitt Chair of American History, delivers the inaugural address.

The Diversity Scholars Program is transferred to OMA&D.

2006. OMA&D and Office of Educational Assessment (OEA) conduct a self-assessment to identify areas of strength, concern, obstacles that prevent OMA&D from working effectively; gauge how well organizational and program goals are being met; and evaluate the expansion of vice provost components.

OMA&D and OEA conduct the UW Study of Attrition and Retention to understand the causes of URM retention patterns.

2007. Dr. Sheila Edwards Lange becomes the seventh vice president for Minority Affairs and the second vice provost for Diversity and strengthens OMA&D's leadership role in making diversity central to campus life, using assessment as a basis for policy and program growth.

UWTV produces a documentary "In Pursuit of Social Justice," an oral history of the early years of diversity efforts at the UW. The documentary wins a Silver Telly and an honorable mention for videography at the 28th Annual Telly Awards.

Community and Public Relations unit is established as part of OMA&D.

2008. OMA&D administration begins to centralize services to undergraduate students by relocating from Schmitz Hall to Mary Gates Hall.

OMA&D receives the Multicultural Alumni Partnership's Samuel E. Kelly Award for outstanding contributions to diversity and educational opportunity.

2009. OMA&D becomes the manager of a National Science Foundation funded program, the Louis Stokes Alliance for Minority Participation, to help double the number of underrepresented minority students earning STEM degrees.

Washington Mathematics Engineering Science Achievement (MESA) joins the OMA&D family of programs after 30 years in the College of Engineering.

Staff Diversity Specialist is transferred to OMA&D.

Gifts to EOP/0MA total $513,889 over the fiscal year, the largest amount to date.

2010. The Department of Education funds a College Assistance Migrant Program providing support to migrant farm worker families in the state.

OMA&D Academic Counseling Services and the EIP/McNair programs move from the third floor of Schmitz Hall to Mary Gates Hall.

OMA&D announces the funding of a program (SSS-STEM) by the US Department of Education to assist low-income and first-generation students in pursuing majors in the sciences.

FEOP Legacy Endowed Scholarship is established.

UW Champions Program is established to serve foster care youth and alumni.

2011. OMA&D assessment unit generates the first of its kind data packet for the Board of Regents titled "Diversity at the University of Washington–All Campuses."

Study abroad programs in Ghana, Barbados, and Australia open for EOP students.

2012. Upward Bound Math-Science is established with US Department of Education grant funding to prepare first-generation and low-income high school students for STEM majors.

A Middle School Outreach program is established.

2013. Study abroad in Iceland opens to EOP students.

A new Ethnic Cultural Center Building, three times the space of the original, opens as the Samuel E. Kelly Ethnic Cultural Center.

2014. Funds raised at the 2014 Celebration reach an all-time high, totaling $300,000.

2015. Forty years after it was first proposed, wəɫəbʔaltxʷ—Intellectual House—opens for use by Native students and tribal communities, as well as UW campus entities.

Study Abroad in Spain opens to EOP students.

Sheila Edwards Lange resigns to become the interim president of Seattle Central College and Gabriel Gallardo is appointed interim vice president and vice provost.

OMA&D partners with UW's School of Medicine Center for Health Equity, Diversity and Inclusion (CEDI), and the School of Dentistry, and secures funds from the US DHHS to create the Health Profession Academy for disadvantaged undergraduate students aspiring to be physicians and dentists.

2016. Rickey L. Hall is appointed the eighth vice president of OMA&D and University Diversity Officer for all three campuses.

The OMA&D Multicultural Outreach Recruitment unit is credited with bringing in the most diverse incoming class in the UW's history.

2017. The Department of Education funds an Upward Bound Program (under the auspices of OMA&D) to serve Kent-Meridian high school low-income students and students who will be the first in their families to graduate college.

2018. Studio Matthews is commissioned to create the OMA&D 50th Anniversary Historical Exhibition, "Revolution and Evolution" which is displayed in the Allen Library for six weeks.

The Black Student Union at UW Seattle establishes an endowed scholarship "to provide financial support for its members who are committed to social justice or are doing work in underrepresented communities."

Appendix A
BSU Reading List

Before the Mayflower – Lerone Bennett

The Militant Black Writer in Africa and America – Mercer Cook and Stephen
E. Henderson

Crisis of the Negro Intellectual – Harold Cruse

Native Son – Richard Wright

The Invisible Man – Ralph Ellison

From Slavery to Freedom – John Hope Franklin

The Autobiography of Malcom X – Alex Haley

A People's History of The United States – Howard Zinn

SNCC, the New Abolitionists – Howard Zinn

The Souls of Black Folk – W.E.B. DuBois

Blues People: Negro Music in White America – Leroi Jones

The Fire Next Time – James Baldwin

Soul on Ice – Eldridge Cleaver

Class Struggle in Africa – Kwame Nkrumah

The Other America – Michael Harrington

Wretched of the Earth – Frantz Fanon

Black Face White Masks – Frantz Fanon

Diary of Che Guevara – Ernesto Guevara

History Will Absolve Me – Fidel Castro

Little Red Book – Mao Tse-Tung

The Spook Who Sat by the Door – Sam Greenlee

Let Rap Rap – H Rap Brown

The Courage to Be – Paul Tillich

Black Reconstruction – W.E.B. DuBois

Soledad Brother – George Jackson

Black Power – Stokely Carmichael

Black Middle Class – E. Franklin Frazier

Why We Can't Wait – Martin Luther King Jr.

Black Rage – Price Cobbs & William H. Grier

Malcolm X Speaks – George Breitman

Black Metropolis: A Study of Negro Life in a Northern City – St. Clair Drake &
  Horace R. Cayton

Slavery by Another Name – Douglas A. Blackmon

Collection of Poems – LeRoi Jones

Works by Nikki Giovanni

Collection of Poems – Don L. Lee

Articles by Amilcar Cabral; Jomo Kenyatta; Ho Chi Minh; Etc.

Appendix B
Biographies of Notable Founders

The paths of all the BSU founders are worthy of note. Those transformative citizens' commitment to caring is reflected in the service-oriented careers many of them chose. They continue to walk the talk in step to serve the people, heeding the reminder— "All Power to the People." All of the BSU founding members received the Charles E. Odegaard Award in 2008.

Royal Alley-Barnes, '73, '74, MAT (UW). First graduate student of renowned artist Jacob Lawrence. Painter and Muralist ("embedded artist") spanning 50 years. Executive director of the Center on Contemporary Art, (CoCA), Seattle. Served as Senior Budget Analyst in the Office of Management and Budget for the City of Seattle; Executive Director of the Langston Hughes Performing Arts Institute, Seattle Parks and Recreation; Professor, Fine Arts Department, Seattle Central College; and Art Director, Extended Services Program, Seattle Public Schools. Received the honor of January 22, 2016, being proclaimed Royal Alley-Barnes Day by Seattle Mayor Murray. Received the 2010 John C. Little Spirit Award and the 2012 Ford Motor Company National Freedom Sister award. Charter member of UW Afro-American Student Society, the forerunner of the 1968 BSU. (See https://www.historylink.org/File/11179 and https://artbeat.seattle.gov/2016/01/25/royal-alley-barnes-day-january-22-2016/ for more information.)

Anita Johnson Connell, '68, '75, MD (UW). OBGYN practice in Seattle since 1982. Delivered youngest son and grandson of Dr. Samuel Kelly (founding OMA vice president). Trained medical assistants. Was a charter member of Afro-American Student Society. (See https://www.washington.edu/omad/2010/04/04/the-power-of-giving-back-alumni-spotlight-dr-anita-johnson-connell/ for more information.)

Eddie Demmings, '75, JD (Rutgers). General Counsel (retired). Served as Associate General Counsel, Senior Assistant General Counsel, Assistant General Counsel (Staff Attorney) District Council 37, AFSCME (American Federation of State, County, and Municipal Employees), New York; intern with Sipser, Weinstock, Harper, Dorn, Leibowitz; Executive Board of the

Founders Day December 22, 2012.

AFL-CIO Lawyer Coordinating Committee; President of the Epilepsy Society of NYC (nine years).

Larry Gossett, '71 (UW). Council member for 26 years, King County, WA. Served as Executive Director, Seattle's Central Area Motivation Program (CAMP); and Supervisor of the Black Student Division, Office of Minority Affairs, UW. Received the 1975 Charles E. Odegaard Award and recognized as 2008 Wondrous 100 Alumnus. 2021 Alumnus Summa Laude Dignatus awardee. Low-income housing building, Gossett Place, named in his honor. Served as President of the 1969 BSU. (See https://www.thehistorymakers. org/biography/larry-gossett-41 for more information.)

Patsy Mose Fletcher, '73, MS (Southern New Hampshire University), MA (Delaware State University). Independent Consultant and Managing Partner, Training, Historical Research & Economic Development (THREAD) LLC; Neighborhood Historic Preservation Coordinator, District of Columbia Office of Planning Historic Preservation Office; Co-founder, DC Community Heritage Project, partnership with DC Humanities Council. Served as an adjunct professor in graduate historic preservation and a community college instructor in African American history and culture. Served as Chief of Staff for public housing authority and Community Development Consultant for public and assisted housing. Author of *Historically African American Leisure Destinations Around Washington, DC* [Arcadia, 2015]. Charter member of UW Afro-American Student Society, the forerunner of the 1968 BSU.

Kathleen Halley, '72,'74, MSW (UW). Social Worker, Virginia County for 20+ years (retired). Served as Legislative Assistant, office of Congressman Mike Lowry; and Family Services staff, City of Seattle. Was a founding member of the 1968 UW BSU and the Seattle Chapter of the Black Panther Party.

William Daniel Keith, '69, '72 MD (UW). Dermatologist for 47 years, Los Angeles, CA, Institute for Aesthetic & Cosmetic Dermatology. Charter member of Afro-American Student Society and founding President of BSU.

Verlaine Keith-Miller, '73, '80 JD (UW). Industrial Appeal Judge (retired), Washington State Board of Appeals. Served to represent plaintiffs in private practice and Assistant Attorney General, Washington State. (See https://www.washington.edu/omad/2018/11/15/omad-mourns-passing-of-alumna-and-founding-bsu-member-verlaine-keith-miller/ for more information.)

Meredith Matthews, '68, '72, MD (UW). Self-employed. Served as Senior Vice President and Chief Medical Officer (retired), Blue Shield of California; Chief Medical Officer, LifeMasters Supported SelfCare, Inc.; Chief Medical Officer, Premera Blue Cross; and Chief Medical Officer, Premera. Charter member of Afro-American Student Society.

Carl Miller,'74 (UW). Trainer, Senior Care Program; Regional Trainer; Licensing Program Analyst, California Department of Social Services. Served as Program Specialist, Employment Program Representative/ Disabled Veterans Outreach (DVOP), Employment Development Department for field offices in Oakland, Berkeley, and Richmond, California; and Student Services Counselor and Minority Recruitment Coordinator, Office of Minority Affairs.

Garry Owens, UW (1968-1972), BA (Hampshire College). Project Manager, City of Seattle (31+years). Served as Youth Program Coordinator, Central Area Motivation Program. Served as State Teen Services Director, LA State Health Department. Served as Board Member, A Territory Resource and Social Justice Fund NW. Was a founding member of the 1968 UW BSU and the Seattle Chapter of the Black Panther Party.

William Stinson, '73, (UW). President (retired), North Pacific Oil and Gas. Served as Consultant, Signal Capital Management; Senior Geophysicist, PGS Oil & Energy; Geophysicist, CGG, France; Senior Geophysicist, ARCO International; and Manager, Ghana National Petroleum Corporation.

Appendix C
Fantastical Notables

Erasmo Gamboa, '70, '73, '85, PhD (UW). Professor Emeritus; Adjunct Professor: History, and Latin American Studies; former Professor, American Ethnic Studies, UW; author, *Mexican Labor and World War II: Braceros in the Pacific Northwest, 1942-1947*, "Nosotros, the Hispanic People of Oregon: Essays and Reflections," *Bracero Railroaders: The Forgotten World War II Story of Mexican Workers in the US West*; Yakima Valley Community College Association Distinguished Alumni Award, 1996; 2007 Distinguished Public Service Award; UW Timeless Award, 2011; leader of the Sea Mar Museum project; Co-Founder, UMAS and MEChA de UW, 1968 SEP cohort.

Mylon Winn, '71, '75, MA (UW), '81, PhD (UW). Professor, Criminology and Justice Studies, California State University, Northridge; former Professor, Department of Public Administration, Nelson Mandela School of Public Policy and Urban Affairs, Southern University, Baton Rouge, LA; former Associate Professor, School of Public and Environmental Affairs, Indiana University, Indianapolis, Indianapolis, IN; former Assistant Professor, Department of Political Science, Miami University, Oxford, OH; former Assistant Professor, Department of Political Science, University of Alabama, Tuscaloosa, AL; one of 257 students who entered UW through the Special Education Program (SEP).

LeRoy McCullough, '72, '74, JD (UW). Served as Judge, King County Superior Court for 27 years; member of the 1968 SEP cohort; served as Chief Judge of the MRJC and presiding Judge of the King County Juvenile Drug Court. Honored as Judge of the Year by the American Board of Trial Advocates and by the King County Bar Association. (See https://spu.edu/acad/school-of-business-and-economics/documents/DSS_McCullough_flyer_Autumn_2017.pdf).

Norman Rice, '72, '74, MPA (UW). Alumnus Summa Laude Dignatus, University of Washington; 49th mayor of Seattle serving two terms from 1990 to 1997 (first Black to serve); former President of US Conference of Mayors; former president, Seattle Foundation; former Seattle City Council member (four terms); former reporter, KOMO-TV and KIXI radio; Odegaard Award Recipient; 2004 UW Communication Alumni Hall of Fame honoree.

Daniel DeSiga, '73. Chicano Artist, former chair of the art department, Colegio Cesar Chavez, Mount Angel Oregon; mural, "Explosion of Chicano Creativity" (named by Roberto Maestas) mounted at El Centro dela Raza (started painting in 1972 and finished in 1997); other works appear in the Denver Art Museum, San Francisco Museum of Art, UCLA Wight Art Gallery, Smithsonian American Art Museum, Washington DC, and Sea Mar Museum of Chicano/a Latino/a Culture; paintings owned by Lou Diamond Phillips, and former President of Mexico, Vicente Fox; art portraying Latinx migrant workers featured in *Los Angeles Times* (1991); paintings appear in textbooks ranging from grade six-twelve, and on one book cover; 1969 SEP enrollee; EOP Recognition Award recipient [*Dian Ver Valen. *Walla Walla Union-Bulletin*, 20 April 2020.] [*http://depts.washington.edu/civilr/DeSiga_interview.htm] [*http://archives.evergreen.edu/1990/1990-51/chicanolatino/artists/daniel_desiga/resume.php]

Ricardo Martinez, '75, '80, JD (UW). Chief United States District Judge for the Western District of Washington; former Assistant Prosecutor, King County Prosecuting Attorney's Office; Odegaard Award recipient, 2018. 1969 SEP enrollee and classmate of Rogelio Riojas.

David Della, '76. Partner, Green Shoots Consulting, LLC; former Principal, Della Strategies; former Public Sector Manager, Waste Management; former Co-Founder/Partner, Global Eco Ventures, LLC; former Principal, Eco Ready LLC; former City Councilmember, City of Seattle; former Director of Policy and Community Affairs; former Community Affairs Manager, United Way of King County; former Executive Director, Washington State Commission on Asian Pacific American Affairs; former Deputy Chief of Staff; former OMA SAB member.

Joanne Harrell, '77, '98, MBA (UW). Senior Director and former General Manager, Microsoft; former President & CEO, United Way of King County; member, UW Board of Regents; Odegaard Award recipient; 2009 UW Communication Alumni Hall of Fame honoree.

Maxine E. Liggins, '79, '85, MD (UW). Area Medical Director, LA County Department of Public Health; Principal Investigator for the first HIV AIDS study; Internist, practicing for 21+ years; first African American female to receive an undergraduate degree in Chemistry at the University of Washington.

Blaine Tamaki, '79, JD (UW). Founder/Owner, Tamaki Law Firm, Yakima, Bellevue; Trial Lawyer of the Year Award recipient, 2012; Board of Regents member. (See https://tamakilaw.com/attorneys/blaine-tamaki/).

Michael P. Anderson, '81, MS (Creighton U.). Served as NASA astronaut, 1st Lieutenant Col.; pilot and instructor pilot, US Air Force; died in 2003 Space Shuttle Columbia tragedy. (See https://en.wikipedia.org/wiki/Michael_P._Anderson).

Leonard Forsman, (Suquamish), '81, (UW). Chair of Suquamish Tribal Council; member of the Council; descendant of the family of Chief Seattle; appointed by President Obama to Advisory Council on Historic Preservation; Board of Regents member. (See also https://www.washington.edu/regents/officers/leonard-forsman/).

Jacinta Titialii-Abbott, '82, '85, JD (UW). Board of Directors, Asian American Justice Center; Board of Directors, Asian & Pacific Island American Scholarship Fund; former Vice President, Tenet Healthcare; former Vice President and General Counsel, Tenet Healthcare.

Nathaniel "Nate" Miles, '82, (UW). Vice President of Strategic Initiatives and former Corporate Director, State Government Affairs Western United States at Eli Lilly and Company; served as Executive Assistant, Washington State Convention Center; Board of Directors member of the UW Foundation, Hightower Petroleum CO., the Pacific Science Center, and IslandWood; Chairman of the Board, Urban League of Metropolitan Seattle, 2014. (See also https://islandwood.org/cst_teamcst_team/nate-miles-vice-president-for-strategic-initiatives-eli-lilly-and-company/).

Gary Holden,'84, Summa Cum Laude, Phi Beta Kappa, PhD (Columbia). Professor, New York University Silver School of Social Work; former faculty member in the Mount Sinai School of Medicine Department of Community Medicine; former editor-in-chief of the Journal of Social Work Education; EOP President's Achievement Award recipient; former OMA SAB member.

Manuel A. Idrogo, '84,'88, MD (UW). Assistant Professor, Department of Family Medicine and Community Health, University of Minnesota

Medical School; advisory faculty and trainer for the World Health Organization worldwide diabetes program implementation. Received the EOP Recognition Award.

Deirdre Raynor,'84, '89', '97, PhD (UW). Associate Professor, Director, Office of Undergraduate Education, UW Tacoma; served as writing tutor and instructor, Office of Minority Affairs Instructional Center.

Kimberly A. Bell, '85, MD (Wisconsin). Master of Medical Management (USC), Regional Medical Director, Team Health West; former Associate Vice President, FHS Inpatient Team, Franciscan Health System; former Regional Medical Director, EmCare; former Medical Director, HCA Centennial Hospital; former Chief of Staff, Providence Hospital; former Associate medical director, Swedish Hospital Medicine; former Chief of Medicine, Medical Director, Providence Medical Center.

Derrick Mar, '85. Chief Technology Officer/VP of Engineering/Advisor, former CIO, Agency eCommerce, Travelport; former Senior Vice President of Engineering & Operations, Scout Analytics; CTO/Co-founder, GridStart, Inc.; Founder/CEO, Universal Software.

Nelson Del Rio, '86, Magna Cum Laude, Phi Beta Kappa, Beta Gamma Sigma, Omicron Delta Epsilon, JD (Harvard). Co-CEO, Board member, Blockable, Inc.; Chairman and President, Prosperity of the Commons International; President, The Del Rio Foundation; Chairman and President, Sonnenblick-Del Rio; Founder and Chairman, Emergent and Intelligence Solutions; Member, State Bar of California, Odegaard Award recipient, President's Achievement Award Recipient; EOP Recognition Award recipient.

Joe Finkbonner (Lummi), '86, '91, MHA (UW). Executive Director, Northwest Portland Area Indian Health Board (NPAIHB); former Director, NW Tribal Epidemiology Center; former EOP Recognition Award Recipient.

Karl Hoffman (Haida/Cherokee), '86, DDS (UW). Owner, Karl Hoffman Dentistry. P.S.; volunteer dentist, Olympia Union Gospel Mission; former officer in the US Commissioned Corps; Co-founder, Thurston County Dental Access Network; 2015 Patients' Choice winner; former EOP Recognition Award recipient.

Marta Reyes Newhart, '86, MBA (Pepperdine). Chief Communications Officer, Carpenter Technology Corporation; former Global Vice President, Johnson Controls; former Chief Marketing & Communication Officer, Suntricity; former Global Vice President, Medtronic; Covidien; former Executive Director, Corporate Communications & Community, The Boeing Company; former EOP Recognition Award recipient.

Townsend Price-Spratlen, '86, '90, PhD (UW). Associate Professor, Sociology, The Ohio State University; book author, *Reconstructing Rage: Transformative Reentry in the Era of Mass Incarceration* (Peter Long Press; former EOP Recognition Award recipient.

Michelle Bonam, '89, MBA/MSE (Penn). Executive Vice President and Chief Human Resources Officer, Global Talent Management; former Vice President, P&O Mars Chocolates North America; former Vice President, Starbucks Coffee Company; former Senior Manager, PepsiCo; former Global Process Owner, Air Products & Chemical Inc.; former Capital Project Manager, The Dow Chemical Company.

Eric Lizarraga Burdge, '89, '96, MD/PhD (Cornell/UW). Surgical Breast Oncologist, Wilkes Barre General Hospital; AR State Air Surgeon, Air National Guard; former attending surgeon and clinical professor, US Air Force.

Wei-Chih Wang, '89, '92, '96, PhD (UW). Research associate professor, UW Department of Mechanical Engineering; adjunct research associate professor, UW Department of Electrical Engineering.

Tri Phan, '90 (UW). Systems Engineer, Boeing Commercial Airplanes; served as Systems Engineer, Connexion by Boeing; Network Management Engineer, Terabeam; Principal Engineer/Engineering Manager, Quintessent Communications, Inc.; Network Management Engineer/Engineering Manager; received EOP Vice President Award.

Michaelanne Ehrenberg, '91, JD (Boston U.). Vice President and Associate General Counsel, Symetra. Served as Partner, Karr Tuttle Campbell; Chief of Staff, Seattle City Councilmember Heidi Wills; Associate, Stafford Frey Cooper; served on the OMA SAB.

Joelle Segawa Kane, '91, JD (U of Hawaii). Partner, Gallagher Kane Amai, AAL, ALC.; served as Partner, Henderson Gallagher & Kane AAL, ALC; Associate, Gallagher & Associate, AAL, ALC; served as an OMA SAB member.

Annie Young-Scrivner, '91, MBA (Minnesota). CEO, Wella Company; former CEO at Godiva Chocolate; former Executive Vice President, Starbucks; former President, Starbucks, Canada; former Region President, China Foods, PepsiCo.

Brent Jones, '92, PhD (UT Austin). Superintendent, Seattle Public Schools; former Chief Strategy and Partnership Officer; former Assistant Superintendent, Seattle Public Schools; former Vice Chancellor, Seattle Community College District; former Vice President, Green River Community College.

Allan Wu, '92, MD (University of Rochester School of Medicine). Chief Medical Officer for the Regenerative Surgery Institute; Managing Partner for Regenerative Resources, LLC; Chief Scientific Officer for StemExo.; Chairman for the Clinical Translation of Stem Cells Summit by Select Biosciences; serves as clinical faculty to the World Stem Cell Summit; has published extensively; member of OMA SAB, 1989; former OMA EOP Recognition Award recipient. (*http://stemcell.ucr.edu/index.php?content=people/faculty/Allan_Wu.html).

Collette Courtion, '94 MBA (Pepperdine). CEO/Founder Joylux, Inc; Marketing & Brand Consultant, Beauty & Brand; former CEO, JeNu Biosciences; former CEO/Founder, Calidora Skin Clinic; former Director of Starbucks Card and Customer Loyalty.

Roy Diaz, '94, '96, '02, MS/PhD/JD (UW). Assistant Vice-President-DIPI International Head of Instrumental Cosmetics & Digital, L'Oréal; Founder, AG Troy, LLC; Founding Partner, Patent Counsel, Patent Preparation & Prosecution, Intellectual Property Law, Diaz/Cook; former Patent Attorney, Patent Portfolio Development, Licensing & Technology, Prosecution Strategies; Intellectual Ventures; former Associate, Patent Litigation & Procurement, Patentability Analysis, Infringement Analysis, Finnegan Henderson; former Intellectual Property Specialist, Technology Patent Process, Terabeam; former UWAA president; Academic Achievement Award recipient.

Wesley K. Thomas (Navajo), '94,'96,'99, PhD (UW). Adjunct Faculty, Social Sciences Division, University of New Mexico-Gallup, NM; Professor Emeritus and Retired Graduate Dean, School of Graduate Studies & Research, Navajo Technical University; former Chair, Center of Dine Studies, Dine College; former Academic Dean, Dine College; former Graduate Faculty, Department of Anthropology, Gender Studies and International Studies, Indiana University, Bloomington; Founding Director of UI First Nations Educational and Cultural Center (*https://icci.indiana.edu/speakers/speakers-2016/thomas.html); former Assistant Professor, Department of Anthropology & American Indian Studies, Idaho State; Native Navajo speaker.

Elva Arredondo, '95, MS/PhD (Duke). Professor, Department of Psychology, and former Associate Professor in the Graduate School of Public Health at San Diego State University (SDSU) and Co-Director of the UCSD/SDSU Joint Doctoral Program of Public Health in Health Behavior; EOP VP Achievement Award recipient; former OMA SAB member.

Rion Ramirez (Turtle Mountain Chippewa Band of Indians), '95, '98 JD (UW). General Counsel, Mashantucket Pequot Tribal Nation; former General Counsel, Port Madison Enterprise in Suquamish, Washington; former Associate, Dorsey & Whitney LLP; former Associate, Schwabe, Williamson & Wyatt, P.C.; former member of President's Commission on White House Fellowships under the Obama Administration.

Antoinette Davis, '96, JD (Seattle U.). Deputy Director, ACLU of WA; former Sr. Staff Attorney, ACLU; former member, Antoinette M. Davis Law, PLCC; former Member, Davis Khan PLLC; former Attorney, Crocker Law Group/Resolve Legal; former Attorney, The Law Offices of Vonda M. Sargent; former VP of Human Resources, Marchex, Inc.; former Corporate Attorney, Labor Ready, Inc.; former Associate Attorney, William Kastner & Gibbs; former Judicial Clerk to Tom Chambers, Washington State Supreme Court.

Tiffany Dufu, '96, '99, MA (UW), Founder & CEO, THE CRU; former Chief Leadership Officer, Levo; former President, The White House Project; former Major Gift Officer, Simmons College; bestselling author of *Drop the Ball: Achieving More by Doing Less*.

Miki Moore Hardisty, '96, MS (UC San Diego). Principal Consultant, Kahale Technology Consulting; former Senior Vice President Product Management and Engineering, LPL Financial; former Director Product Management and Engineering, Dell; former Head of Product and Application, Michael and Susan Dell Foundation; former Director, Product Management and Enterprise Architecture, Dell. Inc.; former Director, Information and Technology, Nationwide Financial.

Terrence Hui, '96, MS (George Mason University), PhD (George Washington University). Senior Data Scientist, GoDaddy; former Data Scientist and Project Manager, Xerox; former Expert Analyst/Team Lead, Acxiom; Senior Analyst, Quinetix; former Team Lead, American Management Systems; former EOP Recognition Award recipient.

David D. Tran, '96, MD/PhD (Mayo Medical School, Rochester, MN). Faculty member, University of Florida; former Director of Neuro-oncology and Assistant Professor, Department of Medicine, Washington University; EOP President's Achievement Award recipient.

Ada Limon, '98, MFA (NYU), US Poet Laureate; author of five books; winner of Chicago Literary Award for Poetry (2003), 2005 House Poetry Prize, 2005 Pearl Poetry Prize; worked for magazines *Martha Stewart Living*, *GQ*, and *Travel + Leisure*.

Mercy Laurino, '98, '16, MS (University of Denver) PhD (UW). President, Professional Society of Genetic Counselors in Asia; Program Manager, Seattle Cancer Care Alliance; Faculty, Genetic Counselor, University of the Philippines Manila; Genetic Counselor, Seattle Cancer Care Alliance; Genetic Counselor, Fred Hutchinson Cancer Research Center; former Clinic Coordinator, Seattle Cancer Care Alliance.

Heather Wilson Ramirez, '98, JD (Seattle U.). Partner, Fiori Law Offices, Inc.; served as Associate Attorney, Lombino Martino, P.S.

Gerado (Jerry) Flores, '99, Principal Mechanical Engineer, NBC Universal Media, LLC; former Sr. Ride Mechanical Lead, Walt Disney Imagineering; former Mechanical Hardware Design & System Integration, Frequentz; former Mechanical Hardware Design & System Lead, Intelligentz; former Staff Mechanical Engineer, NASA Jet Propulsion Laboratory.

Julien L. Pham, '99, MD (UW), MPH (Harvard). President & COO, Genprex, Inc.; former Founding Venture Partner & Advisor, AccelHUB Venture Partners; former Venture Partner, NextGen Venture Partners; former

Founding Board Observer and Chief Medical Officer, RubiconMD; former Founder & Manager, RHINNO (Rapid Health Innovation); former Clinical Faculty, Harvard Medical School.

R. Omar Riojas, '99, JD (Stanford). Partner, Kelly Goldfarb, Huck, Roth, & Riojas, PLLC; former Of Counsel, DLA Piper LLP; former Attorney, Heller Erhman; Board of Directors, Washington State Major League Baseball Stadium Public Facilities District; Member of the Board of Trustees, Swedish Health System; FEOP Board member.

Yael Varnado, '00, MD, (Cornell). Practicing physician at The Johns Hopkins Hospital; board certified anesthesiologist; medical contributor, Today Show, CNN, Dr. Oz, CBS, *The Huffington Post*, *Cosmopolitan*, etc.; EOP President's Achievement Award recipient; affectionately called Dr. V.

John Amaya, '01, '05, JD (UW), LLM (Georgetown Law Center). Senior Enforcement & Investigations Attorney, Homeland Security; former Staff Attorney, Mexican American Legal Defense and Educational Fund; first Latino student to be appointed to UW Board of Regents; former OMA SAB president.

Jennifer Devine, '01, PhD (UC Berkeley). Assistant professor of Geography, Texas State University; Marshall Scholar.

Tyson Marsh, '01, MA (UCLA), PhD (UCLA). Associate Professor and Program Coordinator, UW Bothell; former Associate Professor, Seattle University; former Assistant Professor, University of New Mexico; former Assistant Professor, Educational Leadership and Policy Studies, Iowa State University; former Headmaster, International American School of Alexandria; former OMA SAB member.

Ruchi (Nayyar) Mehta, '01, MD (Ross University School of Medicine). Private practice, Orthopedics and General Pediatrics, Bloomfield, NJ; athletic physician, Bloomfield High School; concussion management fundraising efforts consultant for St. Joseph's Regional High School; Clinical Associate Professor for the Seton Hall School of Medicine, Department of Pediatrics; voted New Jersey Top Kids' Doc for six consecutive years; Suburban Essex Chamber of Commerce New Business Award recipient; Vice President of the Bloomfield Board of Health; founder of All Star Giving Foundation; former Sports Medicine Specialist at the Spine and Orthopedic Center of New Jersey in Jersey City, NJ;

former General Pediatrics Physician, Hackensack Pediatrics, Hackensack, NJ; former OMA SAB member.

Emilyn Alejandro, '02, PhD (University of British Columbia). McKnight Presidential Fellow, Associate Professor; former Assistant Professor, University of Minnesota; former Research Investigator, University of Michigan; Hartwell Foundation Fellow, University of Michigan; NIH, NRSA Predoctoral Fellow, University of British Columbia; Ronald E. McNair Scholar, UW; former OMA SAB member (See https://med.umn.edu/news-events/emilyn-alejandro-phd).

Felix Cabrera, '02, MD (UW), Post-Doctoral Residency Internal Medicine-Primary Care (Yale, IHP Medical Group; former Internal Medicine Hospitalist, Chief Medical Officer, Guam Memorial Hospital Authority; former Internal Medicine Primary Care PMC Isla Health Systems.

Seila Kheang, '02, MS (Carnegie Mellon). Senior Software Engineer, Roku, Inc.; served as Software engineer, Yahoo! Inc.; Software Development Engineer, Microsoft; Senior Software Engineer, Lockheed Martin.

Mariana Loya Linck,' 02, PhD (UC San Diego). Biomedical Engineering Department Advisory Board Member; University of Arkansas, Fayetteville; former Principal R&D Product Development Engineer, Cardiovascular, Medtronic (CA); former R&D Engineer, Science & Technology; former R&D Engineer, Cardiac Rhythm Device Management, Medtronic Vascular.

Angela Rye, '02, JD (Seattle University). Principal/CEO at IMPACT Strategies; political commentator, CNN; former Executive Director/General Counsel, Congressional Black Caucus; former Senior Advisor & Counsel, US House of Representatives, Committee on Homeland Security; former Coordinator, Advocacy and Legislative Affairs, NAFEO (National Association for Equal Opportunity in Higher Education).

Paulette Jordan (Coeur d'Alene) '03, Secretary of the Executive Board, Finance Chair, Northwest Board Member, National Indian Gaming Association; Idaho House of Representatives; Gaming Co-Chair, Affiliated Tribes of Northwest Indians; former Councilwoman, Coeur d'Alene Tribal Council.

Gabriela Condrea, '04, M.Ed. (Chestnut Hill College). Founder/CEO, Team Building in Motion; Creator/Founder, Mingle and Move; Creator/Founder, Connection through Movement; Creator/Founder, TangoStride Technique;

Owner/Tango Instructor, Tango is About the Connection. Author of *When 1+1=1: That "Impossible" Connection*. Served as 8th Grade Language Arts Teacher, Asa Mercer Middle (Seattle Public Schools).

Martha Sandoval, '04, JD (UW). Partner, Perkins Coie LLC; former Counsel, Business Practice Group, Perkins Coie; Pro bono volunteer at Microenterprise Legal clinic; former EOP President's Achievement Award recipient.

Jamal Whitehead, '04, JD (Seattle U.). Shareholder, Schroeter Goldmark & Bender; former Assistant US Attorney for the Western District of Washington; former Senior Trial Attorney, US Equal Opportunity Commission; former Associate Garvey Schubert Barer; former OMA SAB member.

Chalia Stallings-Ala'ilima, '05, '08, JD (UW). Assistant Attorney General, State of Washington, one of the selectees by Attorney General Bob Ferguson to receive the William V. Tanner Award, recognizing attorneys with exceptional achievements early in their careers; 2016 APEX Awards: Excellence in Diversity Award recipient; President of the Loren Miller Bar Association Executive Board, areas of practice include Civil Litigation, Civil Rights, Employment, Government; EOP Gerberding Award recipient; former Costco Scholar. (*https://www.youtube.com/watch?v=6bSSo9dXYbw and *http://www.atg.wa.gov/news/news-releases/eight-attorneys-honored-ag-ferguson-s-william-v-tanner-award).

Sumona Das Gupta, '06, '09, EOP Honors, JD (UW). Pharmacy Compliance and Audit Manager, UW Medicine Pharmacy; former Corporate Compliance and Privacy Analyst, Valley Medical Center; former Corporate and Healthcare Associate, K & L Gates; Co-leader of efforts to establish the Diversity Monument on the UW Seattle campus.

Martin Acevedo, '07, MBA (Seattle U). CEO Global Energy Resources LLC; served as CEO Global Energy Partners, former Managing Partner, Vajra LLC; received the EOP Gerberding Award.

Rachel Gillum, '08, PhD (Stanford). Vice President, Ethical Tech, Salesforce; former Senior Director, Rice Hadley Gates led by Condoleezza Rice, Robert Gates, and Stephen Hadley; Fellow, Immigration Policy Lab, Stanford University; former Research Scholar Consultant, Gallup, Inc.; author, *Muslims in a Post/911 America: A Survey of Attitudes and Beliefs and Their Implications for US National Security Policy*.

Appendix D
The Community of OMA&D

Current as of Spring 2018.

1968 Board of Regents

Drumheller, Joseph

Ellis, James R.

Frayn, R. Mort

King, John L.

Powell, George V.

Rosellini, Leo J.

Shefelman, Harold S.

Willis, Robert J.

First SEP Recruiters

1968

The first student recruiters hired were: Frances Johnson, Eddie Demmings (Seattle), Lyn Ware (Renton), Patricia Honeysuckle (Seattle), Paul Fletcher (Pasco), Thomas McAllister (Seattle), Marcie Hall (Toppenish), and Carmelita Laducer (Toppenish) (Evans, 1968b).

1969–1970 Recruiting Corps

Chicano: Mrs. Irvine Castilleja, Gilbert Garcia, Jesus Lemos, Eron Maltos, Floyd Sandoval, Tomas Sandoval, Judy Briones, Joe Garza, Claudia Harris, Mario Villanueva

Additional recruiters: Jesus Maldonado and Berta Ortega

American Indian: Larry Merculieff, Lloyd Pinkham, Edna Paisano

White: Darcy Drew

Black: Isaac Carter, Verla K. Colman, Richard E Harr, Creed Hubbard, Kathleen Russell, Betty Jean Stokes, Joyce Sims, Tom McAllister, Wanda Mills, Isaac Alexander, Brenda Brock, Deborah Carter, Eddie Demmings

Student Advisory Board (SAB), Charter Members

Ike Alexander, Janice Arnold, Sabino Cabildo, Catalina Cantu, Irene Castilleja, Annie Galarosa, Myron Gibbs, John Gilmore, Curtis Jackson, Linda Jackson, Ruthann Kurose, James Lee, Leonard Luna, Elaine Miller, Lamar Mills, Cal Rodriguez, Eddie Saenz, Jim Tomeo

Ethnic Student Division Founding Staff, 1971

Asian and Poverty Student Division
Supervisor: Mike Castillano
Counselors: Larry Matsuda, Norma Asis
Secretary: Gwen Funi

Black Student Division
Supervisor: Larry Gossett
Counselors: Claude Green, Gertrude Peoples, Eddie Wright, Mary Eltayeb, Lamar Mills
Secretary: Ethel Jackson

American Indian Student Division
Supervisor: Emmett Oliver
Counselors: Don Matheson, Jania Garcia
Secretary: Alice Solomon

Chicano Student Division
Supervisor: Sam Martinez
Counselors: Antonio Cardenas, Raul Anaya, Elda Mendoza, Armando Mendoza
Secretary: Louisa Juarez

Friends of the Educational Opportunity Program Charter Members

Richard Aguirre
William Baker
Fam Bayless
Arthur W. Buerk
David L. Broom
Connie Carter
Tina Dreyer

Betty Drumheller
Charles A. Evans
Jean Farris
Robert L. Flennaugh
Lylia Joyner
Vivian Kelly
Samuel E. Kelly
Dalwyn. Knight
Carl Maxey
Benjamin F, McAdoo
C. Raymond Merriwether
Doris Pade
Stevie Perkins
Eliot C. Read
Don K. Smith
Dan Starr
Kay Wallace
Nancy Weber

EOP Alumni Elected to Prestigious Positions

ASUW Presidency
Judy Nicastro 1992–1993
Franklin Donahoe 1998–1999
Danica You 2001–2002
Alexandra Narvaez 2002–2003 (First Latina)
Cullen White 2006–2007
Anttimo Bennett 2008–2009
Daniele Menez 2016–2017 (First Pacific Islander/Filipina)
Osman Salahuddin 2017–2018 (First Muslim)

EOP Alumni Appointed to UW Board of Regents
John Amaya*
Leonard Forsman
Joanne Harrell
David Moore-Reeploeg*

Darlene Marie Mortel*
Rogelio Riojas
Blaine Tamaki
*Student

Seattle Public School Board
Mary Bass
Alan Sugiyama

City Councils
Desley Brooks, Oakland, CA
David Della, Seattle , WA
Dulce Gutiérrez, Yakima, WA
Jesse Johnson, Federal Way, WA
Theresa Mosqueda, Seattle, WA
Senayet Negusse, SeaTac, WA
Judy Nicastro, Seattle , WA
De'Sean Quinn, Tukwila, WA
Norman Rice, Seattle, WA

Mayor
Norman Rice, Seattle, WA

Washington State Legislature
Jesse Johnson
Kip Tokuda
Javier Valdez
Jesse Wineberry

Other State Legislature
Paulette Jordan, Idaho

OMA&D Administrative Staff
Samuel Kelly (1970–1976) Vice President for Minority Affairs
James H. Collins, assistant vice president, business and finance
William Baker, assistant vice president, supportive services
Bill Hilliard, assistant vice president, supportive services
Mike Castillano, assistant vice president, supportive services
Karen Morell, special assistant to the vice president

Ewaugh F. Fields (1977–1978) Vice President for Minority Affairs
William Baker, assistant vice president for business and finance
Michael A. Castillano, assistant vice president for supportive services
Karen L. Morell, special assistant to the vice president

Herman D. Lujan (1978–1988) Vice President for Minority Affairs
William Baker, assistant vice president for administration and finance,
assistant vice president for administrative services, assistant vice president
for student services, assistant vice president for entry services
Michael A. Castillano, assistant vice president for supportive services
Karen L. Morell, special assistant to the vice president
Nori Mihara, executive staff assistant, assistant to the vice president,
assistant to the vice president for academic services
Millie L. Russell, special assistant to the vice president
Gary Trujillo, budget administrator and special assistant to the vice
president
Steven N. Garcia, assistant to the vice president, assistant to the vice
president for supportive services

Robert Pozos (1988–1989) Vice President for Minority Affairs
Steven N. Garcia, assistant vice president for supportive services
Nori Mihara, assistant vice president for academic services
Millie L. Russell, assistant to the vice president

William L. Baker (1989–1990) Acting Vice President
Nori Mihara, assistant vice president for academic services
Enrique Morales, assistant to the vice president
Millie L. Russell, assistant to the vice president

Myron Apilado (1990–2001) Vice President for Minority Affairs
William L. Baker, assistant (later associate) vice president for student services
Nori Mihara, assistant vice president for academic services
Enrique Morales, assistant to the vice president
Millie L. Russell, assistant to the vice president
Tom Colonnese, assistant vice president for administrative services

Nancy "Rusty" Barceló (2001–2003) Vice President for Minority Affairs
William L. Baker, associate vice president for pre-college program
Tom Colonnese, assistant vice president for administrative services

Enrique Morales, assistant vice president

Emile Pitre, assistant vice president for academic support

Millie L. Russell, assistant to the vice president

Nancy "Rusty" Barceló (2003-2006) Vice President for Minority Affairs and Vice Provost for Diversity

Gabriel Gallardo, assistant to the vice president for new initiatives

Enrique Morales, associate vice president for pre-college access

Emile Pitre, associate vice president for academic advancement and assessment

Delores Larkins, assistant to the vice president

Stephanie Miller, assistant to the vice president

Rosa Ramon, assistant to the vice president

Millie L. Russell, assistant to the vice president

Betty Schmitz, director for center for curriculum transformation

Sheila Edwards Lange (2006–2007) Interim Vice President for Minority Affairs and Vice Provost for Diversity

Enrique Morales, senior associate vice president for pre-college access

Emile Pitre, associate vice president for assessment

Gabriel Gallardo, assistant to the vice president

Delores Larkins, assistant to the vice president

Stephanie Miller, assistant to the vice president

Rosa Ramon, assistant to the vice president

Millie L. Russell, assistant to the vice president

Betty Schmitz, director for center for curriculum transformation

Sheila Edwards Lange (2007–2015) Vice President for Minority Affairs and Vice Provost for Diversity

Luis Fraga, associate vice provost for faculty advancement

Chadwick Allen, associate vice provost for faculty advancement

Enrique Morales, associate president for pre-college access

Patricia Loera, associate vice president for college access

Gabriel Gallardo, associate vice president for Student Success

Emile Pitre, associate vice president for assessment

Jan Kendle, assistant vice president for administration

David Iyall, assistant vice president for advancement

Stephanie Miller, assistant vice president for community and public relations

Steve Woodard, assistant vice president and director/P.I.

Millie L. Russell, assistant to the vice president

Betty Schmitz, director for center for curriculum transformation

Gabriel Gallardo (2015–2016) Interim Vice President for Minority Affairs and Vice Provost for Diversity

Patricia Loera, associate vice president for college access

Chadwick Allen, associate vice provost for faculty advancement

Emile Pitre, senior advisor to the vice president

Jan Kendle, assistant vice president for administration

Stephanie Miller, assistant vice president for community and public relations, assistant vice president

Rickey Hall (2016–present) Vice President for Minority Affairs and Diversity and University Diversity Officer (for all three UW campuses)

Gabriel Gallardo, associate vice president for college success

Patricia Loera, associate vice president for college access

Kristian Wiles, associate vice president for college success

Chadwick Allen, associate vice provost for faculty advancement

Jan Kendle, assistant vice president for administration

Emile Pitre, senior advisor to the vice president

Jeanette James, senior director for strategy and planning

Scot Mar, manager for financial services

OMA(&D) Unit Director/Coordinator (chronological order)

EOP Admissions

Mira Sinco

Jerry Shigaki

Enrique Morales

Recruitment and Outreach/ Multicultural Outreach and Recruitment (MOR)

Enrique Morales

Stephanie Miller

Karl Smith

Stephanie Miller

Cristina Gaeta

Jaime Soto

Resident Release Project
Armando Mendoza
Gordy Graham
Kent Mercer
Jack Eberlein

Correctional Education and Research Program
Karen Morell

Tutorial Office
Jerline Ware
Patricia Clark

Reading/Study Skills
Nathan Ward
Tutorial Center
Alexis Martinez
Nathan Ward

Instructional Center
Nathan Ward
Sandra Madrid
Emile Pitre
Barry Minai
Therese Mar

EOP Counseling Center
Lois Dodson
Fred Henderson
Steve Simeona
Michelle Perez
Alejandro Espania
Robin Neal
Luz Iniguez

Academic Counseling Services
Kristian Wiles

Ethnic Cultural Center and Theater
Roy Flores
Sharon Maeda
John Gilmore
Donald Matt
Charles Canada
Ruben Sierra
Luis Ramirez
Victor Flores
Marisa Herrera
Magdalena Fonseca

Upward Bound
Marguerite Ewing
Karen Morell
Leny Valerio-Buford
Rachel Walker
Roseann London

Trio Training
Karen Morell

Special Services for Disadvantaged Students
William James
Adelusa Judal

Student Support Services (name change)
Roger Grant
Kristian Wiles

Talent Search
William Hodge

Educational Talent Search
Julian Argel
Stephanie Miller
Dina Ibarra

Early Identification Program
Carlene Brown
James Antony
Gabriel Gallardo
Steve Woodard
Gene Kim
Todd Sperry

Early Scholars Outreach Program/Seattle Early Scholars Outreach GEAR UP
Lette Hadgu

Assessment and Research
Gene Kim

Advancement
George Zeno
Greg Lewis
Katherine Day Hase

Champions Program
Melissa Raap

Communications
Erin Rowley
Eric Moss

Health Sciences Center Minority Student Program
Karlotta Rosebaugh
Teri Ward

College Assistance Migrant Program
Martha Estrada
Luz Iniguez
Andres Huante

Louis Alliance for Minority Participation
Stephanie Gardner
June Hairston

MESA
James Dorsey
Gregory L. King

Technology
Peter Scott

Upward Bound Math and Science
Dave Wolzyck

GEAR UP Educator Development Initiative
Roseann London

Tribal Relations
Iisaaksiichaa Ross Braine

Yakima Valley GEAR UP
Louetta Johnson
Conan Viernes

Faculty Advancement
Norma Rodriguez
Simone Willynck

Strategy and Planning
Jeanette James

Wɘłɘbʔaltxʷ - Intellectual House
Iisaaksiichaa Ross Braine

Fiscal Services
Nancy Corning
Scot Mar

Sources

OMA&D Oral History Interviewees

Interviews for this project were conducted jointly by Antoinette Wills and Emile Pitre between 2015 and 2022. (*Sessions conducted by Emile Pitre alone.*) They can be found in the UW Libraries Special Collections: University of Washington Office of Minority Affairs & Diversity oral histories, Accession # 19-018.

Raul Anaya, September 24, 2015

At the time of this interview, Raul Anaya was assistant director of student counseling services at the Office of Minority Affairs & Diversity. His connection to the Office of Minority Affairs began in 1969, when he was a student at Yakima Valley Community College (YVCC).

Myron Apilado, July 13, 2015

Myron Apilado was vice president for minority affairs at the University of Washington 1990–2001, the longest-serving vice president in that role to date.

Rusty Barceló, February 8, 2016

Rusty Barceló was hired as vice president for minority affairs at the University of Washington in 2001. During her five years at the UW, her title changed as the word "diversity" was added; she also was appointed assistant vice provost, to strengthen connections between the Office of Minority Affairs & Diversity and faculty at the UW.

Adrienne Chan, August 14, 2016

Adie Chan spent most of her professional career as a staff member in the Office of Minority Affairs. Hired in 1973 as a tutor in the Tutorial Center—which later became the Instructional Center—she became a counselor in the Asian Student Division in 1974.

Gabriel Gallardo, November 16, 2015

At the time of this interview, Gabriel Gallardo was interim vice president for minority affairs and vice provost for diversity at the University of Washington.

Steven Garcia, September 30, 2015

Steven Garcia was assistant vice president for support services in the Office of Minority Affairs from October 1982 until March 1989. During most of that time he worked with Herman Lujan, who was vice president for minority affairs from 1978 until 1988.

Larry Gossett, June 10, 2016

Larry Gossett was a UW student activist in the Black Student Union and the first director of the Black Student Division in the Office of Minority Affairs at the UW, political activist in the community, and King County Council member from 1993 to 2020.

Lette Hadgu, August 10, 2016

Lette Hadgu joined the Office of Minority Affairs in 1979 as a counselor in the Black Student division. She worked closely with Dr. Millie Russell, assistant to the vice president for minority affairs from 1982 until Russell's retirement in June 2007, particularly on the Early Scholars Outreach Program.

June Hairston, June 6, 2016

At the time of this interview, June Hairston was an academic counselor in the Office of Minority Affairs & Diversity. She joined the Educational Opportunity Program counseling staff in March 1990, shortly after the EOP changed from a practice of ethnic-specific divisions and counseling to multicultural counseling.

Rickey Hall, December 5, 2019

Rickey Hall joined OMA&D in 2016 as vice president for minority affairs and diversity and university diversity officer at the University of Washington.

Bill Hilliard, July 21, 2015

Bill Hilliard was part of the founding staff of what became the Office of Minority Affairs & Diversity. He was hired by the UW in the summer of 1968 to recruit minority and economically disadvantaged students to attend the UW. He played a major role in developing the Educational Opportunity Program, and served as assistant vice president to Sam Kelly, the first vice president for minority affairs at the UW.

Sheila Edwards Lange, August 25, 2015

Sheila Edwards Lange was vice president for minority affairs and vice provost for diversity from July 2007 to August 2015. Lange became acquainted with the Office of Minority Affairs & Diversity while a graduate student at the UW.

Herman Lujan, October 28, 2015

Herman Lujan was vice president for minority affairs at the University of Washington 1978-1988, followed by serving as vice provost for academic affairs 1988-1991.

Larry Matsuda, May 3, 2016

Larry Matsuda worked in the Office of Minority Affairs 1970-1974, first as a counselor then as staff assistant to Bill Hilliard. He then returned to teaching and administration in the Seattle Public Schools, but his connections to the UW remained strong. He joined the board of the UW Alumni Association in 1992 and was elected president for 1996-1997. He and Vivian Lee co-founded the Multicultural Alumni Partnership to promote diversity at the UW and the UWAA.

Tekie Mehary, July 31, 2016

Tekie Mehary received his PhD in forest entomology from the University of Washington, then taught in the College of Forest Resources, the Department of Biology, and the Department of Bioengineering. Although not a staff member, he worked closely with many people in OMA&D toward the common goal of helping students achieve academic success, especially in the biological sciences.

Nori Mihara, February 3, 2016

Nori Mihara served in several OMA roles in the 1970s and 1980s, including as executive staff assistant, special assistant, and assistant vice president to Vice President Herman Lujan with special attention to the Counseling Center, the Instructional Center, and relations with UW faculty members when Mihara became an ex officio member of the Faculty Senate. He later served as an instructor teaching elementary physics in the physics department, and the Instructional Center, and was involved with minority programs in the College of Engineering.

Enrique Morales, July 23, 2015

Enrique Morales had a 34-year career in the OMA, focused on admissions, advising, and administration. He began at the UW as an undergraduate (1972-1977), when he was involved with MEChA (the Chicano Student Movement). He was a graduate student in the School of Social Work for three years (1977–1980), while also working for the state doing probation, parole, and precinct investigations. He joined the OMA staff in 1980 as a recruiter in the Chicano division and took on a variety of roles over the next three decades including recruiting, counseling, admissions, and outreach. He retired in January 2015 as associate vice president for minority affairs and diversity.

Jim Morley, February 24, 2016

Jim Morley spent most of his professional career as a staff member in the OMA. He was hired in November 1974 as an executive staff assistant to Bill Baker, who was then assistant vice president for business and finance. Morely became an English instructor in the Reading Study Skills Center (IC) and later taught there full time until his retirement in 1999.

Karen Morell, April 5, 2016

Karen Morell was one of the early staff members of the OMA, recruited in 1971 by Sam Kelly, the first vice president for minority affairs. She spent four decades in various roles in OMA before retiring from the university. She was instrumentally involved in the Resident Release Project and the Prisoner Education Program (later called Correctional Education and Research), and Upward Bound program, and the TriO Training Program.

Rogelio Riojas, August 4, 2016

His relationship with the UW began in the summer of 1969 when he met student recruiters in Othello, Washington, and was admitted through the Special Education Program. He was a founder and has been CEO of Sea Mar Community Health Centers since receiving his Master of Health Administration degree at the UW in 1977. He was appointed to the UW Board of Regents by Governor Jay Inslee for a six-year term from October 2013 to September 2019.

Mike Tulee, February 4, 2020

At the time of this interview, Mike Tulee was Executive Director of the United Indians of All Tribes Foundation, based in Seattle. He also was a lecturer on the faculty of the Department of American Indian Studies at the UW and an at-large member of the UW Alumni Association. He entered the UW through the Educational Opportunity Program.

Tim Washburn, June 23, 2015

Tim Washburn started working at the UW in 1967 as a systems analyst in the Office of Management Systems and retired in 2005 as assistant vice president for enrollment services. As registrar in 1969, then executive director of admissions and records in 1974, he was directly involved in the university's efforts to expand access to students from underrepresented minority groups as well as economically disadvantaged students.

Personal Communications

Adkins, Carmelita. April 16, 2017.

Alexander, Isaac. April 4, 2017.

Brisker, Emanuel James (E.J.). August 11, 2016; May 14, 2017.

Brown, Carlene. September 5, 2018.

Burkhalter, Gloria. September 29, 2008.

Ceja, Miriam. April 24, 2019.

Crowder, Jesus. July 17, 2019.

Demmings, Eddie. July 6, 2017; September 15, 2020.

Fung, Scott. August 14, 2020.

Garrett, James (Jimmy). February 28, March 3 & March 5, 2017.

Gossett, Larry. June 10, 2016; February 26, August 28, and September 1, 2020.

Hall-McMurtrie, Marcie. March 28, 2017.

Halley, Kathleen. September 2, 2020.

Ibrahim, Anisa. August 14, 2020.

Keith, William Daniel. August 16, 2020.

Kelly, Marcia. April 10, 2018.

Kelly, Sam, April 16, 2004.

Laducer, Carmelita. April 18, 2017.

Leavy, Lee. March 10, 2007.

Locke, Hubert. April 24, 2017.

Mar, Therese. July 31, 2019.

Miller, Carl. November 3, 2016; July 17, 2017; July 12, 2018; September 22, 2019; August 24, 2020.

Morales, Enrique. March 22, 2017.

Owens, Garry. April 28, 2017.

Roberts, Christina. September 18, 2019.

Roberts, Jorge. April 4, 2019.

Salazar, Antonio. November 27 and December 2, 2019.

Seymour, Rachael A. August 4, 2020.

Stern, Robby. April 3, 2017.

Tyler, Kathleen Russell. August 21, 2020.

Viernes, Conan. January 21, 2015.

Walker, Eddie. April 20 & May 1, 2017.

List of Figures

Bibliography

Foreword

Brown, Q. R. "Thanks, Professor Banks: 'The Father of Multicultural Education' is Retiring After 50 Years at the UW." University of Washington Magazine (2018): https://magazine.washington.edu/feature/james-banks-uw-retires-multicultural-education/.

Burch, D. S. & Vander Ploeg, L. "Buffalo Shooting Highlights Rise of Hate Crimes Against Black Americans." The New York Times, (May 16, 2022): https://www.nytimes.com/2022/05/16/us/hate-crimes-black-african-americans.html.

Di Angelo, R. Nice Racism: How Progressive White People Perpetuate Racial Harm. Boston: Beacon Press, 2021.

Fortin, J. "Critical Race Theory: A Brief History." The New York Times. (November 8, 2021): https://www.nytimes.com/article/what-is-critical-race-theory.html.

Harper, S., Foreword, Campus Uprisings: How Student Activists and Collegiate Leaders Resist Racism and Create Hope, ed. Ty-R. M. O. Douglas, K. G. Shockley, and I. Toldson. New York: Teachers College Press, 2020: pp. xiii-xvi.

Kelly, S. E. with Taylor, Q. Dr. Sam: Soldier, Educator, Advocate, Friend: An Autobiography. Seattle & London: University of Washington Press, 2010.

King, J. E. & Akua, C. "Dysconscious Racism and Teacher Education." Encyclopedia of Diversity in Education, vol. 2, ed. J. A. Banks. Los Angeles & London: Sage Publications, 2012: pp. 723-726.

Odegaard, C. E. Pilgrimage Through Universities. Seattle: University of Washington Press, 2000.

Spratlen, T. H. Journey Up from Down South. Eugene, OR: Luminare Press, 2021.

Book

Academic Ranking of World Universities. 2019, http://www.shanghairanking.com/ARWU2019.html.

Adam, B. "Students Block Route 520 in Protest as I-200 Takes Effect." The Daily, December 3, 1998, p. 1.

Ansari, A. "Celebrating 50 Years of Resistance, Community Building, and Resilience." The Daily, May 24, 2018: http://www.dailyuw.com/news/article_6a44f374-5eeb-11e8-bd83-4fc383117f9d.html.

Baker, B., ed. "Janelle Sagmiller." Contact newsletter, Spring 2001, p. 9. Office of Minority Affairs & Diversity archives, Schmitz Hall. University of Washington, Seattle, WA.

Banks, J. "Civic Education for Excellence, Diversity, and Inclusion: Global Perspectives."

Speech delivered for the Samuel E. Kelly Distinguished Lecture Series, University of Washington, Seattle, WA, April 13, 2018.

Berkman, J. "What is EOP? Your Guide to Educational Opportunity Programs." April 11, 2020. https://blog.prepscholar.com/what-is-eop

"Best Colleges." *U.S. News and World Report*, 2017 ed. https://www.usnews.com/best-Colleges.

"Best Colleges." *U.S. News and World Report,* 2018 ed. https://www.usnews.com/best-Colleges.

Biondi, M. *The Black Revolution on Campus.* Berkeley: University of California Press, 2012.

Black Student Union Letter to President Odegaard. May 6, 1968, p. 4. http://depts.washington.edu/labpics/zenPhoto/uw_bsu/uw_library/BSU-Letter-to-Odegaard-May-6-1968.

Bransberger, P. and D. Michelau. "Knocking at the College Door: Projections of High School Graduates." Report for the Western Interstate Commission on Higher Education, December 2016. https://static1.squarespace.com/static/57f269e19de4bb8a69b470ae/t/58d2eb93bf629a4a3878ef3e/1490217882794/Knocking2016FINALFORWEB-revised021717.pdf

Brazil, J. (n.d.). https://en.wikipedia.org/wiki/Joe_Brazil.

Bryant, H. "New Wave of Black Students Hits UW." *Seattle Post-Intelligencer*, September 10, 1968, p. 1.

Bulger, K., "ASUW Committee Stops Short of Resignation Call." *The Daily*, July 9, 1980, p. 3.

Castañeda, O. R., "*Timeline: Movimiento from 1960-1985. Seattle Civil Rights & Labor History Project.*" (n.d.). https://depts.washington.edu/civilr/mecha_timeline.htm

Cataldi, E. F., C. T. Bennett, and X. Chen. "First Generation Students, College Access, Persistence, and Post Bachelor's Outcomes." *Stats in Brief*, US Department of Education, NCES 2018-421, 2018, pp. 6-9. https://nces.ed.gov/pubs2018/2018421.pdf.

Columbia Daily Spectator. Various stories, May1, 1968, pp. 1, 2. http://spectatorarchive.library.columbia.edu/?a=d&d=cs19680501-01.1.1&.

Cornwell, P. "Activist Al Sugiyama Who Empowered Seattle's Asian-American Community, Dies At 67." *Seattle Times*, January 4, 2017. https://www.seattletimes.com/seattle-news/obituaries/activist-al-sugiyama-who-empowered-seattles-asian-american-community-dies-at-67/.

"Council Honors Activist Alan Sugiyama Through Street Naming." *Council Connection*, July 23, 2018. https://council.seattle.gov/2018/07/23/council-honors-activist-alan-sugiyama-through-street-naming/.

Cour, R. "Negro Fund Demanded." *Seattle Post Intelligencer*, May 17, 1968, p. 1.

"UW Vows to Aid Negro Students." *Seattle Post Intelligencer*, May 19, 1968, pp. 1, 10.

Cour, R. and W. A. Evans. "Carmichael Rips into Whites Here." *Seattle Post-Intelligencer*, April 20, 1967, p.1.

Davies, K. "Thompson Resigns from Shifting OMA Program." *The Daily*, October 10, 1978, p. 1.

"Lujan Trying to Promote 'Academic Survival' for OMA." *The Daily*, October 24, 1978, p. 1.

"BSU Members Question Lujan on Minority Affairs." *The Daily*, October 25, 1978, p. 1.

"Thompson Leaves OMA in Protest of Planning Methods." *The Daily*, October 26, 1978, p. 1.

Diversity Appraisal Process and Report. Unpublished report, prepared by N.R. Barceló and the Diversity Appraisal Steering Committee, Office of Minority Affairs & Diversity, 2004, updated January 2006. University of Washington Libraries, Special Collection, Seattle, WA.

Dixon, A. *My People are Rising: Memoir of a Black Panther Party Captain.* Chicago: Haymarket Books, 2012.

Doctor, D. "New Black Image Emerging." *The Daily*, February 15, 1968, p.6.

Dunphy, M. E. "Positions on UW Racial Problems are Laid On Line." *The Seattle Times*, May 19, 1968, p. 4.

Dykeman, D. "To Gain a College Education, an Opportunity for Minorities," *The Daily*, August 19, 1969, p. 6.

"Asian Students Confront SEP." *The Daily*, July 17, 1969b, p. 1.

"Regents Approve Center." *The Daily*, November 29, 1970, p. 8.

Eike, Letoy, ed. "Hoang Nhan Winner of Merage Fellowship of $10,000 Per Year for Two years to Fund Graduate School & Study in China." *Contact* newsletter, Office of Minority Affairs & Diversity archives, Schmitz Hall. University of Washington. 2004, p. 7.

"UW Awarded McNair Postbaccalaureate Achievement Grant." *Contact* newsletter, Winter 1999-2000, p. 8. Office of Minority Affairs & Diversity archives, Schmitz Hall. University of Washington, Seattle, WA.

Eisen, K. "EOP Administrators Defend Program." *The Daily*, May 23, 1980, p. 3.

"EOP Protest Goes On." *The Daily*, May 23, 1980, p. 1.

"EOP Will Be Shut Down Again Today." *The Daily*, June 4, 1980, p. 2.

Elassar, A. "A Somali Refugee Just Became the Director of the Seattle Clinic Where She was Cared for as a Child." *CNN*, October 26, 2019. https://www.cnn.com/2019/10/26/us/somali-refugee-director-seattle-clinic-trnd/index.html.

Emery, J. "Students Have the Right Kind of Friends." *The Seattle Times*, December 11, 1977, B8.

"UW to Begin Honors Program for Minorities." *The Daily*, March 25, 1979, A11.

Evans, C. Minutes of the Senate Executive Committee, May 20, 1968. University of Washington Libraries Special Collection, Charles Evans Papers, Accession # 2598-001, Box 1. University of Washington, Seattle, WA.

Notebook, May 20, 1968. University of Washington Libraries Special Collection, Charles, Evans Papers, Accession # 2598-4, Box 3. University of Washington, Seattle, WA.

Forman, J. "High Tide of Black Resistance." Student Nonviolent Coordinating Committee, 1967. http://www.crmvet.org/docs/67_sncc_forman_tide.pdf.

"Friends of the EOP." *The Washington Alumnus,* February 1972. University of Washington.

Gates, H. L. *The African Americans: Many Rivers to Cross.* PBS series, 2013. https://www.pbs.org/show/african-americans-many-rivers-cross/.

Glover, D. "UW 'credibility gap,' Declares Odegaard." *Seattle Post Intelligencer*, June 10, 2016, 10C.

Gossett, L. *"History, Conflict, Promise: Civil Rights at UW."* Panelist, University of Washington Alumni Association Panel, May 3, 2017. https://www.tvw.org/watch/?eventID= 2017051029.

Guillen, T. "29 Protesters Arrested After Occupying U.W. Minority Office." *The Seattle Times*, May 22, 1980, p. 29.

Haak, D. C., J. HilleRisLambers, E. Pitre, and S. Freeman. "Increased Structure and Active Learning Reduces the Achievement Gap in Introductory Biology." *Science*, 332, 6034, June 3, 2011, pp. 1213-1216.

Hadley, J. "Blacks Want More Help From UW." *Seattle Post Intelligencer*, December 3, 1992, p. B1.

Hannula, D. "U.W. Sit-In 'Just the Beginning' Says Black Student Union President." *The Seattle Times*, May 21, 1968, p. 7.

"U.W. Recruits More Students from Disadvantaged Groups." *The Seattle Times*, July 14, 1968, p. 93.

Haughton, B. "Dean Beckmann Office Trashed During Sit-In." *The Daily*, May 14, 1974, pp. 1, 6.

"Heads/tails—Silenced Warriors and Baby Daddies: Young Fatherhood Among Native American Men." UCSF School of Nursing. 2019. https://nursing.ucsf.edu/news/headstails-silenced-warriors-and-baby-daddies-young-fatherhood-among-native-american-men.

Herrington, L., "Heart of the Matter." *Viewpoint*, Fall 2018, p.15. https://issuu.com/uwalumni/ docs/2018_fall_viewpoint_composite.

Hinckley, Priscilla. "In Pursuit of Social Justice." University of Washington Offices of Student, Affairs and Minority Affairs and Diversity, UWTV, 2007: https://www.youtube.com/watch?v=aVZWgTb2DLs; and extended interview with Verlaine Keith: https://www.youtube.com/watch?v=rpr32-GxqpA.

"History, Conflict, and Promise: Civil Rights at the UW." Panel of UW Alumni civil rights leaders, May 2017. https://www.washington.edu/alumni/events/history-conflict-and-promise-civil-rights-at-theuw/.

Hune, S. and D. T. Takeuchi. "Asian Americans in Washington State: Closing Their Hidden Achievement Gaps." Unpublished report submitted to the Washington State Commission on Asian Pacific American Affairs. University of Washington, Seattle, WA. 2008. https://www.cwu.edu/teaching-learning/sites/cts.cwu.edu.teaching-learning/files/documents/asian_american_achievement_gap_report.pdf.

Jackson, S. (n.d.). https://wikiapediaencyclopaedia.fandom.com/wiki/Samuel_L._Jackson.

Jewel, M., "Pozos' Trips on State Tab Questioned." *The Daily*, June 2, 1989, p.1.

Kelly, S. and Q. Taylor. *Dr. Sam: Soldier, Educator, Advocate, Friend*. Seattle, WA: University of Washington Press, 2010.

Kim, G. and A. Arquiza. *"1969-2017 Autumn Quarter Enrollment by Student Groups."* Unpublished report, Office of Minority Affairs & Diversity, Assessment & Research Unit. University of Washington, Seattle, WA. September 28, 2017.

Knaphus-Soran, E., D. Hiramori, and E. Litzler. "Year 4 Internal Evaluation Report." Center for Evaluation & Research for STEM Equity, Pacific Northwest Louis Stokes Alliance for Minority Participation. University of Washington, Seattle, WA. June 2018.

Kreighbaum, A. "15+ Hours of Work Per Week Can Hold Students Back." Report, *Inside Higher Ed*, August 29, 2017. https://www.insidehighered.com/quicktakes/2017/08/29/report-15-hours-work-week-can-hold-students-back?utm_source=Inside+Higher+Ed&utm_ campaign=e8317ab6e1-.

Lange, S. E. and G. Gallardo. "Self-Assessment Report. Office of Minority Affairs and Diversity: A Collaboration Between the Office of Minority Affairs and the Office of Educational Assessment." Unpublished report, Office of Minority Affairs. University of Washington, Seattle, WA. December 2006.

Lemire, S., C. Snyder, and L. Heuertz. "UW Advising Self-Study Preliminary Report." Unpublished report, University of Washington Office of Educational Assessment. Seattle, WA. 2005. http://depts.washington.edu/assessmt/pdfs/reports/OEAReport0503.pdf.

Lewis, P. "Chicanos Win a Battle in 'War' at U.W." *The Seattle Times*, December 4, 1977, B6.

Long, H. "African Americans Are the Only Racial Group in U.S. Still Making Less Than They Did in 2000." *The Washington Post*, September 15, 2017. https://www-washingtonpost-com.cdn.ampproject.org/c/s/www.washingtonpost.com/amphtml/news/wonk/wp/2017/09/15/african-americans-are-the-only-racial-group-in-u-s-still-making-less-than-they-did-in-2000/?fbclid=IwAR0Yep2DKq0yWAWUySapnTdCovS KoYQNng_hVVHuHvJ-Y7ngNKMVS_sJNyc.

Long, K. "Black Students' Four-hour Sit-in in 1968 Led to Big UW Changes." *The Seattle Times*, May 20, 2018. https://www.seattletimes.com/seattle-news/education/black-students-four-hour-sit-in-in-1968-led-to-big-uw-changes.

Lugo, J. A. "Collaborative and Transformative Learning." *New Learning Environments*, November 24, 2009. http://newlearningenvironmentsnle.blogspot.com/2009/11/collaborative-and-transformative.html.

Mack, K. "Black Women Tell Ordeals in Climbing Out of Cruel Valley." *The Daily*, April 22, 1969, p. 16.

Manning, H. *The Washington Alumnus*, Spring 1968, 58, pp. 14-17.

Matsuda, L. Y. "A Four-Year Longitudinal Study of Variables Related to Academic Success of Normally Inadmissible Students in the Educational Opportunity Program at the University of Washington" Unpublished doctoral dissertation. University of Washington, Seattle, WA. 1978.

Monts, L. Letter in support of the 2001 Brotman Award for Instructional Excellence. See Pitre, E. and R. Stein, Brotman Award for Instructional Excellence supporting documentation. Office of Minority Affairs and Diversity University of Washington Libraries Special Collection. Seattle, WA. 2001.

Moreno, R. and J. Harmon. "An Analysis of Instructional Center Tutoring in Eight Math Courses, 1993-94: Does Tutoring Improve EOP Students' Grades?" Unpublished manuscript, University of Washington Office of Minority Affairs. Seattle, WA. 1997.

National Association of College and University Business Officers and Commonfund Institute. U.S. and Canadian institutions listed by fiscal year (FY) 2015 endowment market value and change in endowment market value from FY2014 to F2015. July 23, 2015. http://www.nacubo.org/Documents/EndowmentFiles/2015_NCSE_Endowment_Market_Values.pdf.

NCAA Graduation Rates. (n.d.). http://www.ncaa.org/about/resources/research/graduation-rates.

"New Card to Ask Each Student's Race." *The Daily*, May 7, 1968, pp. 1, 3.

"New Counselor to Work with Minorities." *The Daily*, November 28, 1967, p. 1.

Norton, D. "Agreement Ends Student Sit-In." *The Seattle Times*, May 21, 1968, p. 5.

Odegaard, C. E. President's report to the faculty senate. University of Washington, Libraries Special Collection, Accession # 2380-005, Box 2. University of Washington. Seattle, WA. April 13, 1965.

"UW President." Black Student Union. University of Washington Libraries Special Collection, UW President, Accession # 1-34, Boxes 68 and 2, Folder 1968. University of Washington, Seattle, WA. April 30, 1968.

"Reply to BSU." *The Daily*. UW President, Board of Deans, Agenda and Minutes 1968-1969. University of Washington Libraries Special, Collection, Accession # 71-034. University of Washington, Seattle, WA. May 10, 1968.

A Pilgrimage Through Universities. Seattle: University of Washington Press, 1968.

Olson, F. "Odegaard Gives Answer to BSU Demands." *The Daily*, May 10, 1968, pp. 1,3.

"Faculty, Staff Asked to Give Hour's Pay for Minorities." *The Daily*, August 1, 1968b, p. 1.

"OMA&D Mourns Passing of Alumna and Founding BSU Member Verlaine Keith-Miller." 2018. https://www.washington.edu/omad/2018/11/15/omad-mourns-passing-of-alumna-and-founding-bsu-member-verlaine-keith-miller/.

Pope, B. (n.d.). http://byronhpope.com/byronhpope.com/About_Me.html.

Pitre, E. "The Instructional Center Chemistry Program: A Longitudinal Evaluation Study." Unpublished manuscript, University of Washington Office of Minority Affairs. Seattle, WA. 1998.

Pitre, E. and N. Stein. Brotman Diversity Award supporting documentation, unpublished, University of Washington Office of Minority Affairs. Seattle, WA. 2001.

Pitre, E., C. H. Beyer, S. Lemire, C. Snyder, and N. Lowell. "UW Study of Attrition and Retention." Unpublished report, University of Washington Office of Educational Assessment and Office of Minority Affairs and Diversity. Seattle, WA. 2006. http://depts.washington.edu/ assessmt/pdfs/reports/OEAReport0609.pdf.

"Preparing for Miss.: Student Reacts to Kidnapping." *Jet Magazine*, July 9, 1964. https://books.google.com/books?hl=En&id=bsEDAAAAMBAJ&q=Brisker#v=snippet&q=Brisker&f= false.

Presidents' reports. University of Washington Libraries Archives. Seattle, WA. 1988/1989-1996/1997.

Reynolds, P. "Diversity: Despite Obstacles, Pozos Hopes to Boost Minority Presence on Campus." *The Daily*, January 3, 1989, p.1.

Rule, M. S. "OMA&D at 50: The People Behind the Movement." *University of Washington Magazine*, March 3, 2018. https://magazine.washington.edu/feature/omad-at-50-people-behind-movement/.

Shallit, B. "Reorganization Plan Combines Ethnic Divisions." *The Daily*, January 13, 1977, p. 1.

"Budget Cuts, Internal Discord Shake EOP." *The Daily*, February 23, 1977, p. 6.

"EOP." *The Daily*, September 28, 1977, p. 12.

"Taking from Peter to Give to Paul: Is the UW Trying to Take it All?" *The Daily*, October 11, 1977, p. 2.

"Counselors Protest Indian Appointment." *The Daily*, November 11, 1977, p. 5.

"Search for Cultural Center Head: New Conflict in Minority Affairs Office" *The Daily*, November 23, 1977, p. 4.

"EOP is in a Troubled Position: Baker Under Attack from BSU." *The Daily*, December 2, 1977, p. 1.

Shideler, J. C. "A Case of Semantics: Walk Out Hits Soul Search." *The Daily*, January 11, 1968, p. 1.

"Soul Search: University Exhibits Subtle Racism." *The Daily*, February 1, 1968, p. 1.

Sibonga, D. *Filipino Forum*, August 15, 1969, 41, p. 8.

Smith, L. "Black Community Power Will End Abuses, Says Carmichael." *The Seattle Times*, April 20, 1967, pp. 5, 7.

Snyder C. and C. H. Beyer. "Focus Group Report." Office of Minority Affairs self-assessment, unpublished report, Office of Educational Assessment. University of Washington, Seattle, WA. June 2006.

"Stanford University Martin Luther King, Jr. Research and Education Institute," Student Nonviolent Coordinating Committee (SNCC). (n.d.). http://kingencyclopedia. stanford.edu/ encyclopedia/encyclopedia/enc_student_nonviolent_coordinating_ committee_sncc/.

Stevens, J. "April 19, 1967: Stokely at Garfield." *The Seattle Star*, 2015. http://www. seattlestar.net/2015/04/april-19-1967-stokely-at-garfield/.

Steward, Mike. "Senate Applauds Brisker and Senate Okays BSU Request." *The Daily*, May 24, 1968, pp. 1, 5.

"Student Diversity in Recruitment, Admission & Support Programs," University of Colorado Boulder. May 10, 2004. https://www.colorado.edu/policies/student-diversity-recruitment-admission-support-programs.

"Task Force Named: Probe of UW Minority Program." *Seattle Post-Intelligencer*, August 20, 1980, p. 2.

The Daily. Photo and caption. University of Washington. February 10, 1966, p.1.

"Opportunity Adrift." *The Education Trust*, January 2010. https://1k9gl1yevnfp2lpq1dhrqe17-wpengine.netdna-ssl.com/wp-content/ uploads/2013/10/Opportunity-Adrift_0.pdf.

"The History of OMA&D: A Talk with Emile Pitre." University of Washington. July 12, 2018. http://www.washington.edu/omad/2018/05/31/historical-talk-with-emile-pitre-highlights-50th-anniversary-celebration/ and https://www.youtube.com/ watch?v=yMD6UstCgCk.

"The Power of Giving Back." Annual Report, Office of Minority Affairs & Diversity, 2009-2010, p. 11. https://s3-us-west-2.amazonaws.com/uw-s3-cdn/wp-content/ uploads/sites/39/2010/07/23190937/09-10_OMAD_annualreport.pdf.

Todd, A. "Black Power Must Grow Further, Says Carmichael." *The Daily*, April 20, 1967, pp. 1, 10.

"University Calls in 1,000 Police to End Demonstrations as Nearly 700 are Arrested and 100 Injured; Violent Solution Follows Failure of Negotiations." *Columbia Daily Spectator*, April 30, 1968, pp. 1, 3. http://spectatorarchive.library.columbia. edu/?a=d&d=cs19680430-01.1.1&.

University of Washington. "Regent Policy 32." Board of Regents Governance policy on admission. February 9, 1979. https://www.washington.edu/admin/rules/policies/BRG/ RP32.html.

University of Washington. "Regent Policy 33." Board of Regents Governance policy on diversity. Formerly numbered Regent Policy No. 11. 1975, 2018. https://www.washington.edu/admin/rules/policies/BRG/RP33.html.

University of Washington Board of Regents, Rogelio Riojas. (n.d.). https://www.washington.edu/regents/officers/rogelio-riojas/.

University of Washington Bulletin. 1964-65. https://www.washington.edu/students/gencat/archive/GenCat1964-65v1.pdf.

University of Washington Bulletin, General Series, 1967-69, No. 1043, pp. 79-261. https://www.washington.edu/students/gencat/archive/GenCat1967-69v1.pdf.

University of Washington Diversity Blueprint, 2015. http://www.washington.edu/diversity/files/2015/02/Diversity-Blueprint.pdf; see also https://www.washington.edu/diversity/diversity-blueprint/.

University of Washington Ethnic Cultural Center Archives. Contact ECC director for access. (n.d.).

University of Washington Office of Minority Affairs. Annual report of the Office of Minority Affairs for the academic year 1970-71. University of Washington Libraries Special Collection, Accession # 95-277, Box VF 2445. University of Washington, Seattle, WA. (n.d.).

Annual report of the Office of Minority Affairs for the academic year 1973-74. University of Washington Libraries Special Collection, Accession # 95-277. University of Washington, Seattle, WA. (n.d.).

Annual reports of the Office of Minority Affairs. Friends of the Educational Opportunity Program newsletter. University of Washington Libraries Special Collection, Accession # 88-030, Boxes 1, 25, 28, 52, 54, 55. University of Washington, Seattle, WA. (n.d.).

"Annual Report." Unpublished report. University of Washington Libraries Special Collection. Seattle, WA. 2004.

Brief for National Conference: Second Annual Conference on Special Emerging Programs in Higher Education, UW, November 7-9, 1974. University of Washington Libraries Special Collection, Accession # 83-027, Box 11. University of Washington, Seattle, WA. (n.d.).

Center for Curriculum Transformation. (n.d.). https://www.washington.edu/omad/ctcenter/history/.

"Final OMA&D Self-Assessment Report." Unpublished report. University of Washington Libraries Special Collection, Seattle, WA. 2006, p. 64, 72, 73.

"Historical Timeline." 2018. https://www.washington.edu/omad/50th/.

"Odegaard Award Winners." (n.d.). https://www.washington.edu/omad/celebration/odegaard-winners.

"SESO GEAR-UP." (n.d.) http://depts.washington.edu/sgearup.

University of Washington Libraries Special, Collection, Accession # 83-027, Box 1. University of Washington, Seattle, WA. (n.d.).

University of Washington Libraries Special Collection, Accession # 83-027, Box 11. University of Washington, Seattle, WA. (n.d.).

Vice President of Minority Affairs. University of Washington Libraries Special Collection, Accession # 88-39, Box 25. University of Washington, Seattle, WA. (n.d.).

Vice President records. University of Washington Libraries Special Collection, Accession # 03-053, Boxes 21, 22. 25, 31, 33, 53. University of Washington, Seattle, WA. (n.d.).

University of Washington Publications. University of Washington Libraries Special Collection, Accession # 02-018, Box 84. University of Washington, Seattle, WA. (n.d.).

University of Washington Registrar's Office. Data Management Services Records. University of Washington Libraries Special Collection, Accession # 04-085, Box 54. Seattle, WA. (n.d.).

UW increases fee ordered to Carmichael. (1967, April 15). *The Seattle Times*, p. 15.

Verbon, D. "BSU Working to Carry Out Its Obligations." *The Daily*, May 22, 1968, p. 1.

Walker, D. L. "The University of Washington Establishment and the Black Student Union Sit-In of 1968." Unpublished master's thesis. University of Washington, Seattle, WA. 1980.

Walker, W. and J. Snell. "Kelly Threatens Resignation as Minority VP." *The Daily*, May 17, 1974, p. 1.

Wang, Z. "Effects of Heterogeneous and Homogeneous Grouping on Student Learning." Unpublished doctoral dissertation. University of North Carolina, Chapel Hill, NC. 2019. https://cdr.lib.unc.edu/indexablecontent/uuid:ac391807-1cca-447e-801d-d65183945ad0

Washington Office of the Superintendent of Public Instruction. Data portal. (n.d.). https://www.k12.wa.us/data-reporting/data-portal; and http://www.k12.wa.us/DataAdmin/Dropout-Grad.aspx.

Credits

Cover
Front a - Courtesy of Steve Ludwig, II
Front b - Courtesy of OMA&D
Back a - Emile Pitre Collection, 130
Back b - Emile Pitre Collection, 04.25.13 014[1]-1

Inside Back Cover
Courtesy of Keoke Silvano, 1.03.14 031

Introduction

10	Emile Pitre Collection
12	Courtesy Larry Gossett
14a	Courtesy Jimmy Garrett
14b	Emile Pitre Collection
15	Courtesy Antonio Salazar
17	Emile Pitre Collection

Chapter 1

18	Emile Pitre Collection, 130
22	University of Washington Libraries, Special Collections, UW Daily 004
24	University of Washington Libraries, Special Collections, UW 41579
26	MOHAI, Seattle Post-Intelligencer Collection, 1200
30	Courtesy Jimmy Garrett
32	Courtesy Steve Ludwig, II
35	Emile Pitre Collection, 20
37-40	Emile Pitre Collection
43	Emile Pitre Collection, 24
47	Emile Pitre Collection, Courtesy of The Seattle Times
48a	MOHAI, Seattle Post-Intelligencer Collection, 1986.5.16852.12
48b	MOHAI, Seattle Post-Intelligencer Collection, 10
50	MOHAI, Seattle Post-Intelligencer Collection, 1986.5.16852.10
52	Emile Pitre Collection, 123
54a	MOHAI, Seattle Post-Intelligencer Collection, 1986.5.16852.5
54b	MOHAI, Seattle Post-Intelligencer Collection, 1986.5.16852.3
60	Emile Pitre Collection, 126
64	MOHAI, Seattle Post-Intelligencer Collection, 26555

Chapter 2

74	University of Washington Libraries, Special Collections, 39189
76	UW Photography Archives, (M12896)-1
80	UW Photography Archives, (M11773)-1
81	Courtesy Larry Matsuda

Chapter 8

Appendix B

Index

Emile Pitre in his apartment posing in front of posters of his favorite activists,
Angela Davis, who spoke truth to power, and one of his favorite jazz musicians,
saxophonist Eric Dolphy. Fall 1968.